Alex Schultz is CMO & VP of Analytics at Meta, overseeing global marketing and analytics. He started his digital marketing career by founding the world's largest paper airplane website. He then joined eBay in 2004, before moving to Meta in 2007. In 2019, the *Financial Times* noted, 'If you joined Facebook at any time over the past decade, Alex Schultz probably had something to do with it.' Named one of the world's most influential CMOs in 2024 by *Forbes*, Schultz is widely credited for helping grow Meta's user base to nearly 3.3 billion daily users globally. His work in the digital marketing sphere is unparalleled – and has significantly influenced the way companies achieve growth in the digital age. He has advised numerous start-ups such as Airbnb and has twice delivered the growth talk for Y Combinator's start-up school series at Stanford. *Click Here* is his second book.

Additional praise for Alex Schultz and

Click Here

'*Click Here* brims with hard-won practical wisdom that illuminates the inner workings of online marketing and makes its profoundly powerful principles and tools accessible to everyone. It's an indispensable field guide for anyone looking to grow a business on the internet.'
KOFI AMOO-GOTTFRIED, CMO – DOORDASH

'No one is better placed to guide marketers through the intricacies of digital media than Alex Schultz. His principles set the standard for our craft, and I can only wish the insights from *Click Here* were available earlier in my career. This is a remarkable narrative that will guide the industry for many years to come.'
KELLY BENNETT, CHAIRMAN – ZALANDO

'A tour de force that equips anyone to become a world-class digital marketer.'
**KYLE DROPP, PHD, CO-FOUNDER
AND PRESIDENT – MORNING CONSULT**

'Few people understand marketing and growth better than Alex, thanks to his years at Facebook, easily one of the most impressive marketing and growth organizations in the world. This book distills that insight into practical, actionable strategies every founder, marketer, and operator needs.'
DANIEL EK, CEO – SPOTIFY

'This is the digital marketing handbook we didn't know we were waiting for. Alex Schultz combines deep experience with a humble, practical approach that's both strategic and hands-on. From targeting and funnel strategy to the rise of AI and connected TV, this book offers clear principles and vibrant examples to guide marketers at any level. It's essential reading for anyone serious about modern marketing.'

JOCHEN KOEDIJK, CMO – EXPEDIA

'This is mandatory reading by one of the most balanced and successful marketers in our global tribe.'

ANTONIO LUCIO, EVP, CMO AND
CORPORATE AFFAIRS OFFICER – HP INC.

'One of the leading thinkers and doers in digital marketing for decades, Alex provides an essential resource for marketers at any level, in any size business, on how to ensure their next dollar spent drives a better return.'

SETH MATLINS, MD – FORBES CMO NETWORK

'Facebook's head of growth/CMO Alex Schultz's book (perhaps the man most responsible for Meta having more users than Christianity) is the best summary of modern performance marketing I've ever read. From high-level first principles to annoying details around correct measurement, it's like doing a daylong download with a God-tier growth marketer.'

ANTONIO GARCÍA MARTÍNEZ,
AUTHOR OF *CHAOS MONKEYS*

'Don't read this book if you're looking for a shortcut. If there was a master's in marketing in a digital age, this is the only textbook you'd have to learn from. Alex Schultz has taken everything he has studied, experimented with, and learned, and synthesized it into an eminently readable yet completely comprehensive tome, peppered with actual cases and examples. If you're looking for double- or triple-digit percentage increases in incremental results, just do exactly what he says. But do all of it.'

ANDREW ROBERTSON, CHAIRMAN – BBDO WORLDWIDE

'I have interviewed fifty of the greatest minds in growth. There is no one like Alex. What *Good to Great is* for business strategy, this is for growth.'
HARRY STEBBINGS, FOUNDER – 20VC

'Whether you're running a small business or scaling a global brand, *Click Here* is the essential guide to what actually works in digital marketing. If you're spending a single dollar advertising online, you should read this book first.'
PAUL TOMS, CMO – WAYFAIR

'If you know nothing about marketing, read this book. If you think you know about marketing, you need to read this book. It's the perfect guide to navigating the future, by learning from the past.'
MATTHEW VAUGHN, FILMMAKER AND FOUNDER – MARV

CLICK HERE

The Art and Science of Digital
Marketing and Advertising

ALEX SCHULTZ

WILDFIRE

First published in 2025 by Wildfire
An imprint of Headline Publishing Group Limited

2

Apart from any use permitted under UK copyright law, this publication may
only be reproduced, stored, or transmitted, in any form, or by any means,
with prior permission in writing of the publishers or, in the case of
reprographic production, in accordance with the terms of licences
issued by the Copyright Licensing Agency.

Cataloguing in Publication Data is available from the British Library

Hardback ISBN 978 1 0354 3409 1
Trade Paperback ISBN 978 1 0354 3410 7

Typeset in 11.5/16 Utopia Std by Six Red Marbles UK, Thetford, Norfolk

Printed and bound in Great Britain by Clays Ltd, Elcograf S.p.A.

Headline's policy is to use papers that are natural, renewable and recyclable
products and made from wood grown in well-managed forests and other
controlled sources. The logging and manufacturing processes are expected
to conform to the environmental regulations of the country of origin.

Headline Publishing Group Limited
An Hachette UK Company
Carmelite House
50 Victoria Embankment
London EC4Y 0DZ

The authorised representative in the EEA is Hachette Ireland,
8 Castlecourt Centre, Dublin 15, D15 XTP3, Ireland (email: info@hbgi.ie)

www.headline.co.uk
www.hachette.co.uk

I dedicate this book to my parents and partner without whose support this could not have happened

Contents

Key Digital Marketing Terminology

ACRUs (activated confirmed registered users) ACRUs have registered, confirmed their account and activated by taking a valid action.

Affiliate marketers Affiliate marketers use their own marketing skills to promote another company's or organization's products and services through affiliate programmes. They are subsequently paid based on actions resulting from those promotions.

API (application programming interface) An API is a way for computer programs to talk to each other.

ARPU (average revenue per user) An ARPU is usually the annual revenue that a company gets, divided by its user base.

Banner ad networks Networks that serve image ads on a site and pay the site's owner a revenue share.

Channel The specific medium used to deliver the ad. Choosing the right channel means asking yourself where you can find users most likely to convert.

Conversion When a user takes a desired action, such as buying a product.

CPC (cost per click) A CPC is typically how much money a click costs a company to buy.

CPA (cost per action) — CPA is a metric that measures the cost of each action driven via a marketing campaign, calculated by dividing total spend by total actions driven.

CPM (costs per mille) — CPM is a metric that describes how much it costs an advertiser for every 1,000 impressions or views of the ad they buy.

Creative — The marketing materials which you are showing users to convince them to take action.

CRO (conversion rate optimization) — CRO is when you optimize a conversion journey to increase the percentage of people who complete it.

CRU (confirmed registered user) — A CRU is a user who has registered and then confirmed their email address or phone number but is yet to activate.

CTR (click-through rate) — CTR is the clicks made by users divided by the impressions of an ad they see. This is usually expressed as a percentage.

Display advertising networks — Companies that aggregate ad spots across a wide range of sites and apps, allowing businesses to buy banner ads from a single source.

DAU (daily active user) — DAU is a metric that counts the number of users active in a given day.

DM (direct mail) — DM constitutes snail mail, email, messaging apps, push notifications, SMS and related channels. It is essentially any channel where you directly reach out to customers.

DSPs (demand-side platforms)	DSPs arrived in the 2010s to simplify ad buying, allowing companies to instruct multiple ad networks at once. This technology enabled real-time bidding on a given impression, based on the targeting data available and how much the advertiser valued it.
EBITDA (earnings before interest, taxes, depreciation and amortization)	EBITDA is a financial term looking at how much profit a company earns before certain important accounting takes place. It is commonly used, although many folks prefer free cash flow.
eCPM (expected or estimated costs per mille)	eCPM is a metric that estimates how much an advertiser might pay for every 1,000 impressions or views of the ad in question.
Holdout	A holdout is a potential customer subjected to randomized control tests. Users in a holdout act as a control group to see how much effect a marketing campaign had, by exposing the true impact of your work on the bottom-line goal metrics. If the users in the holdout end up buying the product or service to the same extent as those who saw the ads, then the ads may not have been all that useful in the first place.
ISOs (individual stock options)	ISOs are stock grants at a given share price.
LTV (lifetime value)	The LTV of a user is the revenue that a user generates in a period of time defined by the company as a lifetime.

MAU (monthly active user)	A MAU is considered 'monthly active' if they have utilized a service at least once over the previous thirty days.
MMM (media mix modelling)	MMM is an analytical method for forecasting the impact of each marketing channel on an outcome.
MTA (mail transfer agent)	MTA is the software or program that is responsible for sending emails from one server to another.
North Star goal	A clear, bright navigational aid that everyone on the team can see and work towards.
NUX (new user experience)	NUX is the experience a company gives to someone immediately after they sign up to their product.
Onsite merchandising	A channel that involves promoting your products or services directly on your own site.
Organic search	A channel that targets users based on the keywords they enter into search engines. Organic search occurs when your site or platform shows up in search engine results without paying for placement or marketing.
Organic social	A channel where your product, service or brand shows up in a social feed, app or site organically, without you having to pay for placement or marketing.
Page rank	A measure of a page's importance. This is determined by how many pages are linked to a page, and how many pages link to those pages.

Paid search	The paid big brother of SEO, this channel involves bidding on keyword terms to appear in the paid search results, also known as SEM (search engine marketing).
Paid social	A channel where you pay to have your product, service or brand show up in a social feed, app or site.
Partner-led channels	Channels that involve working with partner companies to market your service or product. This may include buying ads to promote your product on retail advertising networks run by companies – such as Walmart or Amazon – or using classic web portals to display ads.
P&L (profit and loss)	P&L usually refers to a business group's impact on the company's profits. Often, when you manage a P&L, you are responsible for all profits and losses in your business group, i.e., revenues minus expenses gives either profit or loss.
Pop-over	Ads that pop up all over a website in a full browser window or a JavaScript layer, interrupting users' browsing to get them to see an ad.
Pop-under	Ads that open in a browser window underneath the one the user was actively navigating.
Post-click conversion	A conversion that happens after a user has clicked on an ad and then converts within a defined period of time.

Post-click tracking	A technique used to track user behaviour following their engagement with an ad.
Product-led channels	This involves using your own product as a marketing channel. Offline, product-led channels include branding on the side of your delivery truck or little promotions sticking out into the aisle as you walk around a supermarket. Online means emails, push notifications, merchandising units inside your app or website and navigation elements.
Re-targeting	When someone is shown an ad based on their previous behaviour on an app or website.
ROAS (return on ad spend)	ROAS is similar to ROI. However, it only factors ad spend into the cost, excluding other campaign costs such as creative agency fees.
ROI (return on investment)	ROI is typically expressed as a percentage. It is the dollars returned from a campaign divided by the dollars spent on a campaign, minus 100%. If it is greater than 0%, then the campaign had a positive ROI. If it is less than 0%, the campaign had a negative ROI.
SEM (search engine marketing)	SEM is when you bid on keyword terms to appear in paid search results. This ensures your websites, products and services appear through search engines. This would typically mean working with Google, but there are interesting developments coming with AI and potentially other engines that answer specific questions instead of just providing a page of links.

SEO (search engine optimization)	SEO involves figuring out what keywords your potential customers search for, and how to make sure your brand or site pops up when they do so in the non-ads search results.
Social media marketing	Social media marketing involves utilizing Meta, YouTube, TikTok and all the incredible social media channels that exist now and will exist in the future.
SMBs (small and medium businesses)	Small and medium businesses are businesses that are not big enough to be considered enterprises. It is a very variable line, but it makes up the vast majority of businesses. Typically, SMBs are not publicly traded. If they are traded, they tend to have a small market capitalization.
Targeting	Identifying a specific audience, and the action you trying to influence them to do.
Un-targeting	Excluding specific customers from your ads.

INTRODUCTION

Growth is good. Sometimes I get pushback on this statement, as if it's an endorsement of extreme, unfettered growth at all costs. Certainly, growth comes with its own pitfalls, and when out of control, it must be curtailed. But when summed up across a whole economy, growth improves lives, lifting people out of poverty, providing jobs and funding services through taxes and charity. Lack of growth, or stagnation, leads to the reverse, with such economies experiencing job insecurity, falling standards of living, poorer services and children who are worse off than their parents.

The economy is, of course, made up of businesses, so economic growth is directly impacted by business growth. The sum of growing multiple businesses is what makes a growing economy possible. A growing business lets you explore new opportunities, employ more people, provide for your family and return value to shareholders. A shrinking or stagnating business is constrained in its capabilities, forced to lay people off and often leaves owners with diminishing returns. There is a reciprocity here that cannot go overlooked: as businesses grow, economies grow, and as economies grow, so do businesses. Taken together, business and economic growth results in societal benefits across the board. By supplying the products and services people want and need, and the jobs to produce and provide them, most of us are better off.

Growth is also a choice. Though organic growth is possible, it rarely takes place without concerted effort. This comes down to an individual business's actions as much as it does to the environment in which it operates. An economy should enable businesses to grow. Again, not at all costs, but in a way that allows people across the economic spectrum to thrive. There has been an increase in anti-tech regulation in some places, particularly Europe, and though the long-term consequences are not yet known, it is my personal belief that even if such regulation – on online personalized advertising, for example – is done in good will, the impact is likely to be a drag on business and economic growth.

To succeed, all businesses, organizations, industries and institutions must choose to grow and take action to flourish. Today, there is no better way to do so than through the power of online digital marketing. Marketing remains an integral, almost magical tool to grow the countless businesses that make up the economy. It's part art, part science. To many, a mystery, or worse, a gamble. The goal of this book is to demystify twenty-first-century digital marketing and help you become brilliant at it. The advertising channels that have emerged from digital marketing are tremendous levers to help any business succeed, from a local coffee shop or boutique hotel to a multinational, trillion-dollar market cap tech company. Growth is within reach – all you need to do is grab it.

ENTER MARKETING

In the following pages, I focus on the channels that were born in the 1990s, which came of age in the 2010s and are still developing today, and primarily on the bottom of the marketing funnel (discussed in depth throughout the book). Amazing resources like *Ogilvy on Advertising*, written by the 'Father of Advertising', David Ogilvy, exist for channels before the 1990s, and they are still highly relevant. This book, however, is designed to fill in the gap for more recent developments in the field, like search and social media, which were not prevalent until this century and are now the largest marketing channels on Earth. Whether you are a student just entering the industry, an experienced marketer looking to build out the channels you already use, or a businessperson who wants to leverage the incredible tools available to us all today, the point of this book is to help you achieve a level of growth that would otherwise be impossible.

I know the impact of digital marketing because I have played a role in making it happen, more than once. The first was when, the quarter after I joined eBay in 2004 (the most valuable internet company at the time), the stock price crashed by just under 50 percent. The second was when Facebook – now Meta – stopped growing, shortly after I joined. In both cases, these companies came bouncing back to health, and today are far larger, more profitable and more valuable than when those crises hit – brilliant marketing is one of the main reasons why.

I joined Facebook in 2007 because I believed it would not just be huge, but that it would entirely transform modern advertising. Facebook's user IDs would allow advertisers to measure the impact of their ads online by comparing the behaviour of those users who saw the ads and those who didn't, also known as 'holdouts'. In essence, 'holdouts' are potential customers that act as a control group to see how much effect a marketing campaign truly had. If the holdouts end up buying the product or service to the same extent as those who saw the ads, then the ads may not have been all that useful in the first place.

While I worked at eBay, I and many of my colleagues across the industry grew frustrated that we couldn't look at the behaviour of user-level holdouts on our search and affiliate marketing. I was convinced we were undervaluing internet marketing as a channel; only focusing on the last click of a person who converted by buying a product or service, and saying it was because of an ad. What I would have liked to have done was to investigate the incremental impact of a channel on consumers over a longer period, which is possible through testing and experiments, many of which are discussed throughout this book. I believed that studying, or running, holdouts over a long timeframe (more than a year) would become possible, and in doing so we could better understand and harness the long-term value of marketing.

I also felt Facebook would be able to give superpowers to small and medium businesses (SMBs) to help them drive growth, superpowers that historically only big businesses could afford. Large companies could buy ad spots on tailored TV shows, such as *RuPaul's Drag Race* for gay men like myself, or run campaigns in custom print and digital media, like *Attitude*, the popular British gay lifestyle magazine, but SMBs were not positioned to buy these ads.

Thanks to digital marketing, and especially social media, SMBs could now target as many people in those audiences as they could afford to, testing their way in rather than being restricted to buying a big ad spot that might not move the needle. This approach would allow businesses to exist that couldn't have previously, and grow further than they could have ever imagined. Digital marketing didn't just level the playing field, it created a new one – an egalitarian pitch where almost anyone could figure out a way to reach their intended audience, no matter how broad or niche, allowing niche businesses to exist that couldn't otherwise.

At Meta, I started helping small businesses to use our pages product and buy self-service advertising, allowing them to place ads on our platform without having to work directly with an ad salesperson, making the process quick and efficient. This approach worked especially well when we focused on upselling those businesses already using our products to adopt more tools. From there I helped our search engine optimization (SEO) teams to grow our new users by 100x from non-brand SEO, an approach that does not use specific brand or product names in its keyword search. I was also part of the initial leadership of the Growth team set up under Chamath Palihapitiya, the VP of platform and monetization at the time, in 2007. Since then I have taken on more responsibility, including running our data science and data engineering teams, and became Meta's CMO in 2020.

My whole life I have enjoyed online marketing and analytics, and I see them as two sides of the same coin. They were my hobbies at high school, a useful income generator at university and the mainstay of my career ever since. On top of eBay and Meta, I have advised a number of startups as a growth consultant, both formally and informally, and in businesses small and large, including Airbnb and Coursera.

Great marketing can lead to 10- or 100-fold differences in outcomes. In the late 1990s and early 2000s, while eBay debated whether to open up to SEO, Amazon built a marketplace and dominated Google search results for items they sell themselves or that third parties sell through their marketplace. I'd much prefer Amazon's position today over eBay's. As Snapchat built an incredible social media success, they did not employ an aggressive growth approach, leaving room for competitors – TikTok found product market fit and bought billions of paid marketing, allowing them to grow aggressively. As with Amazon over eBay, I prefer the business TikTok built over Snapchat. In both cases, and many more, great marketing led to material differences, a competitive advantage that I want to help you capture. It starts with two guiding principles.

GUIDING PRINCIPLES

There are two guiding principles for this book.

The first is that *tools evolve, but principles are timeless.* No matter the technology, it's always still marketing. Having been a physics student before entering the field, I had to learn the principles from scratch. Books like *Ogilvy on Advertising* provided advice that could be applied to each new endeavour I undertook, regardless of when or with what tools. That has remained true throughout my career.

Sometimes when folks look at new tools, however, they get lost in the complexity of the technology. Take push notifications for mobile apps. How do you build an app? How do you prompt for push permission? How do you register a push token? How do you send a notification in the first place? They might ask all these questions – and many companies did when push notifications became popular – without stepping back and thinking of the timeless marketing principles that would actually make the tool effective.

For me, marketing push notifications are the latest in a long line of descendants of direct mailing, David Ogilvy's 'first love and secret weapon'. In the 1980s and 1990s, those direct mailings were sent by post. When the letters arrived on someone's doorstep, they needed to compel that person to open them, read them and then take action. The address had to be current – a logistical nightmare – and as a marketer you needed to justify the incremental benefit because you paid for each letter sent. In the 1990s and early 2000s, direct mailing went digital. Emails were free, and the perfect subject line could tempt people to open them. Still, you needed the right email addresses, and your message could be marked as spam, which meant you essentially could never deliver an email to that address again.

In the 2000s and 2010s, marketers like myself started to layer in SMS. With text messages, we had less room to get our point across and, unlike email – but very much like the post – we had to pay to send them. We still needed up-to-date addresses (phone numbers) and had to measure the incremental impact of sending the messages – and again, being marked as spam was an issue.

Today, in the 2020s, we have push notifications. The principles on delivery, measurement and impact have remained timeless across these channels. And guess what? Whatever new channel comes along, these principles will still stand. This guiding principle holds true across most of our work in online marketing. Recognizing these commonalities will help you leverage the collective marketing knowledge developed over decades, even if the tools to utilize it seem overwhelming at first.

The second guiding principle is that *incremental results are everything*. An incremental result is one that you can prove happened because of your actions. In other words, if you hadn't done the marketing, would anything have happened? Ideally the answer is no. But generally, if we appropriately self-scrutinize, the answer is yes, and the real question is how much (if any) less would have happened without that marketing?

One of the most canonical examples of this guiding principle is the online search work by Professor Steve Tadelis, of the University of California, Berkeley, when he was at eBay, years after I left the company. The company had bought the keyword 'eBay' so ads for the online marketplace appeared when you searched for the word. Tadelis hypothesized that those users who clicked on the ad would have converted without eBay buying the ad. Therefore, it was paying to acquire users who would have converted regardless. He then ran experiments that proved the vast majority of users eBay's internet marketing team thought were coming from the search term 'eBay' would have come to and used the platform anyway. The company was wasting money buying ads that were doing next to nothing for them – according to this research, they were not generating many incremental results to those that would have happened without the marketing in the first place. This is the core difference between tracking what happens after someone clicks on your ad versus running proper experiments to see what impact your ad created.

Fraud is another reason tracking incremental results is so important. Uber is my favorite example here. During the late-2010s land grab for ride booking apps, they spent hundreds of millions of dollars on ads. In 2017 their CMO, Kevin Frisch, found that when he turned off some of the ads that supposedly drove their growth, there was no actual drop in growth. Shocked, he dug into the data further and realized that a group of companies was using Uber's tracking improperly, taking credit for user registrations and defrauding Uber of millions in the process. Uber won a resulting court case, and saved the company hundreds of millions of dollars over the years to come. (It is rare that these fights become public and so this case is a favourite because some details, at least, are publicly available to discuss.)

These two guiding principles – *tools evolve, but principles are timeless* and *incremental results are everything* – have served me throughout my career, and they remain relevant no matter the scale of your business. And though this is advice I often give, it really only scratches the surface of the awe-inspiring powers of digital marketing. The details of the practice are complex and nuanced, and to just give you these two principles and send you on your way would be misleading. Yes, they guide me in all my work, but to really tackle all the ins and outs of digital marketing requires a full book – like the one you hold in your hands right now.

WHY WRITE THIS BOOK?

When I started to think about writing this book, everyone I talked to – from friends who are experts in the internet marketing industry, to book publishers, to business school professors, to other business leaders not tightly tied to internet marketing – said there was a gap in this topic. There was nowhere you could go to learn the basics of digital marketing for the internet age, and I agreed. I am regularly asked for a resource to share, but I've never been able to find one I wholeheartedly believe in. There are countless books on traditional creative and brand marketing, including the legendary Ogilvy book I reference throughout this book, but a comprehensive good book on digital marketing doesn't, in my opinion, exist. But it should. Not only is this a major industry, but as a tool, anyone can access growth through digital marketing, as long as they know how to use it. That fact, more than any, inspired me to write this book. I also felt I was a good candidate for the job, and I wanted to give back to the industry that has given so much to me.

In fact, my background in online marketing starts far earlier than my jobs with eBay and Meta, and it stemmed, somewhat, from necessity. My parents gave me an awesome upbringing. I am lucky they understood the benefit of a good education, and I am endlessly fortunate that they were able to provide one for me by making sacrifices and sending me to a great private school. By the end of my high school, though, my family's financial situation had changed, and money was tighter still. I needed a scholarship to continue at the school (which I won and am forever grateful for) and gained a needs-tested bursary, another type of scholarship, to get started at Cambridge University. (These factors changed my life, and for that reason I am proud to say all of my royalties from this book will be going to charities to help others get the best possible education without having to worry about money.)

Although my parents would have put themselves under more stress to help me pay for university, I was determined to self-fund my life after high school. On top of the bursary, I still needed spending money, textbooks and the ability to pay for my rowing career (kit, travel and training camps added up). To do so, I took my small GeoCities website about paper airplanes, among other topics, which I had used to make a little money on the side, and turned it from a hobby into a real income generator. In the 1990s, GeoCities was one of the few hosting services where you could set up your own website, a somewhat Wild West precursor to the standardized, sleek sites of today.

My site surprisingly started to get visitors from search engines, at that time mostly AltaVista, and all on my paper airplanes section because someone had added a link to it on their, far more popular, website. It was a revelation – the link was more valuable for the search ranking power it gave me than for the direct visitors clicking on it. I wanted to get more visitors and so, over time, I learned SEO. My experience with the site exposed me to SEO's power, and I was able to use SEO to rank first in Google for 'Paper Airplanes'.

Over time, I created more websites, which were user-generated, one on making cocktails, another on butterfly tattoos. Both ranked highly in Google for terms with large volumes of searches. When these sites began getting more traffic, I added ads to them from banner advertising networks and, eventually, Google AdSense. This resulted in thousands, and then tens of thousands, of dollars of revenue. It even resulted in me writing my first book, on paper airplanes, which sold (I am told) 150,000 copies.

The move from running sites for fun to understanding SEO and choosing topics where I could add value, but also win significant traffic and make real money from ads, was foundational for me. Everything I learned through that experience was the basis for my career today and that training is, mostly, still relevant. Importantly, it was also a turning point in my career path. I had been planning on becoming an academic and rower, but I found a passion for digital marketing and analytics. I decided to make my hobby my career, and I know I'm incredibly lucky to be one of the small group of people who can say that.

By promoting my websites, I learned which online marketing techniques drove impact. I found that, often, impact could be attributed to a new digital marketing action that didn't have any incremental effect on the bottom line. The fact that the outcomes were integral to my quality of life caused the lessons I learned to really stick. When I started at eBay in the UK, I noticed that many business and marketing leaders did not follow what would become my second guiding principle. They rarely considered whether the actions they took were driving incremental results or were just busy work. Without this scrutiny, large marketing programmes (like partnerships with specific websites or buying the keyword 'eBay' from search engines) delivered *nothing*, and fraud – which could amount to many millions of dollars – went unnoticed. Meanwhile, affiliate marketers took credit for conversions (like new user registrations) that would have happened without them anyhow.

You may be familiar with the John Wanamaker quote: 'Half the money I spend on advertising is wasted; the trouble is I don't know which half.' In fact, the problem expressed by this turn-of-the-twentieth-century businessman and marketing pioneer is much greater – in some instances it is the entirety of a marketing channel that gets wasted. Clearly the tools have changed, moving from offline to digital marketing, but need for incremental returns has stayed the same.

So how do we solve that problem? In many ways, it's the same approach I took to running my GeoCities websites in the 1990s and websites in the 2000s – testing. This concept is one I spend a lot of time on in the book, so I won't belabour it here, but the fundamental point is that testing is key. These tests can be super-clever and multivariate, using advanced statistics, or they can be as simple as a before and after comparison, and everything in between. If you lead a large business growing just a few percent year over year, then you probably care about small effect sizes (e.g., growing year-on-year revenue 0.5 percent faster). But for most business owners and leaders, if you need a data scientist and microscope to find out if your marketing had an impact, I can save you a lot of time, money and effort – it didn't. In terms of timeless principles, this topic was explored over a hundred years ago by Claude C. Hopkins in *Scientific Advertising*. Again, though the tools may have changed, Hopkins's principles of split testing and tracking remain the same.

BASICS, INFRASTRUCTURE AND CHANNELS

This book is based on my over twenty years of experience, high-lighting the most applicable, actionable lessons I've learned. My goal here is to ensure readers gain a basic grounding in how to correctly measure the incremental impact of digital marketing and can use digital marketing tools to be successful in any of the new channels that have grown up this century. As such, the book is split into three main parts: the basics, which walks through my high-level view of how to think about marketing; the infrastructure, necessary to setting up any successful internet marketing operation; and the channels, consisting of detailed descriptions of the current main channels of online marketing and how to best leverage them.

Nothing matters more in online marketing than getting the basics right. Too often I consult with startups and companies that lack clarity on the actual goal of their marketing efforts, especially at the most basic level. For example, as a travel company or small hotel, are you trying to maximize revenue or occupancy? If one person at the company advocates for steep discounting to drive occupancy, while another refuses since this approach will not maximize revenue, you clearly have a problem. Both are correct, and both feel they are doing what they were told to, but that's because leadership hadn't clarified the most basic goal. So, in Part I: **The Basics**, I address the most foundational principles, including conversion (What are you trying to get people to do?); channel (Where are you trying to find them to convert them?); targeting (Who are you trying to get to do it?); and creative (What are you showing them to convince them to take action?).

Next up, in Part II: **The Infrastructure**, I move to the infrastructure that needs to be in place in order to make things happen. One initial note on this topic: today's marketing technology, unfortunately, is often presented in a way that scares or overwhelms those without a technical background. I am not a genius programmer by anyone's definition – I learned coding PHP and MySQL from a book aptly titled *PHP and MySQL for Dummies,* but I have some programming skills. I think you should too because some technical proficiency is necessary (especially in situations where you find yourself in a room with twenty engineers).

That being said, you don't need to get beyond the level of a 'for Dummies' book to be useful in directing the work or even implementing it for most small businesses. So, Part II explains what it takes to set up the technology, teams and talent to be a successful internet marketer, including how to perform incrementality measurements, what skills to look for in agencies and team members, and how to work with cross-functional partners. I hope it does it in an accessible way that will help anyone be able to set up a team, small or large, to build the infrastructure that enables incredible digital marketing.

Part III: **The Channels** provides an in-depth exploration of the four most important channels of online marketing:

- **Product-led channels:** Using your own product as a marketing channel. Offline, product-led channels include branding on the side of your delivery truck or little promotions sticking out into the aisle as you walk around a supermarket. Online, this means emails, push notifications, merchandising units inside your app or website and navigation elements.
- **Partner-led channels:** Working with affiliates to market your service or product. This channel may include buying ads to promote your product on retail advertising networks run by companies such as Walmart or Amazon, or using classic web portals to display ads.
- **Search marketing:** Ensuring your websites, products and services appear through search engines. These days, that mostly means working with Google, but there are interesting developments coming with AI and potentially other engines that answer specific questions, as compared to just providing a page of links. I believe in that transition classic search marketing will still matter as its principles will hold true, even as the tool changes in the AI future.
- **Social media marketing:** My home turf, and now the largest channel in online marketing, utilizing Meta, YouTube, TikTok and all the incredible social media channels that exist now and will exist in the future.

I present the timeless principles of these channels, their history, and modern examples that will illustrate how you can get the most from each one in your own marketing efforts.

THE NEW GOLDEN AGE OF MARKETING

My hope with this book is not just that I can give you a flavour of the journey I embarked on at the beginning of my career, but that I can empower you with the techniques and tactics to make the most of your business, company, organization, or even self through the undeniable power of online digital marketing. Whether big or small, new or old, anyone can leverage these tools to be successful.

The internet has spawned a new golden age of marketing tools to help you reach your maximum growth potential. It has given small and medium businesses opportunities that only huge companies could previously access. Today, you can connect with people around the world more efficiently than ever before, providing them with the products and services that can help them lead their best lives, even in small niches. This book provides ideas and knowledge for anyone who wants to leverage digital marketing as a tool to get better results. When you understand the tools, the timeless principles behind them, and the actual, incremental results those tools drive, you can not only allocate your time and budget effectively, but also advocate for investment with your peers, colleagues, CEO and finance departments.

Again, growth is good. A rising tide lifts all boats. Growth is also a choice. Today, one of the most effective paths to growth is the always-evolving online marketing world. I'm honoured to be your guide on this journey. Let's get started.

1

THE BASICS

Mastering the basics of any discipline is key to success.* In general, the most effective business marketing to clients we do at my day job is when we get them to adopt the basic best practices they are not already using. For example, one of our most successful suggestions has been that the creative must match the channel: if a business is showing an ad in one of our video channels, we tell them to not just make a video, but also shoot it in the orientation the viewer has their phone and include music like the videos before and after it. (Such marketing has provided Meta with extra revenue during my time as CMO.) The truth is, in my experience, no business is perfect at implementing the basic best practices.

In fact, as I wrote the chapters you are about to read, I repeatedly kicked myself as I thought of examples where my teams and I were not getting the basics right. Implementing best practices across a thousand people is hard, and if we were to do everything outlined in this part of the book alone, we'd get materially better at what we do. Throughout my career, every time I have zoomed in from high-level strategy and grounded myself in the basics, two great things have always taken place: I've delivered better results with my team, and I've found inspiration that has helped me move that larger strategy forward. The basics matter – do them well and they will reward you at any scale.

* At times, this book refers to, discusses or suggests data tracking, collection and use, which should always be read and understood to be in the context of companies working with their lawyers, legal and compliance departments to ensure that all such practices comply with all applicable laws and regulations. This book reflects the author's personal views and experiences and not those of any company.

The most basic advice is to be clear on your goal and how you will measure if you have achieved it. Note, goals are not metrics – metrics describe goals. After identifying your goal, ask, what marketing do you need to achieve that goal? Start with the marketing funnel: are enough relevant people even aware your product or company exists? If they are, then work through to getting them to take action, and understand why they haven't previously.

Once you have diagnosed what you are trying to do, how you'll measure it and where in the funnel you have issues, I will dive into details on how to practically implement your measurement. Doing so allows you to drive incremental results, optimize your conversion flow, target the people you want to convert and then show them digital marketing that will make them convert in the right channel, with the right message, at the right time.

1. THE NORTH STAR

Great growth requires great marketing, and great marketing requires clarity on what you are trying to achieve – the main goal at hand. I refer to this goal as a North Star, a clear, bright navigational aid that everyone on the team can see and work towards. This means that a goal, and a metric to measure progress towards that goal, are both essential. You, your team and your entire organization need to be aligned on that North Star. It could be as simple as 'maximize income' or as high-minded as 'connect the world online' (Facebook's goal when I began there in 2007). If done right, the North Star will be ambitious and clarifying.

NORTH STAR METRICS

The greatest threat to your North Star is your number two goal. This second goal is often a good thing to work on – it might even be *better* than the North Star. But flipping back and forth between the North Star and your second goal means you are splitting resources, probably competing internally and failing at both. Unfortunately, it can be hard to maintain the disciplined leadership to make sure your people and teams use the North Star to question everything they do and that their actions align with that ultimate goal. Great goals have real tradeoffs, and as my former colleague Deb Liu likes to say, 'It isn't prioritization if it doesn't hurt.'

When a North Star is complex, detail matters. 'Connect the world online' is a wonderful North Star, but break it down and questions arise. For example, are these online users registered users or are they monthly, weekly or daily active users? Does 'the world' mean only current online users, or does this imply expanding the internet? What even defines 'active' to begin with – a logged-in visit, a post, a like? The metric to gauge success must also be crystal clear. For example, the goal for revenue might be 'annual revenue' or 'annual free cash flow' or 'annual EBITDA (earnings before interest, taxes, depreciation and amortization)'. Or the metric could be quarterly, not annual, or a five-year plan.

The metric for Facebook was monthly active users (MAU). A user was considered 'monthly active' if they had logged into the service at least once in the last thirty days. Revenue must be in service of driving that goal. And that meant revenue couldn't be made in a way that reduced MAU by, for example, running paid ads that annoyed users so much they stopped using the site. This settled a lot of disagreements on how to make money.

That's one of the most inspired ideas Mark Zuckerberg had in the early days of Facebook. He made it clear that MAU would serve the North Star goal of connecting the world online. This North Star has continued to inform the company and its culture; it is fundamental to our entire marketing philosophy, from how we plan campaigns to how we attract new users across platforms. But, at the time we formed it, there was no guarantee it would work and many investors and talking heads thought the top focus should be revenue. Of course, they were wrong.

CONNECTING THE WORLD ONLINE

Shortly before I joined Facebook, the company almost sold to Yahoo! At that point Mark's leadership team were very keen on the exit, but Mark determined they would not sell. His goal was to connect the world through social media – and he believed the best way to do this was as an independent company – not to quickly exit and become wealthy. This plan was not universally popular, and many executives left. I joined in the aftermath of this shakeup as a naive man in my early twenties; I thought it was obvious Facebook was awesome and would be used by the whole world, so it would be absolutely foolish to sell.

I now see that this decision involved a difficult tradeoff. There was no guarantee Facebook would make money from an, as yet, unproven business model. Typically, the goal of a startup is to grow, sell and make investors, employees and founders rich. Today, twenty years on, it feels natural that a mission-oriented business could work, and that Facebook would be huge and valuable, but at that time it was a bold bet. Coming out of that moment, though, I entered a company that had a North Star goal that was forged in fire.

Not only was the North Star clear, so was the metric that measured it. As mentioned, this metric was MAU, and though that may seem standard now, it was unusual at the time. Most people then quoted registered users - the number of people signed up for a given platform - to describe their user base. Of course, someone could be registered and not have used the service for months or years, so this was mostly a vanity metric. Mark and Facebook were the first large company that completely did away with that metric for public reporting, and it truly moved the industry forward.

The combination of the goal and metric was extremely clarifying for my and my teams' work, and it settled many arguments without needing to escalate them to Mark for a decision. With less debate and more action, we were able to move faster and get things done quickly. For example, our North Star helped us make decisions about our monetization product that stopped us from making revenue decisions recklessly. At the time, the company needed money - we weren't profitable, so we needed our ad product to succeed. The ads team had lots of ideas on how to do this.

One idea was to try out 'homepage takeovers', which other

social media companies were selling. In a homepage takeover, an ad that could simply not be ignored would appear on the homepage of a site, dominating it entirely. On MySpace, for example, I remember an ad in which the Hulk 'smashed through' the homepage, jumbling up icons and bouncing the text and other features around for a few seconds. These takeovers made the companies a lot of money, but they harmed the user experience, blocking new users on those days from ramping up their usage and connecting with friends. Since that hurt the MAU, this extreme monetization option was proposed and killed without senior review as far as I could tell (and so were hundreds of others). This led to an ad system that has little tax on user engagement and, indeed, for many users, is a positive.

MOVE FAST AND STAY ALIGNED

The other reason the MAU metric was so clarifying was that many colleagues felt you couldn't be counted as an active user if you only visited the site once a month. They felt only daily active users (DAU) was a valid way of counting actives. There is some merit to this idea, but I disagreed overall, as I still do. DAU is more a measure of usage and engagement, while MAU is a measure of people using your service. MAU is the skin in the game that gives you an option to upsell someone to use your service more heavily. With DAU, you have already won most of the battle in getting someone ramped up to be fully engaged with your service.

The way we worked, and how most companies I've advised work, is that we designed the product for ourselves and we became power users. This gave us insights that we likely wouldn't have had otherwise. Take notification defaults. We found that notification defaults set for someone who engaged with the site throughout the day would have to be different than for someone who only visited once a day, or who was just starting to use the site.

The notification experience is very different between those two sets. If you are just ramping up on using a service, you want to know everything that's happening. The notification for the first ever like you receive, for example, is a deeply meaningful experience. If on the other hand you have made a post on which you got a thousand likes, you really want to mute those notifications, or your phone will be unusable. A focus on MAU forced us to confront the marginal user who did not use our products like we did, and they still provide a counterbalance to this day on such decisions.

One caveat: the MAU metric could, of course, be abused. We could count a single click on an email as 'being active', and in response, send loads of emails that get one click from the recipients, but that delivers nothing for us in the long term. Sure, it might look good in the short term for MAU, but in the long run you are not adding actual value. Still, I have seen approaches like this done in various companies and teams both deliberately to game a metric and accidentally from inexperienced folks. So, we did have a metric to act as a guardrail too, which was to take into account the percentage of MAU who were *weekly* active. This consideration helped us to stop acquiring low-quality or low-engaged MAU, deliberately or not. (I discuss guardrail metrics in more detail in Chapter 7 on measurement.)

With a clear North Star of connecting the world and a simple metric that properly described it with MAU, we were able to move fast and stay aligned with what our leadership wanted us to deliver, without endless meetings, reviews and escalations. This approach doesn't just apply to those teams and companies involved in digital marketing – it's important for everyone. Do the work to develop a clear North Star goal and metric to describe it and you set yourself up for success in everything that follows.

2. THE MARKETING FUNNEL

The marketing funnel is an old concept – but far from outdated. The original idea is widely attributed to Elias St Elmo Lewis who created the 'AIDA' model – Awareness, Intention, Decision, Action – right around the turn of the twentieth century. In time, the model would develop into a funnel, with awareness at the top and each subsequent stage moving 'down' the funnel. There are many different versions of the funnel out there, but I especially like the original. I see it as a description of where your target audience is overall, as compared to a tool for understanding any individual person.

I use the funnel to think about the right campaign at the right time in your company's, product's or service's existence. For example, if someone is not aware of your product, you probably shouldn't be focusing on convincing them that the price point is right. Rather, you should be making them aware of your product as an option that exists and that would be useful for them. Now, there is debate about the funnel – marketing folks argue how much it is actually used in decision making, how effective a model it truly is and which version is the best. In my opinion, the AIDA version is an excellent, accessible way to help plan campaigns and is foundational in understanding marketing as a whole, and digital marketing in particular.

THE AIDA MODEL

My personal favourite version of the funnel, shown below, is a mildly modified version of Elias St Elmo Lewis's AIDA: 'awareness' to 'intention' to 'decision' to 'action', with a loop of 'word of mouth' – if you give people a great experience, they will talk about it and promote it.

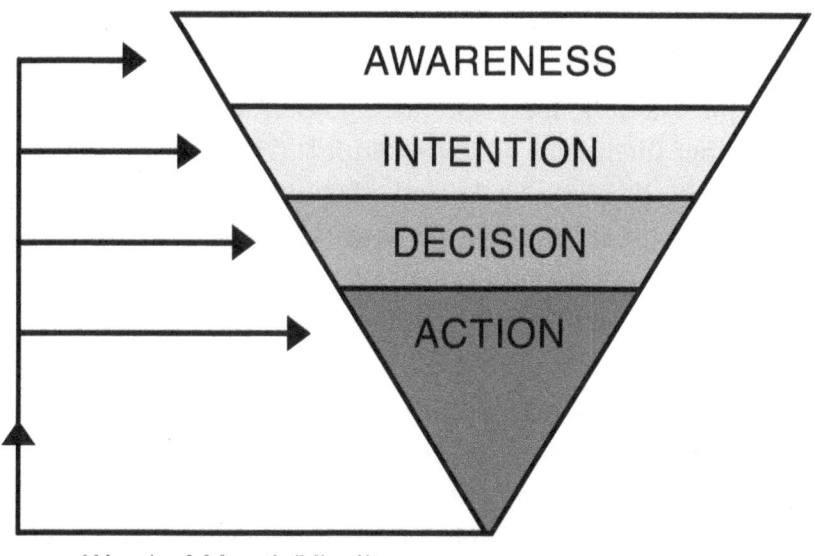

Word of Mouth/Virality

The marketing funnel

- **Awareness**: Do people know you have a product or service they might want to use?
- **Intention**: Do they have a desire, or intention, to use your product?
- **Decision**: Are they over the hump in their desire and intention and do they just need to find the time to convert desire into action?
- **Action**: Did they take the action you wanted?

- **Word of mouth/Virality**: Did they tell people about your product, whether positively or negatively? This aspect impacts each level above it.

Some marketers believe 'awareness' to 'consideration' to 'conversion' to 'loyalty' better reflects the customer journey. Others, including many members of my team, are fans of throwing 'preference' in the mix. But I stand by AIDA, with the word-of-mouth loop.

Regardless of which version you prefer, you need to remember that humans don't necessarily follow the stages of the funnel in perfect sequence. They move forwards and backwards. They may, for example, forget products and services exist, only to remember them later on. (*How Brands Grow: What Marketers Don't Know* by Byron Sharp and other books in the series cover the topic in great detail.) Humans are imperfect and unpredictable, and so are models of their individual behaviour. As large groups, however, they can be quite predictable in useful ways.

Humanity generally responds well to being modelled in this way. Having a mental model of how the masses, or just a large group of people you're targeting, might behave as a whole is super-valuable for producing the right campaign at the right time in the existence of your product. I often use the model to set marketing strategy and advocate for the work I want to do. For example, in 2025 we need to promote awareness for RayBan Meta glasses in the US – less than half of Americans know they exist, but when they are made aware of the product, their likelihood of buying them goes up dramatically.

Instagram in the US, however, has a different issue for non-users. Awareness in the US is close to 100 percent, but amongst non-users the intention to use the app is low. So our marketing needs to focus on convincing people who don't use Instagram that there's a good reason for them to start using it. This simple approach clearly steers our work, and it can be relevant to your offerings, whether building awareness in one small town or marketing a new or existing product globally.

Different stages of the funnel will become more important at different stages of a company's life cycle. For example, when we were growing WhatsApp in the USA in 2024, we had an awareness issue. Maybe half of people in the US were aware of the app, whereas just about everyone in the US was aware of Facebook. Today, Facebook has a consideration issue, among people who don't use it, but not an awareness issue. As a result, we take different approaches for each of those brands to drive growth.

POOL SIZE

The funnel should first be used to evaluate the size of the pool at each of the four stages, or levels. This evaluation allows you to know which level has the most opportunity for growth. With that in mind, let's think about each one in turn, and what it implies for a marketing campaign:

- **Awareness** – When introducing people to your product, you want to create a simple message, then run it in whichever channels overlap best with your target audience. For example, for WhatsApp in the USA, our message was that the app is a more private alternative to iMessage that allows you to send messages easily across devices. We ran that message everywhere, from television ads to ads in our other products.

- **Intention** – Here you get a bit more pointed, amplifying the problem you are solving for the consumers you are trying to attract. When you understand and speak to their pain points or provide them with a benefit they're looking for, you can create a desire for your product. For

WhatsApp in the USA, we also ran ads that emphasized the problem of interoperability across iOS and Android devices and how WhatsApp solved that issue.

- **Decision** – Once you have people considering your product but they haven't yet decided, you need to help push them over that hump. This is where price point, for example, could play a major role. Ads for RayBan Meta glasses noting that they start at $299 are likely to help those potential customers who are through the awareness and intention levels to now reach a decision. We run those ads more online and use more direct response-heavy channels here, as well as in store merchandising.

- **Action** – Getting potential buyers to this level is a result of direct response campaigns with clear 'buy now', 'register now' or similar calls to action. These ads should be run as close as possible to the 'place' the person will take action. For example, if we want someone to import contact information to find their friends currently using the product, we will promote that function inside our apps when a new user registers, a point at which they are likely thinking about adding friends or seeing who else they know currently uses the product.

A famous example of understanding your pool size is found in GoDaddy, who knew they had only a small pool of people aware of domain name hosting as a business. They singlehandedly grew the internet domain selling and hosting industry through their annual Super Bowl ads. In fact, they were so effective, the rest of the industry barely bothered with the awareness level at the top of the funnel. As the industry leader of domain registry and hosting, GoDaddy had increased the size of the awareness pool, not just for them, but for the whole industry.

This growth led the rest of the players to focus on winning customers at the bottom of the funnel. Because the pool of customers who now wanted a domain name was so large, all the other domain registry companies could succeed by just competing with GoDaddy further down the funnel at the action stage, where many of the customers, mostly small businesses, were researching the best deal before purchasing.

But that initial awareness was key because once people understood domain registry and hosting as a service they could easily purchase, they were quickly converted through the rest of the funnel. Awareness led immediately to intention for small business owners – they could see how important a web presence would be to future business.

What became the campaigning ground amongst GoDaddy's competitors was getting potential customers to consider them at the decision level and then get them to take action. They did this by buying ads in places where customers were doing their research on web hosting and domains. Unsurprisingly, a lot of this research took place online, so GoDaddy's competitors placed ads in search results and on websites where people would go to look into the best available tools. At the decision and action stages the ads focused – and still do – on comparative features available, such as more storage space for files, and price point, including starting discounts.

There are well-known companies in various industries for whom awareness is not an issue. Take car companies. Mercedes have huge awareness, but they still need to convince the next car buyer why they should buy them over Audi or BMW. This means their marketing is generally focused further down the funnel as well. Still, understanding how to move people all the way down the funnel – from awareness to action – remains important for any business.

MOVING DOWN THE FUNNEL

Imagine running a small hotel on the coast of England in a holiday destination like North Norfolk. As the summer holidays approach, lots of people are in the market for a seaside getaway. Pretty much everyone is aware they could take a holiday in the UK, but do they know about North Norfolk (or when they hear 'Norfolk' do they think Norfolk, VA in the States)? And if they do, are they aware of your hotel?

You could try to move the people aware of the holiday region down the funnel into action by working on top-of-funnel marketing and PR. To be honest, though, that's a huge uphill struggle for any small hotel on its own. Instead, you should start with building a broader *awareness* about the area. This may mean banding together with the local tourist industry or local government and trade organizations to create a campaign like 'Visit Norfolk'. These collective efforts can help move prospective visitors down the funnel – individual players likely cannot.

Once you've created awareness about the region, you can then focus on selling a stay at your hotel, not just a stay in Norfolk. This means moving people further down the funnel towards intention and decision. For example, maybe a group of people have stumbled across your hotel on Booking.com or through a Google search, or maybe they have stayed with you before and you have their email addresses or WhatsApp details. Now you want to get them to seriously consider you for their holiday.

To do so, you might promote reviews of your hotel to this group. This can be done through a few routes. For example, you could email your existing customer list or message them through WhatsApp to remind them of your existence and highlight the best reviews you've received. You could also buy ads on Google, to ensure your hotel comes up in various online searches, and on Expedia, Booking.com and any other travel sites you are listed on. These ads could start tailored for people searching for your small geographic area at first, in this case North Norfolk, and gradually expand the geographic region until you get a large enough volume of customers. You could also post testimonials that are fun, interesting and compelling on social media, perhaps even walk-throughs, capitalizing on the latest viral craze, and then boost them as promoted posts.

After intention and decision, those people on the cusp of booking a hotel in North Norfolk for vacation are reaching the demand fulfilment stage, moving from decision to action. Now you want to be right there when they make the purchase, so the conversion is with you and not with the hotel down the street. Here, you focus on big, direct response calls to action, such as providing a discount if they book now. This can take place within whatever platforms you use for booking, such as your listing page on Booking.com, or when you are messaging with them on WhatsApp following your earlier outreach campaign.

It doesn't matter if you are a massive company with four billion people using your services or a bed and breakfast in North Norfolk with twelve rooms to fill – the principle is the same, and the funnel works. Once your potential customer takes action and becomes an actual customer, the experience you provide will generate the word-of-mouth buzz you'll want to achieve. You can only get to that point once you've directed them through the funnel.

STAY FOCUSED AND SAVE MONEY

Where people are in the funnel will inform everything from your channels to your creative to your landing pages. Done smartly, your targeting will hand people off through a user journey as you see their behaviours evolve. When users are at specific points in the funnel, you will often use the same channels but in different ways. For example, you wouldn't target someone who is only at the awareness level of the funnel with a display ad offering a 'book now' discount. That would be the wrong message and unlikely to spur action. But you might serve them up a 'visit Norfolk' ad. They first need to get down that funnel, where they are right on the cusp of buying, before a call to action will be effective.

The funnel is a great model, and it should be used by businesses of all sizes as they consider what marketing campaigns they need to run. Practically, you can do this by:

1. **Researching your funnel**. As an SMB, this research will mostly take place by talking to people around the town and following your gut. As a larger company, this involves running surveys or commissioning research from a reputable provider to understand the amount of people at each level in the funnel.

2. **Applying logic to think through where you have opportunity**. Identify where there are big decreases in numbers between levels in the funnel and adjust your focus accordingly.

3. **Planning out some campaigns based on the suggestions in this chapter**. Start wherever you feel most comfortable and apply the lessons that work best for your business.

4. **Running the campaigns**. Then iterate based on the results!

I'll be the first to admit that the funnel is far from perfect; a model that perfectly captures all human behaviour is a nirvana or holy grail no one has ever, or will ever, achieve. But you can always strive to be a little closer to perfection, and when used properly, the funnel will save you time, money and effort by making sure you remain focused on what matters the most to your business at any given stage.

3. CONVERSION – UNDERSTAND IT, LOG IT, OPTIMIZE IT

All marketing is about selling, whether you take a long view of building brand awareness at the top of the funnel or a short-term focus on driving the bottom of the funnel. This principle has been true as long as marketing has existed. In short, you have to get results. If you are doing online, direct response marketing, like the type described throughout this book, you want people to take an action on your site or app. In the parlance of the field, you want them to 'convert'. Conversion is the 'action' at the bottom of the marketing funnel, when the prospective customer has purchased the product or service you are selling and become a true customer.

As the tools for selling have changed, for most online marketing you will want to drive someone to fill out some online form to convert. This form may be as simple as providing their email, phone number and password or as complicated as a full insurance contract. In this contemporary context, conversion can be defined in several ways, but purchases, installs, registrations and leads are four of the most common I deal with. For example, if you are Amazon.com, conversion may mean selling this book (please!), or for a travel site like Booking.com or Expedia.com, it could mean getting someone to book a stay. For a game developer or social media company, conversion might take place when someone downloads the app (install) and creates an account (registration). Last, for an auto dealership, scheduling a test drive with the customer may be considered a conversion. Subsequently, the customer could be fully converted offline.

The heart of conversion comes down to two main factors, which are covered throughout this chapter: first, you must correctly track your conversions, both technically and logically, to ensure you are achieving your North Star goal and moving your metric. Second, it's imperative to learn how to perform 'conversion rate optimization' (CRO), increasing the percentage of people who convert to the action you want them to take.

Before I start any campaign, I make sure I:

1. Know what the conversion is we are supposed to drive.

2. Ensure the conversion is thoroughly logged with all the data we need, meaning it can be tracked and recorded by the marketing technology as we make progress.

3. Use that logging to understand the conversion flow.

4. Come to an opinion if the funnel itself needs improvement.

Without these four steps, everything fails; you can do the most magnificently effective marketing but if the conversion step of the marketing funnel is broken it will all be worthless. Mediocre marketing with a great conversion flow is way better than brilliant marketing with a broken one. Still, it can be tricky - the conversions you need to optimize to drive the biggest results are typically not as simple as they first appear.

GET THE ACCOUNTING RIGHT

The first step before I start any campaign - know what the conversion is we are supposed to drive - sounds so simple that, reading that step above, you may have thought I was, well, a dummy. The fact is, though this always feels simple, it's usually far from it. For example, if you are trying to grow MAU for Facebook as your North Star, then you just drive registrations, right? Throughout my career, thoughts like this one have tripped me up. Here's an example of why.

In 2008 Danny Ferrante, who as of 2025 leads core data science and user research for Meta, introduced the concept of growth accounting to Facebook. I had not previously had any experience with growth accounting, either at eBay or at the various companies I consulted with, before, and during my time at Facebook. (Today, the concept is widely used, but at the time it wasn't, and I'm grateful to Danny for making me see the world in a new way.) Growth accounting is a method of analysing how specific factors affect growth. To utilize this method at Facebook, we had to first define three metrics:

1. **Acquisition** – Newly acquired monthly active users.

2. **Churned users** – Users who were last active thirty-one days ago, so not monthly active (the industry standard is to define a month as thirty days, which is irritating since some people only use a service on weekends or weekdays, so a multiple of seven would really help).

3. **Resurrected users** – Users who were active today but were counted as inactive users yesterday, meaning they had not been active in the previous thirty days.

We then created the following accounting equation:

+ Acquisitions
- Churn
+ Resurrections
= Net Growth

Before we landed on this equation, we had thought that we only had to focus on acquisitions and churn, creating an equation that did not include resurrections (acquisitions – churn = net growth). But what we found was that churn and resurrections *dwarfed* acquisition; they were both double the size of acquisition in absolute numbers.

That meant that if we had a 1 percent impact on each row of the equation, the impacts of a 1 percent improvement in churn or resurrection were twice as big as a 1 percent impact on acquisitions. This created a totally different context for us surrounding our conversion events, which we had previously focused on acquiring new users by driving registration. Since our goal was to drive net growth, our conversion event could no longer focus solely on acquisition – our growth accounting equation showed that we had to think far harder about churn prevention and resurrection of inactive accounts.

Getting this accounting right changed our understanding of what our most important conversion events were for our North Star goal and metric. For growing Facebook, and any product I have worked on with an active user base, the answer wasn't (and still isn't) as simple as 'drive registrations' as the conversion event. Without taking the time to understand the actual conversion we were supposed to drive, we would have missed a major piece of the puzzle and growth would have been way lower, or we could have even declined.

HAVE YOU DEFINED YOUR CONVERSION CORRECTLY?

So, we have selected that acquisition and resurrection are the most important conversion actions to track for MAU in this example (note, churn isn't a conversion action; it is the absence of actions, as you reverse it through getting a resurrection). The next question is: are you defining those actions correctly? The fact of the matter is that not all conversions are equal. Some leads are more likely to convert to sales than others. Some registrations are more likely to retain and have a higher lifetime value. You can, of course, just stick at defining a conversion at the highest level, but if you dig a little deeper, you will find that a small amount of work can make the conversions you are optimizing for way more valuable. I learned this lesson earlier in my career while working on affiliate marketing at eBay. The company had, understandably, started with the simplest answer to defining conversion, but as we got more advanced and understood our craft better, we realized there was a better one.

When I first worked as an affiliate for eBay, they were tracking registered users and confirmed registered users (CRUs). A CRU was someone who had registered and then confirmed their email address. Just as I joined eBay they switched to activated confirmed registered users (ACRUs). These were users who had registered, confirmed and bid on an item, bought an item or posted one for sale. This was a brilliant move by eBay and, at the time, ground-breaking. It gave them the right conversions, ones that activated and solidified the right incentives for affiliates by paying them for users who activated. I got to watch them make this change as an affiliate and then observed the positive benefits by joining as an employee. One result of this change was the volume of CRUs began decreasing when we started optimizing for ACRUs.

This decline happened for a few reasons, but there were two big ones in particular. First, we saw a large set of affiliates stop working with us who were driving CRUs with a low activation rate to ACRUs. Second, we changed our landing pages for when users were searching for an item from the registration form – which maximized conversion to CRUs – to the search results page for whatever they were searching for. This included creating many new tools and publishing best practices for affiliates doing search, encouraging them to link to dynamic landing pages related to search queries. Doing so maximized users' likelihood of completing an action and hence becoming an ACRU (discussed further in depth later in this chapter). Shifting from just confirmed registrations to activated confirmed registrations altered our channel strategy and our landing page strategy, and the new approach drove much better results.

Another great example of why focusing on the right conversion, and not just the 'first-glance' simple conversion, can be found in how Facebook dealt with contact importers. In Facebook's early days, to grow our user base, we needed people to import their email address books and then send invites to their friends to join. It seemed easy for the team working on this project to get contacts imported and invites sent, but it turned out there were a lot more steps between sending an invite and landing an active registered user.

To understand these steps the team had to track which users began using the platform after clicking on an invite. This enabled the team to understand the full conversion process, tracking the metrics they aimed to drive and using the right tools to know how they were progressing. Overall, the team had to change their behaviours to focus on what happened after an invite was sent, and whether a conversion took place or not. For example, at that time, a material number of invites were timing out, not sending and being lost. In response, the team built logging, storage and retries to make sure the invites were sent and received. When they had only focused on sending invites, and the registration team had only looked at converting registrations, these issues had been overlooked.

Time and time again, I have found that deep consideration reveals what to optimize at every step in the user journey and causes people to focus on what matters most towards the end goal. For example, you don't want registrations, you want registrations that lead to active users who stick around and have a high lifetime value. You don't want contacts imported, you want people to register from the invites sent to them. You don't want weak leads, you want leads with potential.

In most cases online, it is possible to make your conversion event the actual action you want to take place. This is a key part of the basics, because your success and growth are built on the foundations of defining your conversion event. From there, you must track the right metrics because every subsequent optimization will amplify your decision, good or bad.

HAVE YOU LOGGED THE CONVERSION CORRECTLY?

After defining your conversion, the next step is to properly and thoroughly log the data. Again, this may seem ridiculously basic – I even hesitated to include it here – but correctly logging the conversion will save you countless headaches. Not correctly doing so has caused more fundamental problems in my career than any clever ideas have ever given me benefits. So please, heed my warning.

Before Facebook went public, we tracked active users primarily through server-side logging. For the web, this was essentially the same as the client side in all cases, no major discrepancies. As mobile apps grew, however, a pernicious logging issue developed where the app would pre-fetch data, so it was ready to start at a moment's notice. Specifically, this 'pre-fetching' primed the app each day by requesting certain data, such as the first few news feed stories or notifications that would load, so there would only be a tiny time gap between the moment users opened the app and the first interactions they had with the platform.

This feature was great for user experience, but when we checked server-side user counts (the number of users we thought were interacting with the app based on calls to the Facebook servers) against client-side user counts, we found a greater than 10 percent discrepancy. With client-side counts, we only logged actions an actual person took in our app (on the client side) and sent that data separately to the server. We were diligent with this metric as it was to be our core reported user metric when we went public. The reason for this elevation in the metric is that the team that implemented pre-fetching was not aware they were calling code that previously was used to log if a user was active because it had to be triggered by a user action. So when that code was called, even though now it didn't require a user action, we logged that the user had been active that day.

As a result, we created a list of actions that could be considered active and only counted users as active if they performed them. Then we also kept both channels of logging (server and client) live and monitored for discrepancies. We then investigated any substantial change in those discrepancies in case any new logging bugs were added to one channel or the other. Active users – monthly or daily – was our longest-used and most important metric and yet, even four years into working on it, I learned there was a double-digit issue in the number, which we then had to fix.

This issue illustrates two key points. First, if you want to track active users as your conversion event, you need to make sure your logging is actually tracking something triggered by a human action and not an app calling code on the server automatically. Second, you should always try to have two independent paths of logging on critical metrics; I have carried this tenet through into so much work, and often the second path is just sampled logging, a logging method that helps support your main path through logging only a certain portion of activity.

For example, for video ads, we count those users who view an ad longer than three seconds as a three-second video view (a standard industry metric). For this metric we have one path of logging that logs only the frame after three seconds. This main path saves resources by logging a tiny fraction of all frames. We then have a second path of logging, the sample logging, that for one view in, say, 10,000 logs every frame. This is then compared to the standard path of logging to see if there is any unexpected difference detected. If there is, we take actions to get rid of that difference and ensure we are tracking this conversion event (viewing a video for three seconds) correctly.

When the purchase of a product or service is the conversion event, a common issue arises in logging sales revenue without accounting for chargebacks. A chargeback is when someone reverses a charge on their credit card after a purchase has been made. This can be due to a bad retail experience, an honest mistake, directly nefarious behaviour or, of course, a stolen credit card.

Logging purchases without chargebacks has come up repeatedly in my career. I first encountered this problem at eBay in 2005 when an affiliate marketer encouraged thousands of users to do chargebacks, causing us to realize this was an issue we needed to care about. Still, the problem persists in my work. In fact, in 2024, while working on our e-commerce site selling Quest headsets directly, we made a mistake by not tracking the conversions of chargebacks. They gradually grew to such an extent our entire judgement of return on investment (ROI) was wrong.

As you can see, twenty years into my journey I'm still leading teams that make the same mistakes from time to time. The main point I want to stress, though, aside from the fact that mistakes happen, is to just care about logging the conversion correctly. Try to get it right and check in on the tracking periodically. And please, don't be daunted. Getting the tracking right is a critical step in getting the basics right, and once you have it down, everything that comes after will be that much easier.

UNDERSTAND YOUR WHOLE CONVERSION FLOW

After recognizing the conversions to track and how to log them successfully, you must understand the flow to making the conversion happen, including every step in that conversion journey. When you are at the action step of the AIDA marketing funnel, you want to make sure nothing gets in the user's way from taking the conversion action. This can only be done if you know how they got there, and how you can help get them to convert.

At Facebook, we were very lucky, again, to work with Danny Ferrante, who ensured we had detailed logging throughout any conversion flow, and who built a system to help everyone else at Meta to do it. For example, the conversion flow for converting an inactive user to an active user through email marketing could look like this:

1. An action is performed for which you wish to notify the inactive user.
2. Action is logged.
3. Action is extracted and transferred to the marketing database.
4. Email is generated.
5. Email is sent to mail transfer agent (MTA), the program that sends the emails.
6. Mail transfer agent attempts to send email and succeeds or fails.

7. Email is opened.
8. Email is clicked.
9. User lands on landing page.
10. User logs in, driving a conversion and becoming an active user.

It's important to include this level of detail, even it seems like overkill. Otherwise, you will miss something important.

As discussed, when we first put this logging in place, we found that there was a huge drop-off between step 4 and step 5, even though it should have been small at that stage. We went to investigate. The issue was quite technical, and all this work was done with product managers and engineers who helped explain to me what was going on at each stage. It pays to listen: I came in with a basic understanding of code and left with a detailed understanding of how our invites system worked.

What we found was that these invites were being sent to the asynchronous tier, a part of our infrastructure that executed actions that did not have to happen at the exact instant they were triggered. In other words, they could happen with a delay. In this case, the invites were queued up so they could be sent over time, since they weren't required to happen instantly. This allowed the large workload of sending millions of invites to happen more smoothly over a day, as compared to instantaneously. This delay gave our infrastructure some breathing room so our systems could work at the average load instead of having to be built up to work at the peak load, which would be taxing on the infrastructure. This approach also meant we would need fewer machines; it was cheaper and a good business decision too.

The issue, however, was that invites were held only in temporary memory and not in permanent memory. This asynchronous tier was low priority and would encounter an error that forced it to restart – in other words, crash – more frequently than other tiers.

As a result, the messages that were trying to be sent were never transferred to the MTA, and hence never sent.

We got a great boost in the effectiveness of our invites (tens of percents) when we found and fixed that issue. This was done by creating a permanent database, logging when a send had succeeded and just working through that invite list in order, with absolutely no need to know if there was a system crash or not. This goes to show how important the details are, and why it's necessary to be specific in your conversion flow steps. Write them down, share them with the team and follow them closely. A truly great digital direct response marketer cares about the details and fights for every inch when trying to get conversion. Understanding the whole conversion flow is part and parcel of winning that fight.

REDUCE FRICTION WHEREVER YOU CAN

Once all the back end, infrastructural and tracking components of conversion are in place, you must make sure the user-facing component is as good as possible. This whole approach to conversion can be summarized as: the journey from click to conversion should be as short as possible but no shorter. To do this you need to answer the following two questions:

1. What is the page the user should land on, when sent to your site?
2. How hard is it for them to complete the actions they wanted to do on that page?

In other words, what does the person you are trying to get to convert see and how can you optimize the experience?

First and foremost, consider what the user will see when they arrive at your landing page. As mentioned, at eBay, with CRUs, as an affiliate I remember the best landing page was always the registration form. I tried every other landing page going but could never beat the registration form for getting people to register and convert. When eBay switched to ACRUs, the landing page that won for paid search became the e-commerce search result page. If a person searched for 'electric kettle', it was important they saw electric kettles so they could decide to bid for or 'Buy it now' and actually activate – not just register and confirm, which as CRUs was all they had previously done.

Switching the landing page dropped CRU conversions but drove up ACRU conversions. Weirdly, at Facebook, we saw quite the reverse. We tried the same approach of landing people on search result pages when they searched for people's names on Google, helping them to directly find those people on Facebook. This always underperformed landing on the registration page for long-term monthly active users.

I believe two factors led to this difference. First, users couldn't find the actual 'Joe Smith' they were looking for in public search, whereas on eBay they easily found generic listings that perfectly matched their search for 'Hotpoint washing machine' or similar. So while the eBay search landing page reduced friction, Meta's increased it. Second, Facebook's new user experience (NUX) was itself a lower-friction way to find friends than using our search function. Users were more likely to find friends via contact importing or pending friend requests from people who had invited them to join.

As you can see, choosing the right metric for your business matters for determining the landing page in your conversion flow, as does your specific business and new user experience. There are rules of thumb, but the most important one is to log and test to find out what works for *you*. The answer was completely different for the two different internet giants I worked for, even when both optimized for active users.

Another place to reduce friction in regard to the landing page is to ensure it is easy for users to do what they want on that landing page. Just shortening forms and making the experience simpler is super-important. Shorter forms tend to have higher conversion rates. This is received wisdom at this point, but forms still tend to end up too long. To get them down to size, you must shorten the conversion flow. Often, the best way to do so results from fundamentally creative, generative thinking.

For example, looking at every new channel and tool as an opportunity is key here. Computer technology is always breaking new ground and doing new things we never thought possible. With that in mind, here are some examples of creative approaches that might help start you in the right direction towards a shorter form and simplified conversion flow:

- Can you confirm an email address at the same moment as you contact-import? Someone has just proven to you they own the email and password – why do it twice? If someone has just authorized that they own the email address through the Hotmail API, for example, then there's no need to send them an email to have them confirm. (An API is an application programming interface, which is a way for computer programs to talk to each other.)

- Can you have someone type a message reply inside the notification they receive, completely removing a click and an app launch, thereby reducing friction? Today, Meta does this with the WhatsApp notifications in Windows on desktop, cutting a whole step from the conversion flow and improving message sends.

- Can you get the conversion action inside the creative itself? At Facebook, when we promoted contact importers, for example, we put the authorization into the banner ad rather than having users click through to a landing page first. This gave us a massive increase in conversion rate. Gmail, Yahoo! and Hotmail allowed you to do something similar, using a button to call their API. Other providers used their login fields with usernames and passwords.

- Can you buy an ad where the conversion form is in the ad or on the third-party site, not even on your own? We loved this idea so much that we created ad types where the whole conversion happens at once. For example, 'lead gen ads' allow you to buy an ad where the consumer fills out the form to become a lead for a product by clicking a submit button in the ad – that's the entire form. Similarly, with our click-to-messaging ads, the conversion action is to send a message that's one click from the ad to starting a message thread, an approach often used for commerce in South-East Asia.

These are not the only ways to be creative in this area, of course, just examples of useful approaches that will hopefully inspire you as you brainstorm your conversion flows and how you can make them shorter.

Other times, though, the ability, or inability, to create shorter forms and conversion flows is not about creativity. For example, forms may end up too long as teams with competing goals try to use the same form to make progress, even if the impact is marginal improvements for one team and completely fundamental to the success of another.

At every company I have advised, consulted with or worked at, multiple teams try to co-opt the registration or new user flow to some extent. And at any company, all these teams are well intentioned. They might have a goal to drive up buyer feedback to increase trust on the platform. Or they might have a goal to get a profile completed so search will work better. Or maybe their aim is a higher resolution picture upload so items will be sold at a higher rate. Each of these is a noble goal, but if you don't have clarity of priority order, and which one has true primacy, you will get a form or flow designed by committee and politics that will be mediocre at best.

PRIORITIZE AND SIMPLIFY

Pick a primary goal far down the funnel that is hard to argue with. Then be ruthless at holding that goal, only adding elements to the conversion flow that don't hurt the primary goal. Measure this with a randomized controlled experiment, then maintain a holdout (a group of users who don't get the new add-on) to make sure there is no regression.

Periodically, you also need to just revisit the whole conversion flow and make sure a company priority that is no longer relevant isn't just hanging out in there. I've seen this at every large company I've been involved with, as have all of my colleagues at other companies. For example, Google surely worsened conversion flow when they introduced Google+ into every flow in the company, or recently inserted Google Meet into every calendar invite. Even if these moves were meant to fulfil a strategic priority, at some point they likely needed to be cleaned up or removed when those projects failed or were deprioritized.

As you work to improve conversion, though, note that despite explaining in detail the benefits of a shorter form, it must be said that shorter isn't always better. You can be too short. The brilliant Brian Hale, who now runs growth at DoorDash and was my right hand on product growth for over a decade, led a team to discover this for our simple 'boost as an ad' feature, where you could pay to turn a post into an ad with one click.

Adding in more advanced targeting options in that purchase flow added a lot of pixels and lengthened the process meaningfully, but it also drove up conversions and revenue. Optimize, shorten and reduce friction for sure, but remember, just as with conversion overall, a form should be as short as possible, but no shorter.

4. TARGETING – HOW DO WE TARGET THE PEOPLE WE WANT?

Targeting is the act of getting the right user to see your ad at the right time. This has been the holy grail of marketing for as long as I can remember, exemplified by the mantra 'right user, right ad, right time'. Some folks in the field, whom I deeply respect, feel there shouldn't be such a focus on targeting, but I, respectfully, disagree. My whole career has boiled down to targeting. Whether keyword-based or user-based hasn't mattered. There has always been an edge in online marketing that comes from segmenting the audience. When doing so, you can then show these different segments different ads, emphasizing what is most likely to speak to each group.

Though there are a number of approaches to targeting, they can broadly be broken down into 'behavioural targeting' and 'demographic targeting'. Behavioural targeting beats demographic targeting every day. For example, even with something as basic as geography, there are Americans living in the UK who will buy a product from a US company even if, by nature, the company selling that product has excluded the UK from its targeting. Similarly, targeting based on a demographic like gender is faulty as well. Though it would seem simpler to market men's clothes to men and women's clothes to women, it's also likely to be less effective. There are of course women who buy men's products, either for themselves or as gifts for their spouse or partner, and vice versa, so the simple answer above of just showing women's clothes to women isn't as powerful as behavioural targeting. In the long term, the advantage any company will have over the ad system they buy from – and consequently their competition who are able to buy from the same ad system – is not something simple like demographics. The advantage comes from more proprietary information. Behavioural data tends to fit better with that than demographic data.

Sometimes behavioural targeting is denounced as going too far, but in my work, we have shown time and time again that people prefer more personalized ads that are more relevant to them to the sort of generic ads that work when targeting is taken away. Targeting, when done right, is a win-win-win-win: people get better experiences, companies get better ROI more business is stimulated, growing the economy and providing jobs, and the ad companies make more money to fund building products people love.

TARGETING HAS ALWAYS BEEN A THING

I sometimes see folks, even within the marketing field, act as if targeting is new. But those of us who have come up as internet marketers over the past twenty years need to better understand the history of marketing, and probably the history of technology more generally as well. We need to realize we didn't invent *everything*, despite the great advancements made in our industry since the turn of the twenty-first century. The tools with which we do targeting have changed, and many modern tools are way better than what we had before. Still, this goes back to my first guiding principle: tools evolve, but principles are timeless. Targeting the right ad to the right person at the right time has always been the name of the game, and it will continue to be so, likely until the end of time.

At the most basic level, wherever and whenever you bought an ad in the past was targeting. If you bought an ad in a high-end broadsheet vs a tabloid newspaper, you were targeting, on average, people in different income brackets. If you bought billboards in a football stadium in the 1960s, you were targeting men (it still skews that way today). If you bought a TV ad in a daytime soap opera in the 1990s, you'd mostly be marketing your product to housewives. Take that a step further, and the *Days of Our Lives* viewership would be mostly white housewives, that of telenovelas mostly Latin American, and that of K-Dramas the Korean community. This type of targeting was effective and quite granular, but it had, and still has, a few issues:

1. It is typically just demographic, not behavioural, though there are a few exceptions – gardeners, for example, usually watch gardening programmes, but aren't necessarily a demographic in the strict sense.

2. It is only affordable for large companies or organizations. At best, SMBs could mostly do geo targeting by buying in local papers, but the options were fairly limited.

3. It has significant leakage, meaning you may be targeting all people in Philadelphia with a local radio ad but people on the internet are listening to that station on the other side of the country. Leakage here is people outside your target audience seeing your ad. Cinemas and billboards don't move, but radio and TV can be picked up over long distances.

4. The audiences are too broad, making them inaccurate – plenty of wealthy people bought tabloid magazines, for example, and plenty of non-Latin Americans love telenovelas.

On leakage, my favourite story was working on measuring eBay UK's first TV campaign. The whole team excitedly gathered in a pub in the target geographic area to watch the ad air. The ad break came and went, and no ad was shown. We were all upset and confused. Had we mucked up? Had we been ripped off? It turned out the satellite or cable station through which the pub was showing the channel was downloading the stream from Wales and broadcasting it to the whole UK. We had devised a clever geo holdout for the ad, not showing it in Wales and then looking for uplift. Our first attempt to view our own ad had landed us in the holdout group despite being in the test region. Cleanliness of test and control is a problem everywhere, but it is easier with a lot of online direct response channels that do not rely only on classic demographic targeting.

Bear in mind, I am not saying you shouldn't use these techniques or channels. Far from it. Not only are they the foundation of modern targeting, but they are also still useful. You just need to understand their limitations. To this day, my team and I buy a lot of ads with this targeting and are pleased with the results. For example, during our big push in 2023 to accelerate the growth of WhatsApp in the USA, we found traditional channels were more effective than digital. Few people in America were aware of WhatsApp, and it was so geographically skewed that the targeting was granular and easy. The longform offline ads creative was super-effective as well.

The right campaign at that time for our company was awareness, the first step in the marketing funnel. We therefore shut down direct response marketing in favour of brand-awareness targeting. Subsequently, as we have succeeded in making people in the USA aware of WhatsApp, we have found that combining traditional top-of-funnel awareness channels – like TV and billboards – with typically bottom-of-the-funnel action-based digital channels supercharges the impact. Bringing the two together, at the right time, can be a boon for your business.

THE WEB'S NEW WAYS TO TARGET

In the earliest days of web targeting, online was the same as offline. You would buy on certain sites like you would buy in certain newspapers or magazines. Often those sites were run by the same publishing group or broadcaster and were additions to your existing media buys.

The first huge step-up in web targeting was contextual advertising, in which ads that appear on a site are related to the content being shown. For example, if you visit a paper airplane website, you might be shown an ad for a book on paper airplanes. Contrary to popular opinion, this approach wasn't pioneered by Google, but by a marketing company called Overture, whose business model is documented as inspiring Google's business today, and others like them. The easiest version was based on what the users were searching for. They were shown ads for the words they had just typed in the search box (I'll go into loads of depth on this topic in Chapter 13, on search). A harder version was matching ads to the page a user was visiting, though if the visit started from a search referral, and the person serving the ad was the search engine in question, it was fairly easy as well.

In building modern targeting at Facebook, we realized people's browsing behaviour could tell us a lot about their likelihood to click on an ad. We used this behaviour together with contextual information to show the right ad at the right time to the right user. For example, the ad you show a user on their first page view when they visit your site or app will be quite different from the ad you show them on their fiftieth page view in the same visit, even if the content is the same.

My first experience with this concept was when I ran Google AdSense on my hobby websites while at university. Google AdSense is a program that allows websites to monetize their sites by running ads served up through Google. (I am grateful to Google and YouTube revenue share, both of which really improved my life in my twenties and gave me my start in online marketing.) In running AdSense on my site, I also used banner ad networks, networks that serve image ads on a site and pay the site's owner a revenue share.

I had a hypothesis that click-through rates (CTR) and costs per mille (CPM) would be higher from search on the first couple of pages in a visit. CTRs are the clicks or impressions created by a user interacting with the website – a click is the actual action of clicking on the ad, an impression is counted as when they open the page and see the ad – while CPMs, where 'mille' is Latin for 1,000, is a metric that describes how much it costs an advertiser for every 1,000 impressions, or for every 1,000 views of the ad they buy.

Since search would show users ads for the same term they just searched for, it made sense that click-through would be more likely. The CPMs would then be higher from the banner ads on your later ad impressions in a given site visit. The search CPMs are driven by CTR (as they are pay per click ads) and the CTRs on ads served by the search engine drop further the more page views deep into a visit a user is when they arrive from search. The banner ad CPMs stayed constant because they are unrelated to the referring search; they are not bought on a pay per click basis and the user has not seen the best banner ads until you actually serve the banner ad in place of AdSense. I tagged my AdSense positions in this way and found the data agreed with the hypothesis. The data in the graph below shows a clear decline in CTR with depth of visit, with CTR on the y axis and number of impressions deep into the visit on the x axis

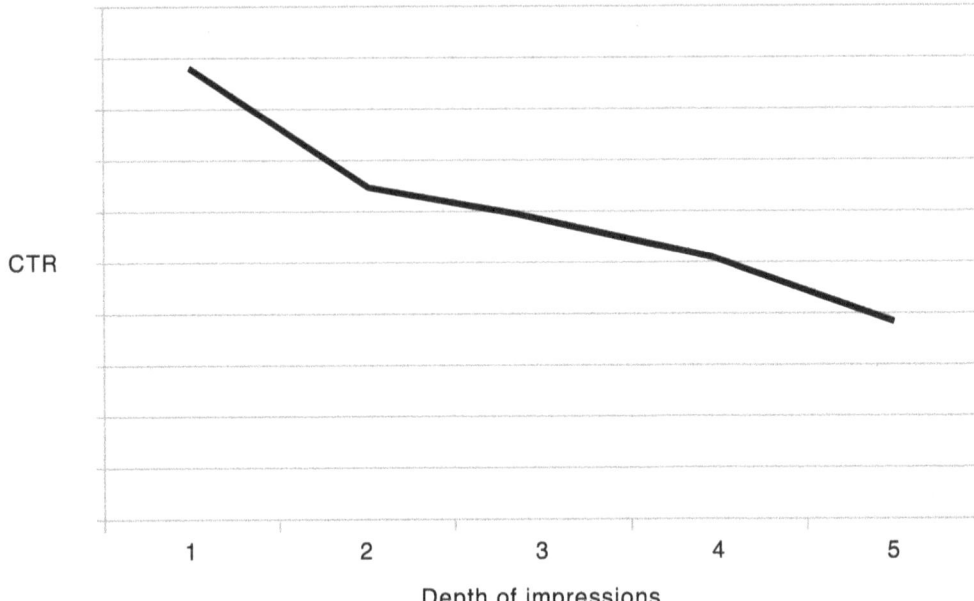

CTR of AdSense ads, depth of visit, January 2010

(i.e., the first page view, the second page view, and on). As a result, I started serving AdSense ads first and banner inventory ads last in a user journey.

I found that Google already optimized against this decline even back then in the 2000s. In the next graph, I tracked the percentage of impressions where Google AdSense would actually serve, or place, an ad on my site. You can see this rapidly dropped off on the fifth page view in a person's journey through my site. That meant AdSense was not serving ads at that point, so they weren't using the space, but clients could tell AdSense what to use in their place. I asked them to automatically fill those slots with the banner ad networks, allowing me to continue making revenue from another ad source. So, for me, Google would fill 90 percent of ads for the first four page views on the site but then drop off and fill with remnant banner ad networks.

This data is hardly a revelation; in fact, it is fundamental to how behavioural targeting for advertising networks works. Understanding and optimizing for this process has become standard practice now. The concept of 'remnant inventory' – unsold ad space on a site that is filled with secondary ads – has become commonplace. With remnant inventory, which is always the umpteenth page view on a site, search ads and contextual ads work less well and behavioural ads tend to win more, since they are unrelated to the click from a search engine that drove the user to the site. To me, this is a foundational element of showing ads on a website or app, and a clear example of how targeting today is more advanced and effective than what came before.

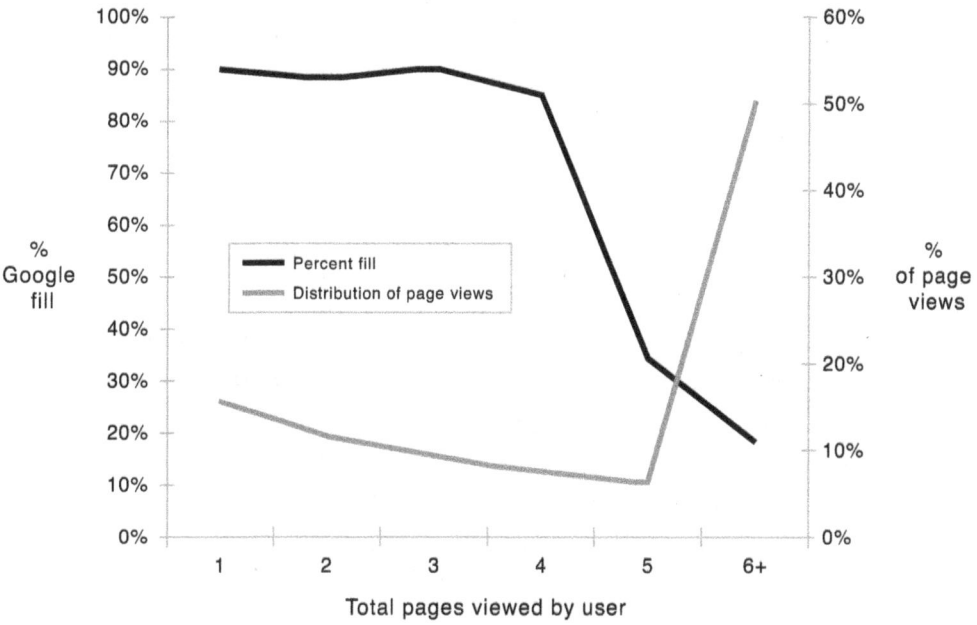

Remnant ad use based on total pages viewed

Something else I learned during this time that has continued to influence my marketing approach was targeting by time of day, widely referred to as day parting. I found that if someone is browsing the web late at night, searching for and visiting review websites looking to buy, say, a kettle, they converted at a higher rate than someone shopping online during the daytime. I have always positively thought that they must be motivated shoppers to be searching at that time of night, but other people have suggested a lot of them may just be, well, drunk. I leave you to decide, but either way, it's a useful bit of info when considering your targeting approach.

The ability to form hypotheses for what would work on targeting in a new channel and test if you were right was extremely important for marketers trying out the new channels in those early days of companies like Google and Facebook – and extremely lucrative. I would also note this was mirrored in capabilities on people's own websites for onsite merchandising, which I will dig into later, not just banner advertising and paid search. Many other insights have been gleaned through testing these types of hypotheses over the years and have improved targeting and returns.

The group that experimented with this type of targeting the hardest was affiliate marketers. Affiliate marketers use their own platforms to promote another company's or organization's products and services and are then paid for actions that occur as a result of those ads. They may also work directly for you on certain projects. For example, you could offer them terms to help register users, and then they take actions at their discretion to land those registrations. (I describe affiliate marketers in a bit more depth in the next chapter on channels and then a lot of depth in Chapter 12.)

To this day, affiliate marketers are some of the most cutting-edge folks in the industry. They are more nimble than big companies, but they sometimes have budgets of a similar size. They can also instantly apply what they've learned from one industry to another, such as travel to e-commerce, because for them it's all just a question of where they can make the most money. I had a lot of fun in the affiliate world back in the early 2000s, and learned so much from those folks. But as the web evolved, so did targeting, and the emergence of social media and new platforms opened up a whole new behavioural-focused world.

RE-TARGETING, UN-TARGETING AND DATA QUALITY

The next era in web targeting was the shift to behavioural, taking in more context than someone's current browsing session on a given site. The approach, in my opinion, was broadly started by email marketers and onsite merchandisers, consisting of both engineering teams and marketers. It built on the foundations of database marketing and snail-mail campaigns going back decades. A customer ID and some data was all that was necessary to send potential customers mail or an ad online. Initially, these ads were sent through the post, then email. Over time, however, it became clear that banner ads, based on what users just did on the internet or even on their behaviour over time across many channels, was a better option.

When social media started, it was a simple demographic targeting medium, just with higher fidelity than the original web and the old-school targeting of TV shows and magazines. The era of behavioural-based targeting was huge for all those companies on the internet who were not selling search ads. It also enabled such non-search properties (everything from Facebook to Amazon) to start competing meaningfully with search for ad dollars. This development was huge because it was now possible to sub divide demographics using behavioural targeting.

For example, think about men's grooming. You could target men who had previously bought or recently searched for a razor.

Clearly this avoids trying to sell razors to men with beards, but if they just browsed for razors on your site, it also allows you to target people who are in the market for one right now and interested in looking for one online. Now broaden this idea to every possible subcategory you can think of. Suddenly, you go from generic ads to men aged 22–29 to a completely custom set of ads based on that person's behaviour that are the most relevant.

As you can see, this approach creates a better, more relevant browsing experience, allows website owners to have higher converting ads and enables companies to have more performant advertising. This to me is part of the core promise of behavioural advertising – done responsibly, it is better for everyone. This modern behavioural targeting approach relies on three fundamentals: re-targeting, un-targeting and data quality. Once you understand them, you will get the best possible results from today's targeting tools.

Re-targeting

Re-targeting is basically the most common form of behavioural targeting for this era. Re-targeting is when someone is shown an ad based on their previous behaviour on an app or website. The simplest and easiest example is conversion drop-off. Say someone has come to your website searching for a holiday package in the Seychelles islands but hasn't bought one. Then when that person went to another travel site like Booking.com, it might note that they just browsed for that Seychelles holiday. This was all possible because of a piece of code called a pixel. The pixel was usually a 1x1 pixel image, or a single pixel on a website (hence why the code is called a 'pixel'). Sometimes, the pixel was a 1x1 pixel iFrame, or an 'inline frame', an HTML element that allows you to display content from another website within your own page. The pixel would load on the webpage the user was viewing within a site, and drop a piece of tracking code called a cookie onto that person's browser.

Although more complex in reality, simply stated, this cookie would carry a 'label' for the person that linked to information about the person's visit to that site. Then when the user went to another site, that cookie would go along for the ride. The ad network wouldn't typically have the information associated with the label, it would just be a label to them. You, as the website owner, would be the one who knew what the label meant and could then instruct the ad network to act when they saw that label again. For example, 'Please show this person an ad for discounted flights to the Seychelles.'

Over time, the process became more advanced, especially once demand-side platforms (DSPs) came along. Instead of just one ad network you could instruct, DSPs are broker in-betweens that instruct multiple ad networks at once. A DSP goes out to everyone selling ads and says via APIs (the application programming interfaces mentioned earlier), 'If you see this user on your service I will pay you X amount to show them this ad about the Seychelles on Booking.com' or some other travel site (although I believe Booking.com were the best in the world in the early days of re-targeting).

This would result in that person seeing ads from your company for the Seychelles on almost any website they visited. The downside was that this got annoying for the potential customer if they'd already bought the holiday, shoe, jacket, or whatever product or service they first browsed for – they'd continue to be chased around the web by the same ad for days. It was also a huge waste of money for the advertiser. As a result, you also needed un-targeting.

Un-targeting

I like relevant ads a lot, but it frustrates me to be chased around the web by ads for something I've already bought from the store where I bought it. This is where un-targeting comes in. When the customer takes the desired action, the website in question should fire a pixel again. This time it should call their DSP or other vendor to tag the user and have them cancel all purchase orders with all networks they are buying from on your behalf. My head of media regularly tells me his job is not re-targeting or behavioural targeting as much as it is just un-targeting, as we're trying to market to the people who don't use Facebook, Instagram or WhatsApp in the mid-2020s, not those who do.

Data quality

The effectiveness of re-targeting and un-targeting all boils down to the data you are feeding to your partners. It needs to be good, and the partners in turn must use it well and compliantly. This is another place where technical skill and creativity come together. Technical skill is necessary to implement these tools, and as a direct response marketer operating at the decision and action stages of the marketing funnel you need to be big on details.

Creativity is needed to think through what data to send to the ad networks and DSPs and how much to bid to show an ad to a person who has that data associated with them. For example, someone who has browsed a search page for the Seychelles versus a specific hotel should probably be tagged differently on intent, and you should bid different amounts on those tags – depending on where they are in the funnel, you might be willing to pay more because they are more likely to convert.

When using behavioural data, there are a host of questions to consider. Here are just a few to inspire you and get your thoughts going as you aim to create an effective marketing campaign:

- What do you feature in the ad? The specific hotel they browsed? A generic ad about hotels in the Seychelles? An ad for a different hotel that typically gets a higher conversion rate? What's the right play?

- Should you upsell the next product in the journey? Say they have already purchased a hotel stay on your site, should you now be promoting flights? And if they have a reservation at the hotel and have bought flights on your site, is it time to upsell them on excursions and daytrips?

- How should you treat someone logged in to your site as compared to someone who is not logged in? Should you bid more on them because they have a lower-friction conversion flow without login? Or bid less because they are likely to use your site anyway and so the conversion won't be incremental?

- How should you treat someone with a valid stored credit card versus someone who is using a new card? Perhaps advertising to them is less incremental because they are 90 percent likely to buy from you anyway. Or maybe this has such a high conversion rate because the conversion flow will be shorter, as they do not need to fill in credit card details, and that increased conversion rate will make up for lower incrementality.

Remember, incrementality is everything, so you must always ask how that applies at any given stage of conversion.

There are so many ways to be creative with your bids and

data, and this was especially the case in the early days of online targeting. It's still worth understanding this process and using these lessons, even as we're entering a brand-new era in targeting thanks to AI.

AUTO-OPTIMIZING CAMPAIGNS

As I think about modern targeting and where it is headed in the future, AI systems are getting smarter and doing more of the targeting and, in most cases, doing it well. I only see AI getting better, allowing you to further automate and optimize targeting. What will matter most moving forward then is what data you give these systems, what they might be trying to do on your behalf and how to make sure you are giving them the right information to do their jobs well.

Channels evolve and mature, and as stated in my first guiding principle, though these tools evolve, the principles remain timeless. In the early days of targeting, as with many new tools and technologies, you could find opportunities to capitalize on as everyone was still discovering how it all worked. In the later stages, it gets harder to find an edge as the channels build in best practices and become standardized. In general, this has happened with the whole realm of targeting. You can still differentiate yourself through technical skill and proficiency, and when new tools emerge there is space to make progress, but these aren't the early days, and this isn't the Wild West any more.

For example, there are laws in place stating how you can target and track users and how you can use their data. Platforms have cracked down on cookies and other tracking tools. There are now platform restrictions and settled civil society positions on what are reasonable business practices. I don't agree with every decision made by platforms, all civil society pressure and even every law, but net-net I think the progress here has been positive. Even though it may be somewhat limiting for how marketers can use data without expressed permission, it is easier to do business with a clear set of rules and a level playing field between advertisers, if not platforms.

As a result of these clarified rules, the best practices are also becoming clearer, and the big players have built most of these into auto-optimized ad campaigns. Auto-optimized ad campaigns are those that use AI to automatically target the people who should be getting your ad based on the data you have provided. Auto-optimization is a huge boon for SMBs because they no longer need an expert in every platform to get good results from each one. They just need to correctly leverage the auto-optimization. To do that, whether you are an SMB or a large multi-national, you must properly send the data that the services need.

Typically, this process works along the following lines: you upload a list or tag a list through some form of server-side API or client-side pixel (though these are less popular these days) of who you want to acquire, and they start doing a lot of the work for you. The search engines generate suggested keyword lists or even completely automate the buying for you. This could begin by you sharing your URL with them, after which they suggest how to start. The DSPs and social media companies will then, using AI, automatically create lookalike audiences for you, similar to the ones you've told them to find with the data you have given them, combined with their proprietary first-party data, obtained with consent where required. The more information you send them about what else people do around your site – such as what they browse, what they search for, what they are purchasing – the better, as long as you are always in compliance with applicable laws, of course. This allows them to refine their models on who visits but doesn't convert, who is part of the way through their journey to convert and so on. Good data, with as much context as possible, and permission to use it, helps machines make better decisions.

Even with the huge campaigns I run, we mostly use these auto-optimization tools now and focus carefully on sending them the right data and setting the right cost per action (CPA) targets. (CPA measures the cost of an action you have driven via a marketing campaign by dividing total spend by total actions driven.) Similar to routine computer programming, very few people ever touch machine code any more or really have to think about how memory is used or processors work, especially compared to, say, fifty years ago. The same has happened with targeting – much of it's been obfuscated by good frameworks that make targeting more effective but reduce comparative advantage for people who were brilliant at the base levels of this tool.

TIMELESS TARGETING

Even with all the advancements over the past twenty years, and the era of AI, targeting is still a valuable tool and skill that allows new ideas to emerge, especially with the ad channels owned by a business such as email, notifications and onsite merchandising. That said, targeting is a much smaller comparative advantage now when buying ads from the larger platforms. The key is adopting the new features and technology well. One of the best new features Meta offers today is 'Value optimization' campaigns where, for each conversion, you can tell us how much it is worth to you. The increase in return on ad spend (ROAS) is double-digit uplifts, but the adoption rate of this tool for those who can use it is low. This is often the case when new features are added, which means being on top of the technology, finding what works and adopting it can be a huge advantage here.

Fundamentally, targeting is still about showing the right user the right ad at the right time. This used to be granular, limited and mostly only available to large companies with big budgets. The internet turned that on its head and gave small businesses superpowers alongside the large ones. In the early days we learned a lot through trial and error but, as targeting became standard, clear best practices were adopted, and they are being implemented in today's major automated ad systems. Taking advantage of these advancements is easy in theory, as long as you continue to share good data with them and stay on top of the changing trends and tools.

5. CHANNELS – WHICH CHANNELS WILL BE MOST EFFECTIVE?

In the end, all online marketing is delivered through a channel. That channel may be an email, website or app that you own and operate. It might be a third party, search or social, whether paid or organic, affiliates or display ad networks. Or the channel could be something new, like a retail ad network, the kind Amazon and Walmart have, or an app store ad network like Google's or Apple's. More channels will come into being, while others will become irrelevant, like the old web portals where I started my career.

Once you know where in the funnel you are playing, what your conversion action is and what tools and data you have in your arsenal to target ads to customers, you need to think hard about which channels are going to be most effective with your set of parameters. A high-level understanding of the channels will help you decide where to focus your efforts. Most of the rest of this book is based around channels, so I won't go into too much depth here, but before I go any further, I want to make sure you have a high-level guide across channels so you can begin thinking about what will work best for you.

'WHICH CHANNEL SHOULD I USE?'

Perhaps the most daunting question facing anyone getting started in online marketing is, 'Which channel should I use?'

There are so many, and each has its individual nuances, making it hard to know where to begin. Usually, if you are just launching a business or dipping your toe into digital marketing, you probably don't have infinite resources and you can't simply sample every channel. Similarly, just picking any channel has a huge sense of FOMO associated with it. What if you don't pick the most effective channel for your business, but a competitor chooses the right one?

The inverse FOMO effect works too: when a channel is working well, you might begin to wonder if you should maximize it, or if you should be trying out another one to see if the grass is greener. I particularly love the framing I first heard from Harry Stebbings, a venture capitalist (VC) and podcaster from '20VC', a podcast focused on startups. He described how 'channel market fit' is real and you should not take it for granted when you find it!

So how do you get started with a particular channel, when do you explore others and when do you exploit? (Explore and exploit are concepts in computer science. Explore is finding all possible solutions to a problem; exploit is, once you have found one, getting the most from that solution.) I think about it as a process that takes the following steps:

1. Assess the market and copy what other people with businesses like yours are doing.
2. If you can't copy, explore your options with affiliate marketers.
3. If that doesn't fit your model, systematically explore others – make testing count.
4. When you find a channel that works, double down. Again, channel market fit is real.
5. Rinse and repeat. New channels emerge, old ones die and products change. Go back to the start, see what other

businesses are doing that you haven't tried yet. You don't have to be the first to use a channel or approach, so you can still copy one of your competitors as they get good and test new channels with affiliates.

Since step 4 is just about scaling and step 5 is to return to step 1, let's consider the first three steps in further detail, as they are the main components of the channel decision process.

ASSESS THE MARKET

First, assess the market. What channels do other companies in your industry use? This might seem basic, but many people don't actually do it. If established players use a particular channel time and again, it is probably for good reason. Still, once you know what approach they are taking, you can still make your own decisions. Are you going to use that collective, Darwinianly selected wisdom, or do you feel you have a unique way to use a channel no one has thought about or used before?

For example, Dollar Shave Club used social media (You-Tube and Facebook mostly) to run a comedic video that went viral, broke through and gave them free awareness advertising that Gillette had never achieved. Coupling that with a new business model and some standard social media lead-generating ads helped them rewrite a category and later sell for a billion dollars. So though you can survey the market and copy the best practices, there are also opportunities to do something totally new. Regardless of the approach, you need to be deliberate in which channel you use and keep your eyes wide open as to why and how.

When you are taking a totally new approach, like I did with Facebook in 2007, you don't have a playbook to follow. As a result, you have two options: you can either use affiliates to explore the space or systematically and logically explore the space yourself.

WORK WITH AFFILIATES

The affiliate route provides a huge opportunity for any business. Affiliate marketing offers a way to define your conversion event while a wide range of affiliates drive conversions for you. Generally speaking, if you're a new business and want to try several different channels, going through a third-party affiliate is a great approach. Not only do you get to try out lots of different channels but there are also fraud protections in place to hopefully make sure you don't get duped or ripped off. Unfortunately, you still need to be on guard. I will go into this in depth in Chapter 12, on partner-led channels, but in affiliate marketing you are partnering with a lot more groups than, say, just search or social, and not all those partners are from large, reputable companies. As such, fraud is a risk in the affiliate channel that you have to keep in mind.

The difficulty with affiliates is that you have to have an attractive enough offering, or in other words, appear to be able to pay enough. So, if you are a small player, getting affiliates to try to market you may not be within reach. If you do, however, manage to attract the best affiliates, you'll find a wealth of opportunities. There are typically affiliates who work in all channels and who will provide you with expertise based on their experience to assess channel market fit for your business, advice you won't likely have in-house. They then experiment to see if they can make the channel work for you. From there, they run a scaled campaign for you in that channel.

For many businesses, it will then just make good business

sense to let the affiliates keep running the campaign, paying them and the network the margin to operate, and saving yourself the cost and management of doing this in-house, and less effectively at that. For other businesses, though, the channels discovered become too strategically important for them, and they must bring them in-house, as eBay did after I left.

SYSTEMATICALLY EXPLORE OTHER CHANNELS

In addition to, or instead of, working with affiliates, you can experiment with different channels yourself. To do this quickly, you typically need to be a large, well-resourced company. Still, SMBs can take this approach if they explore one, or a few, at a time. Looking closely at what has worked for other SMBs and competitors in their space will allow them to prioritize what channels to test. When I joined Facebook, I tried out all the channels I could, over about six months to a year, aiming to grow advertisers and users. I did the same explorations twice for these different goals because the way the channels responded to a North Star of advertiser growth versus a North Star of user growth was quite different.

I felt affiliates were too high risk. With so many conversions, it would have been easy for nefarious third parties to defraud us. We were already large and well funded, so we'd be an obvious target, but we didn't have the resources to stand up to that potential fraud ourselves. Uber fell foul of this issue at a similar point in their existence with a banner advertising partner, not even a full affiliate programme. In the end, I just didn't feel we had the resources to work well with affiliates. At the same time, I had a logical structure to explore how to get companies to buy ads and to get users to sign up to Facebook.

The first product I promoted was our self-service ads. Logically, I felt our best advertising customers would be on our own site (later, this concept would be formalized as the KX funnel after Kang Xing Jin, an early leader of ads engineering at Facebook in 2007). So, we started with onsite ads. Once I felt that channel was in good shape, it was time to try another one. We decided to go to the biggest place to buy ads on the internet – Google. Next, since I still felt our best customers would be on our site, onsite, in-product promotion seemed an obvious channel. I left this channel until last because I could try the first two with very limited engineering support, but onsite linking required engineers to change the core product. Therefore, I needed to get credibility with the other channels before I could convince them to take action.

To go from thinking to execution on onsite ads, we initially bought the standard ads available to us, which were fine, but we wanted to get better ones. To do this, we created custom audiences, a targeted list of users based on our specific objectives. We initially used custom audiences to promote our ads products to small businesses on our site that already had an organic presence with a Facebook page (I believe Danny Ferrante, mentioned earlier, did this because he got excited about the idea and was helping work on ads). Custom audiences became far bigger when Meta later created a public product utilizing the approach for our customers.

On Google, we bought all the terms around advertising and promoting your small business, and we defended our brand keyword, meaning we bought the keyword 'Facebook ads'. This move was controversial because many marketing folks feel such a purchase will not deliver incremental results (which, as I state in the second guiding principle, are everything). In our testing, though, it was just incremental enough, because most, but not all, of those conversions would have happened anyway without us buying the phrase.

We also basically copied all the keywords we could find that Google bought themselves. We found these keywords in two ways. First, we just searched ourselves on Google to see when these keywords showed up, a somewhat low-tech, straightforward process anyone could use. Second, we used off-the-shelf competitive analytics tools that told us how sites got their visitors, including keywords.

Once our two largest paid channels were operating well, we analysed where the organic traffic was coming from. It turned out that a lot of links on our own service were getting page administrators to buy ads. That was when we recommended building more in-product links to promote ads. We mostly decided to add more links in the right context for a business. For example, we suggested adding links where users were in the unpaid business interfaces (i.e., they had a presence like a page or profile that did not require them to buy ads). This channel was incredibly effective, and with the three combined – Facebook ads, Google ads and product-led growth – we landed our first million active advertisers for Facebook. In short, we got there by following scale, using targeting advantages, seeing what the other players like Google did and optimizing on what we found through our analytics.

As you can see, we moved from easy to hard channels to execute, based on how independent we could be. We then executed on those channels using analytics to find the best keywords to buy, or links to build, and we weren't afraid to do a lot of manual work ourselves, like those Google searches. This approach works if you are a multi-billion-dollar company or a small business. The scale will vary, but it's important to note there were only two or three of us who did all the work to start – you don't need a huge staff or budget to incorporate this approach. It might take some time, but it will be worth it as you develop and scale.

New channels will come along all the time, but this logical

way of thinking about them has served me and those I advise well: big channels generally work better for a reason, so start with the more established ones. Other companies like yours skew their budget to one channel or another for a reason, so use that data. For example, LinkedIn may not have the scale of Instagram, but it does have an engaged business audience in a corporate mindset when using it, so it would likely be a great place for a business cards company to market itself.

That said, it isn't a given that the small niche site you found will be good just because you found it. Be thoughtful and logically plan out why the outcome will be different for you than for the rest of the industry so far. In my experience, it takes more work to try out a small, less established platform than to onboard and test a larger, more established one. And the chances to get results are far greater when you use a big, established channel. My boss, Facebook COO Javier Olivan, regularly says, 'Common sense is the least common of all senses,' and sadly that's been my experience. I've seen huge amounts of money and time wasted because of people not thinking through the simple points above.

One last interesting point on testing channels comes from a conversation I had with the brilliant Matt Schenker, a legendary commentator and connector in the marketing industry who runs the AdWeek conference amongst other things. Ten years ago, mobile itself was a channel. You'd have search marketing, social marketing, affiliate marketing and mobile booths at most online marketing conferences. Now, mobile is a surface for those existing channels, and it is fully and deeply integrated into all of them. This is the natural order and speaks to my belief that, in marketing, when new technologies and channels emerge, they are treated as distinct. As they mature, they get subsumed, becoming a part of the existing bigger picture. By thinking through and understanding how common approaches and frameworks work, we can adopt them as they come along and play a larger role in our everyday work.

A HIGH-LEVEL OVERVIEW OF CHANNELS

Though you may have already established which channels work for you, or which channels you want to try out, it's important to recognize how many are out there, what they are good for and when you should use them. I often come back to this mental model of each channel, and hopefully it's helpful for you as you think through your choices. There is a detailed run-through of each of them in Part III, but understanding the basics is necessary first.

Affiliates – This is the channel of channels. Affiliate marketing lets you experiment and learn a great deal, especially early on, because there are countless affiliates who use many different channels. The one issue is you have to market yourself to affiliates to get them to work with you. To be successful here you must make sure your compensation model is right. Affiliates do exactly what you pay them for and it is pretty binary – either you pay enough and it scales or you don't and it does nothing. Finally, as discussed, affiliate marketing does have issues with fraud since they have licence to take any approach they want to lead to a conversion action.

Organic search – Organic search is when your site or platform shows up in a search engine's results without paying for the placement or marketing. This often is referred to as 'search engine optimization' (SEO). SEO involves figuring out what keywords your potential customers search for, and how to make sure your brand or site pops up when they do so in the non-ads search results. The most important thing here is keyword research: where do you want to appear and how much competition is there for those keywords? Once those keywords are in place, you need to have content that targets for those words. From there, you need to have linking, both internal, to help show search engines which content is important in your site, and external, to show your site matters. Finally, you have to correctly optimize the page that you want to rank itself both in code and in text.

Paid search – Paid search is the paid big brother of SEO. Bidding on keyword terms to appear in the paid search results is known as 'search engine marketing' or SEM. This channel is best when you are not a totally new category, so people are, at a minimum, already searching online to find solutions to the problem you solve. However, keyword research and targeting is difficult with this channel. Especially if you are small and new, the search engines can't just recommend targeting, or do it for you, because there is only so much data for you and your site. Note, understanding what happens with the marketing team bidding on your brand name is important, so make sure it's incremental and tracked distinctly from the rest of the campaign.

Organic social – This channel is one in which your product, service or brand shows up in a social feed, app or site, without paying for that placement or marketing. Keep in mind, your content needs to be interesting for a user to interact with it and take action. The distribution of your content, however, is tied to whether the system thinks that content is interesting. This basically depends on whether someone else found it interesting, as in they paused on your content, clicked on it or interacted with it in some way.

You can achieve this in two ways: come up with how to do this directly yourself or pay for talent and work with an account or creator who already has a lot of distribution and knows how to build up a following.

Paid social – I consider paid social the pinnacle of all we've learned in building online marketing channels to date. This is the best channel for most businesses to get started in generating leads. In this channel, you pay to have your product, service or brand show up in a social feed, app or site. Setting up a conversion action, piping through the conversion and value data and letting the sites auto-optimize for you is a great way to begin. If you couple that approach with a compelling organic social approach, you can boost your content or ads and the results will be turbocharged. You don't even need a website to get started. In fact, in many countries people have completely skipped the website altogether and just have social media and messaging presences. This is a great channel for businesses big and small, as you can start with any size budget.

Direct mail (DM) – I categorize snail mail, email, messaging apps, push notifications, SMS and related channels all under 'direct mail', as in each one you are directly reaching out to potential customers. You get different responses by channel based on age: younger people are more inclined to use messaging apps, SMS and push, while older folks tend to use email and even snail mail more often. Broadly, the most important aspects of DM are deliverability (do you have the right address and does it get there?), targeting (what does your database know and how can you use that information well?) and timing (are you following timeliness and doing notification-style messaging, which is on average, far more effective than newsletter or just emailing?).

Onsite merchandising – This channel consists of promoting your products or services directly on your site. Targeting with onsite merchandising is more or less the same here as with DM, but you have to think deeply about how to integrate into product and make your offerings persistent (even if small), contextually relevant and personalized. I believe the line between product and promotion is blurred in a web product, and that's OK, but marketers and product people should embrace that fact and work together.

Display advertising networks – In this channel, businesses buy banner ads from companies that aggregate ad spots across a wide range of sites and apps or one site or app they own. At the high end, there are high-quality targeting options with auto-optimizing campaigns, just like with the top search engines and social media sites. At the low end are an array of banner ad networks on forums and similar sites. No matter what end you're operating at, you will have to deal with a lot of potential fraud. With that in mind, make sure to work with a good aggregator, focus on data quality and have your team keep a sceptic's eye on the lower-end sites for fraud. I bucket the emerging retail ad networks and app store ads in this channel, as they behave similarly to the web portals of old, but I am sure a good argument could be made that they are their own channels and will become more important over time. In 2025 these are, in my opinion, the fastest-evolving, newest scaled channels in the mix.

Across all channels, you need to think carefully about budget optimization. Make sure you are looking at both marginal and incremental ROI, not just looking at average ROI for each channel. All the channels above compete with each other actively, so never consider them siloed – look at them and optimize them as a whole.

FOLLOW THE STEPS

There are a lot of great channels, and it can be daunting to think about them. If you feel overwhelmed when starting out, come back to my earlier advice: start by looking for what works in your industry already and find what competitors use successfully. Beyond that, try channels that have the best chance of being high scale and easy to use at first, such as paid social with Meta and search with Google. Only once you have exhausted that approach should you try to attack the long tail of smaller sites and channels.

As you decide on which channels to use, and what work best for you, keep your eye on incrementality. I've raised a number of potential pitfalls – such as bidding on your brand name or affiliate fraud – that risk making your returns far lower than you could achieve. As such, you must remember the second guiding principle and carefully track the incremental conversions you get, not just those that were attributed to someone clicking on your ad.

6. CREATIVE – WHICH CREATIVE WILL CONVINCE THOSE FOLKS TO CLICK?

In the end, as much as I love all the theory, logic and code in the preceding pages, at some point you have to bring it all together and actually show someone an ad. At this stage, you are hopefully clear on your goal and the metric that describes it. By now, you should have looked at the marketing funnel and begun planning the right campaign for your company at its current stage. You need to already know who your target audience is and have a good idea on how to reach them, both with clever targeting and appropriate channel selection, showing the right ad to the right person at the right time. That's where creative comes in: the right ad!

THE FOUR PS OF CREATIVE

Creative is the blanket term for the design of your ad, and how it looks, sounds and appears. As I think about creative, for digital marketing, there are four principles that cut across all channels. Creative should be prominent, personalized, persistent and performant:

- **Prominent** – Subtle creative that doesn't get seen doesn't work. A right-hand, full-page newspaper ad in colour is way more expensive than left hand below the fold in greyscale, as it should be. This principle applies to the new tools too. Your ad must be seen to work.

- **Personalized** – People will respond better to content that is more relevant and personal to them than generic. On the internet, when you show someone an ad, you will already know something about them – always use that information to show them a better ad!

- **Persistent** – If you can find a place where it is natural to keep reminding people of the action you want them to take, then continue using it. This approach is most likely to be possible in the in-product channel and, importantly, requires subtle creative choices to be able to be truly persistent.

- **Performant** – It needs to work. It sounds so basic, but your ad needs to load, fast, when someone comes to a site. You may have bought the best placement prominently at the top of the page and perfectly personalized the ad, but it won't matter if the person viewing the page has scrolled past it before it is visible. This happens a lot.

There is so much space to be creative and take new approaches, especially with today's technology. The brilliant Netflix CMO Kelly Bennett, for example, completely restructured their marketing away from over-optimizing against direct response marketing, made Netflix realize all marketing performed and brought a healthy balance across their entire marketing funnel, driving a lot of growth. As part of this, he tried a lot of creative online and off but made sure it was all supportive of the Netflix brand when he did so. Generally, we are not in a measure-twice, cut-once industry. It's important to try lots of different creative, test the results, see what works and double down on those that do. In fact, you must do that to be successful.

David Ogilvy said, 'If it doesn't sell, it isn't creative,' and I couldn't agree more. You need to measure results, and your creative needs to work driving conversions. If it doesn't, it's not creative. Building on the work of my predecessors, I have grown our creative team into a multi-award-winning organization. In 2024 alone we won eighty-eight awards for creativity, including a Grand Prix at the Cannes Festival of Advertising and five other Grand Prix across various awards shows, culminating in best in-house agency at the London International Awards.

The thing that makes me the proudest is what the leader of our Creative teams, Tom Markham, said: 'Focus on the results and the awards follow.' Our creative works: it gets results and its integrity is respected and award-winning. We've proven such win-wins are possible, even in a team run by a numbers nerd like myself. Still, you only get the chance to be truly creative if you get great results. With that in mind, let's take a look at the four Ps in turn.

Prominent

I always joke that my career has been all about big green buttons. In the early part of my time at Facebook, we developed the concept of a 'big green button' test. We would promote a product, say, contact importers, with a prominent promotion, often using a big green button image or icon, so we'd take awareness and navigation issues off the table. This would generally be only a small-reach test, in which you just try your ad out on a small number of people, but it was a good way to understand how compelling the promotion had been for those users who had seen it.

This approach gets at two important points about creative for direct response marketing that are consistently a struggle across my industry. The first is that creative needs to actually be seen. Too often, people mistake creative for being a piece of art rather than a tool that has a job to do – that job is to get people to take action. The second is that people need to know they can click to actually take action. Among brand folks, the joke is often that the CMO is always asking for a bigger logo; in direct response, we are always asking for a bigger button. Creative and the click target must be prominent.

Personalized

Creative should be personalized. Every time you can make a promotion more personal to an individual you get better results. You treat them with respect, give them a better experience and hence get better results. Generally, I think this makes sense. In my experience, if you actually think about someone when you ask them for something to their face, they will be more likely to respond positively if you greet them by name and remember their personal context. Historically, ad campaigns couldn't be all that personalized, but with the advent of the internet, people expect user interfaces, including ads, to be tailored to them. I have found that if you are going to show people ads, en masse, nothing will annoy them more than irrelevant, un-personalized, generic ads.

With personalization, the content should be relevant to the person seeing it. My favourite example of this rule is from my early career at eBay; it is also an example of why diversity matters. I was asked to work on making our onsite merchandising more effective. One hypothesis I had was that a lot of goods are gendered – with male and female versions of the same products, like shoes, jackets or razors – and people would buy more of a given product if they saw someone of their own gender using it or wearing it. Twenty years ago, eBay didn't have a lot of gender data, so we rarely had the opportunity to use it, but when we did, we saw better performance.

I used eBay's existing data set for gender to see what first names were associated with what gender. I then took that data and predicted the gender for all other users based on their first name. Having done that, we targeted certain ads to women (including women's golf clubs, razors and clothing) and certain ads to men (including men's golf clubs, razors and clothing). The results were fascinating. In the tests, we saw uplift for women but not men. We had a predominantly male design team, and by default we had previously only included male products in our testing. So, customizing the ads for men didn't matter – but for women it gave us a double-digit CTR uplift.

This type of personalization is true for using these banner ads for onsite merchandising and direct mail or for display advertising across the web targeted at the same people. Explaining how we drove these results was also a great talking point at events when convincing people to come work with us! It showed the impact you could have if you brought your unique insight to the table and how data could prove that insight mattered. Today, I expect these results would absolutely work on social media marketing, but you don't need to do gender prediction since people typically include it in their profiles and actually expect you to give them relevant ads. Personalization is a cross-channel win.

Over time, targeting and creative experiments showed me that the best personalization is behavioural, and behavioural data contains so much more insight than just the simple behaviour it tracks. Take the above example. When women are clicking on women's products, if we just behaviourally show them other products like those they had clicked on, we will not only get gender-relevant ads but we will also get ads that are relevant to the specific items they are browsing for at that time.

You have surely experienced behavioural creative in action. You browse a pair of shoes on a shoe retailer like Zappos and the rest of the day you are being chased by those shoes around the web. When you add an item to your shopping cart on an e-commerce product, you might get a reminder email or notification later to say you have left something in your cart. Or when you add a new contact on a social media product like LinkedIn, immediately the People You May Know (PYMK) unit appears with refreshed, relevant suggestions based on the contact you just added. This technique is amazingly effective, as it is timely, relevant and totally personalized on the consumer's behaviour. When done right, over time, it can actually be seen by users and the company you work for as a product. (I'll discuss this idea more in the in-product merchandising section in Chapter 11.)

Triggered creative is a form of personalizing creative based on a person's behaviour but, I would argue, distinct from behavioural because it is triggered by an action that isn't performed by the person who is being marketed to. For example, say, as a marketer, you have a sale on your site, and you send an email about the sale to people you think will be interested. Another example is thinking through what you should notify people about in terms of actions taken on their account, such as, for a social media site, which notifications are turned on by default for new users (a deliberate decision I'll explore more later).

No matter the creative, the best responds to the context in which it appears. If you are in a search results page, for example, a banner ad would be totally incongruous, but a text and link-based ad that looks like a search result would be appropriate. Similarly, if you are inserting an ad in a series of short-form, sound-on vertical videos, having a static image with no sound would seem out of place. When search marketers first started using dynamic keyword insertion (inserting keywords in a search result based on what the user was searching for) in Google AdWords, Google didn't have a product to help in the process. We just did it manually by uploading ads with the keywords in them. Eventually, Google rolled out a dedicated dynamic keyword insertion product and performance on these ads shot up.

At eBay, we went a bit over the top with that idea and bought, and dynamically inserted, every keyword users searched for on the service. This led to some issues when people searched for 'dead babies' (the name of a book, film and song, all of which you could buy on eBay) or other potentially offensive content. You can't predict why people search for something, and some people searching for this expression were not searching for the book, film or song. That meant they were very offended when we seemed to be suggesting that they buy 'dead babies'. We had to develop filters and stop words (i.e., words we never want to buy) to never use, but this was a powerful approach. The ad contained the word you were searching for and showed the contextual relevance. The secret behind AdSense is the same – a travel ad will do better on a travel site and an e-commerce ad on a shopping-related site. So, your ad should fit the channel it is used in and hence be personalized to the current browsing behaviour of the user. Within that constraint you should be as creative and personalized as possible.

Finally, with personalization, using someone's actual name matters and is, I think, polite. If you are sending someone an email, it is totally reasonable to write 'Hi Alex,' at the start of the email. It performs better – I've heard loads of theories why – and it also just seems the right thing to do if someone took the time to enter their name in a form on your site or product.

Persistent

Persistence can be tricky. Send too many emails or use the same banner ad too often and negative outcomes are likely. They may be low cost, such as wasting a portion of your budget, or high cost, such as causing people to opt out of your email campaigns or block your ads. So, I want to start by stressing that creative should be persistent – not ridiculous.

That said, I believe in persistence in every channel. If you want to, for example, grow a new feature within your app, you need prominence and personalization but, above all, you want to create a persistent place where people can find it. In my opinion, this is an example of the classic marketing funnel, moving people from awareness to action. The first few times someone visits your app, they are likely trying to accomplish a specific task or job. The next time they open they app, they may notice a new navigation element, becoming aware of the new product. They may be intrigued by it, but they still have to go and do their job (driving intention). When they have spare time, they might think 'oh, I'll check out that new product' (decision). But if you only advertise the new product with a banner ad with an impression cap (limit on the number of impressions any one person can see), they might never find it again, blocking the action stage in the AIDA funnel. An appropriately persistent navigation element will avoid this fate, making it hugely valuable.

So often in my career I have seen people focus on big banner ads and offsite marketing campaigns for a new feature and just miss the basics of making it easy to navigate to persistently. At Facebook, we did a huge marketing campaign for Facebook live video to get folks to use it, even including TV ads and out-of-home ads (ads that are outdoors like billboards on a motorway), and saw marginal lift. We then changed the entry point to include it in the interface where users created a post at the top of newsfeed, and the live video usage surged – people knew where it was and found it.

There is a ton of competition for people's attention in every channel. Persistence is key to breaking through their competing priorities – and your competition – and driving them down the marketing funnel from awareness to action. You also need to be channel-aware in how you deliver persistence. In search, you want to show up every time someone searches, but there are limited tools to affect the search results. In onsite merchandising, a persistent unchanging navigational element is best (if, again, it is prominent enough). Beyond those two channels, you have to be even smarter about persistence.

Outside of product linking and merchandising, the single most important creative aspect for persistence is to make sure you rotate your creative and don't just show people the same precise ad over and over again.

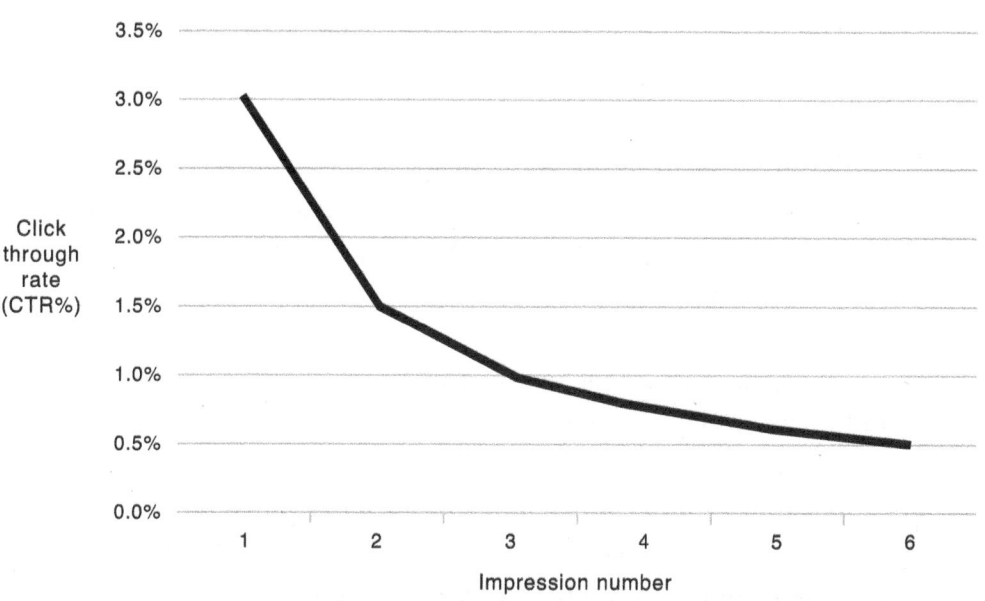

CTR decline over number of impressions

The above figure is stylized but it is what I have seen repeatedly in my career. It doesn't matter if you are promoting a listing on a travel site, suggesting an account or friend to follow on social media, promoting an item to buy on an e-commerce site, running a banner ad to acquire a new user or sending an email to resurrect someone who hasn't come back to your product in a while, CTR drops the more times someone sees the same piece of creative. So how do you counter this potential predicament? There are three main ways:

1. Creative rotation (based on user actions).
2. Behavioural-based creative.
3. Triggered.

Creative rotation (based on user actions) was the first technique I learned. At that stage, in the early 2000s, it was simple but revolutionary, and it gave me double-digit uplifts in performance from our marketing campaigns across multiple channels and companies. For each piece of creative, you must log how many times it has been seen by a user. Then you look at the CTR for all first impressions of that creative, all second impressions, all third impressions and so on. This will give you your own version of the graph above. You must develop these graphs robustly for each of your creative variants. Then you show the creative with the highest CTR until its CTR (say, on impression three) falls below the second highest CTR creative – then you show that one.

The great news is that now most platforms build this approach in for you, and all you have to do is upload lots of creative variants. From there, they will pick the best for you, put them in the right sequence and change that sequence as needed. When you are relying on home-built solutions, though – for email or onsite merchandising – this CTR decline is something you need to consider closely.

It can also be important in understanding why an automated channel isn't showing a piece of creative you really love or is behaving in a weird way. Lots of strange things can happen: you might suddenly go from receiving thousands of impressions a day to zero impressions a day without yourself making a clear change. This may be the result of it actually crossing a CTR threshold with the ad-serving platform and they chose to no longer show it automatically. Sometimes, you have to force it to break out of a trap the ad-serving system catches itself in, which doesn't give you the best possible result even if it is a good result (a local minima but not the global maximum). The best way I know to do that is usually to try the new creative in a fresh campaign, then see what happens when you add other creative variants, hopefully leading to more clicks or impressions.

Performant

This may sound ridiculously basic, but your ad must load before the person you want to see it has scrolled past and moved on. As the web has progressed to mobile and mobile has progressed to apps, performance has remained a constant in my experience. As marketers, we like to have the coolest and best creative going. That almost always means more pixels, more frames and fundamentally more data. But in email marketing, your email needs to work even if the recipients don't load the images, as many people won't. In push notifications, the text cannot spill over what is easily read in a pop-up notification. And in SMS in particular, the link needs to not spill over SMS segments, causing it to be impossible to click because it is cut in half. The basics really matter (again), so how do you solve these types of issues?

The most important place to begin is working with and through the people on your team. It is a special creative or designer who thinks about load times or the quality of phone processors in their work. Building a culture in which caring about performance is seen as mastery of your craft, and is then celebrated, is probably the single most effective way to make sure you get performant creative. Beyond that, making sure you have different sizes and renderings of your creative that you target to people based on their connection speed and phone type (using header data and response data) is the way to make this work. If you don't have access to that information, you can roughly approximate it geographically. For example, rural areas and low-and-middle income countries typically have less reliable networks, along with lower-performance phones.

One example of this issue I struggled with was when I worked with an excellent design team who had a value they called 'craft'. This value materialized through smooth, beautiful, animated transitions between screens and was an absolutely gorgeous sight to behold, at least on a top-end iPhone. But with a low-end Android, the animations degraded dramatically. This meant features of their app were unusable and the whole app was slow and clunky. Showing them data about the problem did not help them understand the issue. But recording images of the app on a low-end phone and showing them the actual user experience was a game-changer. Seeing the degraded quality created a visceral understanding of the issue. From that point forward, that team cared about performance as part of the craft.

For over a decade now, the Facebook Lite app, which takes up less space and uses less data than the Facebook app, has allowed users with lower-end phones to have an excellent experience, so our full-fat app can serve the highest-end phones without us leaving the lower-end phones (and network bandwidth) behind. Today's Facebook Lite wouldn't run well on the phones it was originally launched for over a decade ago, but it has more usage than ever because it acts as a product for the lowest-end phones used at any time, which themselves get better over time, like a moving layer.

Another good example of performance is just making sure the creative fits on the screen. Again, this sounds so basic, but it has repeatedly come up as an issue in campaigns and products I have worked on. Not all phones have the same screen size and not all windows on a computer are full screen. You have to remember this when you are running your ads and considering how your conversion form will respond.

For example, we used to serve an ad to get people to fill out a survey. Over time we made the conversion event happen in the ad (which, as discussed, is an awesome form of conversion rate optimization). Instead of saying 'click here to fill out a survey', users could immediately start filling out the survey with the question and response inline. However, the design of the app changed; the iFrame the survey appeared in was smaller than the survey's first step, hiding the top box of the survey options (I believe only on some devices). This caused our brand metrics to crater right as we launched a new newsfeed design that required the new iFrame. We decided the new design was so bad we had to roll it back. It took some time before we found that the actual issue was the survey promotion unit, resulting in us getting fewer top-box answers – that redesigned feed was not nearly as big a problem as we'd thought. As you can see, though thinking about performance isn't sexy and is regularly overlooked, it's always important.

CREATIVE MATTERS

Creative is a lot more than a simple banner ad; it is tied to the channel you are using, and in our world of online marketing it can be aware and respond to its context. This context includes what page the ad is on, what the person seeing it has done before and details about their connection and device. This information gives countless opportunities for doing incredibly interesting creative.

I encourage you to try a lot of creative. As you do, don't forget to break it down into thinking about prominence, personalization, persistence and performant. Make sure an ad is prominent enough that it will be seen in position and design. Ensure it is personalized to the person viewing it (ideally on behaviour not demographic) and, often, its context. Make it appear persistently enough that it will break through and be noticed in a busy environment. Then, finally, have creative that is performant and loads so it can be seen. If you consistently follow this approach, then I believe you will put yourself on a path to great results.

I would like to end on one cautionary note. Your creative must represent your brand. Some teams act like the conversion is all that matters and debase the brand to get short-term gains. Netflix, for example, would show ads promising a price discount and using a sexy image from a film that didn't build, or harmed, their long-term brand, even if it drove short-term results. These users would also be price-sensitive and retain less well. This balance of short-term gains vs long-term brand strategy is hard to measure and comes down to judgement. It is a balance I continually have to strike and one that led Kelly Bennett, while still at Netflix, to turn off all direct response marketing for Netflix for a period because they had gone too far. This was a brave move for a tech company and my understanding is it worked to reset the culture in marketing. Creative must have constraints. So, please don't use this chapter as an example for clicks and conversions at any cost. That kind of thinking can put you on a path to a terrible long-term outcome.

2

THE INFRASTRUCTURE

I once heard someone describe the act of building a skyscraper as a lot of time messing around in a hole until, suddenly, the towering building shoots up. That's because the infrastructure needs to be put in place before the first steel beam: power cables, utilities, sewage, foundations and more. If you don't spend enough time in the hole before you build your beautiful edifice, you will have a lot of problems down the line. The same is true of online marketing: you need the right infrastructure to build your hugely performant, impactful digital marketing programme.

The goal of this part of the book is to help you set up that infrastructure. This boils down to the right measurement and the right team. With measurement, the second guiding principle of this book is key: incrementality is everything. So, how do you ensure you are getting incremental results? You must move beyond the basics of the North Star and its metrics and run great experiments. Experiments allow you to understand the incremental results you are driving, both overall as a programme, and for the last dollar you spent, which is generally less impactful than the first dollar. In this part, I describe how to build the metrics, measure lifetime value, and design synthetic and actual controls. We'll explore various kinds of experiments from pre/post to AB testing, and discuss other tools you need to measure impact and explain your work to your company's other teams.

No infrastructure, however, is more important than your team – if you are going to be successful at any meaningful scale, you can't simply do it alone. You will need a mixture of employees, agencies and partner teams inside your company to produce the best work. To that end, I explain how to build the best team and how to get hired onto one that will allow you to develop the best career possible in this industry.

The final chapter in this part covers how to work well internally. In many ways, that is the most critical piece of all the infrastructure. In companies big and small, you need to work with others – unfortunately, marketing's reputation for rigour is not uniformly good, which makes this hard. I share how to show colleagues the impact you have and inspire them to do more marketing as well. After all, collaborating with others not only contributes to marketing's success; it helps make the work rewarding and, at times, even fun.

7. MEASUREMENT

Not everything that matters can be measured, and not everything that can be measured matters. I deeply believe in measurement but always hold that thought close to my chest. It is so easy to go too far and reduce your possible impact by being too much of a measurement purist without acknowledging the practicalities of the real world. You should keep your approach simple. Have one goal metric that describes your North Star goal. Other metrics are necessary to understand how well you are executing, but don't confuse those with the North Star metric. Metrics, when they become targets, often become co-opted, gamed and hacked. To that end, you must understand how to set goals and create telemetry and guardrail metrics to avoid these issues. These metrics – goals, telemetry and guardrail – must complement one another.

Once you have great metrics, you can track if you have incrementally moved them. There are various tools to do this; some are blunter, like turning campaigns on and off and seeing what happens, and others are more nuanced, like randomized controlled testing, in which you test offerings or approaches using an experiment group and a control group, both chosen at random. Choosing the right experimental tool for the right job is important. Ideally, every campaign would have a long-term randomized controlled test, where some people see an ad, for example, and some don't, that runs essentially forever. This would allow you to uncover how your goal metric moves for those who experience the ad versus those who don't.

The world, however, isn't perfect, and the tools to perform testing vary. Some don't allow user-level holdouts; some campaigns would need so large a holdout you would materially harm your core goal. This chapter therefore aims to help you choose when to use what tool. I love experimentation, I love the rigour, I love knowing we did something that mattered and wasn't just busy work, and I love the defensibility it gives my work. But always remember, if you need a data scientist and a microscope to determine if your marketing had an impact, well then, it didn't.

Once you have experimental results, you usually need to scale them to large-scale decisions. Again, theoretically you should have long-term user-level holdouts through randomized control tests to expose the true impact of your work on the bottom-line goal metrics. As a practical matter, though, this just isn't possible. So typically, you must run a small or timebound experiment to validate your hypothesis that a certain campaign will have an impact, like adding 10 percent more new registrations. Then you take those experimental results and use them to model the incremental impact of your campaign for the next period, using other metrics like post-click conversions. This is the only practical way to run most campaigns, and it is a totally valid approach if you periodically validate that your original experimental results still hold true.

When I became head of marketing at Meta, many folks at the company and throughout the marketing industry were concerned. In the industry, I was described as a 'numbers nerd' (a badge I hold proudly, as you know) replacing a 'rockstar marketer'. Internally, I was told by one senior executive that 'creative people are different than numbers people – they put their heart and soul into their work'. Generally, I got a sense that my industry and Meta colleagues were concerned about the heartless, evil queen of numbers (me) destroying creativity. Hopefully, I have already put the outcomes of this alarmism to bed in the creativity chapter, but I'll admit I think this fear of the tyranny of numbers is well founded. With that in mind, think about the following points as you work through and implement this chapter. First, no measurement is perfect, and many crucial outcomes can't be measured at all. Don't let perfect measurement be the enemy of great impact or let it stop you from trying logical ideas, even if the results can never be measured. Second, embrace failure. I don't trust a team that never fail in their goals – either they are measuring wrong or the goals they set are far too easy to reach. Celebrate people trying, failing and getting better, or measurement might cause a culture of fear, destroying your long-term effectiveness.

KEEP IT SIMPLE, STUPID

In my opinion, the core of measurement is that you should know what can be measured and what cannot. This is so simple to say, but so hard to do. It's an idea that I have always stressed when taking on new teams. I often found that they tried to measure *everything*, assuming that's what I wanted because of my reputation for caring about measurement and because of my title as head of analytics. In the process, these teams contorted themselves into strange positions. For example, one team tried to measure the impact of a meeting where we invited a hundred clients to launch a product. There is no way we could statistically, significantly measure the impact of that meeting, but the team thought that's what I wanted, without talking to me, so they tried.

This was my fault, but it was a huge shock to me that all kinds of words and desires were put in my mouth that didn't line up with what I wanted or believed, or even said as far as I can remember. I saw this happen again when Meta performed budget cuts in 2022 and 2023, but this time the over-measurement was turbocharged. The remaining marketing team tried to please finance with measurements to protect their budgets and jobs.

Sometimes this meant we were so scared of not showing measurable results that we reduced creativity and risk-taking. We delivered on our core jobs, but looking back I wonder if we missed potential upside because of this. All of this was upsetting and, again, my fault. I have continually tried to fight this mindset and rectify this mistake and still have to do so to this day.

Today, I tell teams that they should measure what can be measured really well, then be clear when something can't be measured. If they do the first part well, then they will be trusted in their opinions on the second. If they do the first part badly and basic measurement can be criticized and pulled apart, they will never be trusted on the second. This has unlocked our ability to do amazing things.

A great example here can be found in my team that handle large-scale marketing campaigns to accelerate the growth of WhatsApp in the US. These campaigns are run across all the major media channels with designated market area (DMA), or geographic area, level and user-level randomized controlled tests. The key metric here is monthly active users, and the team have performed well on their contribution to driving incremental MAU of WhatsApp. They were also well measured on improving awareness, consideration and belief in WhatsApp's privacy.

In this case, awareness and consideration are telemetry – the metrics around a metric target that describe how you achieved it or didn't – for how we drove our key goal metric of active users. Privacy is a guardrail – a constraint that, in this case, tracks the brand strategy – to make sure people believed what we were promoting about the brand. This measurement was validated by product and finance teams, and the outcomes were considered to have worthwhile impact and be methodologically bulletproof.

This is also a great example of a team with range. That same team produced a documentary on how the Afghan Women's Football team used WhatsApp to communicate as they fled the Taliban. They also organized a promotion in which Lewis Hamilton – the greatest F1 driver of all time – did donuts on Fifth Avenue in New York, while a go-kart shaped like the WhatsApp sports car emoji drove next to him. Unsurprisingly, the short film and PR stunt weren't measurable on the final impact on active users, but we could prove they got reach and people saw them.

A team that is great at measurement and has real impact on the bottom line doesn't have to only take one approach or the other. Large-scale, measurable campaigns and cool stunts and one-offs both work. We can only truly measure the final impact on active users of the first one, but my team has space to do the others because we've measured the first so well and taken action on the data.

SIMPLIFY

For measurement, simplicity is beauty. As discussed, you always need a clear North Star metric. In my experience, there are three that have been most important in my work, depending on time and place: change perception, get active users and drive revenue. Note, you should pick one, not try to do all of them at once. You usually need lots of other metrics for telemetry to tell you why you succeeded or failed and how efficient you were, even if you did succeed. These other metrics will help you optimize your work.

Still, these metrics must never be confused with the one North Star metric. This sounds simple but you will always have multiple stakeholders, and their definitions of success will all vary slightly, and sometimes fundamentally. I have regularly seen teams throw every metric into the mix to please everyone, thinking there is no cost to this approach. What they should have done is have the hard conversation up front as to what could and could not be measured, and what the North Star goal means in practice. Too many metrics leads to confusion around what actions to take as it is rare for all metrics to move in sync. When it comes to optimizing a campaign as it runs, the direction of optimization can become confused without one North Star metric, and execution is harmed. You can also badly damage the judgement of the campaign if you give different leaders the ability to disagree on whether or not it succeeded based on the metrics that they individually value the most.

For example, it would be easy to set active users and sent messages as the two top-level goals for a WhatsApp campaign in the USA. Both matter, and even if you get more active users, if they send most of their messages via iMessage, then you are still losing. As a team, you could easily give in and set both metrics as top-priority goals. The issue here is that new users usually don't send a lot of messages for some time until they've ramped up. That means it would be perfectly normal to move active users by, say, a couple of percentage points (which currently means a couple of million users) but see no statistically significant difference in sent messages.

In that case, the executive who wanted to see more users would declare the campaign a success; the one who wanted more sent messages would declare it a failure. Worse still, to drive sent messages, you will generally be most effective if you get power users to send more, whereas to get more active users, you want sceptical users with low consideration of your product to try them. You don't need any fancy research to know those two metrics would result in totally different media channel optimizations and approaches, including in-product and online for power users and offline or off product for non-users.

What looks like a harmless agreement to take two top metrics for a campaign to perhaps placate two executives with slightly different views then ends up driving massively conflicted and different behaviours down the line for the campaign. I use this example, in part, because Will Cathcart, who runs WhatsApp, has actually been one of the most data-literate and best partners I have ever worked with and didn't let this happen.

So, keep it simple: measure what can be measured well and acknowledge what can't be. Get respect for that measurement, providing air cover for some of the less measurable campaigns or one-off promotions. Make sure you have a clear North Star metric, because even small, seemingly harmless metric additions can paralyse a team and cripple good execution. In data, the simpler the better and the more beautiful it is. Finally, try to depressurize failure – the point of measurement is to know how you did and iterate based on that. It's a simple plan, but sometimes fear and the impact of failure make it hard to execute.

DON'T KILL RISK-TAKING WITH MEASUREMENT

Something I try – though still struggle – to do is make sure everyone on my team knows that failure is expected. I explain that I won't believe them if they only bring me success stories, because, as discussed, that means either the goals were too easy or the team measured incorrectly. A favourite example of mine here is from 2023–24, when we ran a series of marketing events. At the events, we discussed direct response marketing with experts from our company and partners in front of an audience of thousands of marketers around the world.

In the first series of events while I managed the team, held in 2023, we invited digital direct response marketers selected by our sales leaders. But at the end of the 2023 series, we showed no uplift in our tests, whereas most of our other events showed clear revenue lift in their wake. We scrutinized this finding and realized we had invited people who had already implemented all our best practices. Even though they loved the summit in survey responses, we were just confirming for them that they were taking the right approach, and they were not changing their behaviours. We had been preaching to the choir.

So, for the second year, 2024, we changed the heuristic. We invited direct response marketers who did *not* adhere to our best practices. As you'd expect, in 2024, we got better results. This is what you should be looking for: failure, learning and iteration. I try hard in all-hands and Q&As and other media to celebrate these examples, because we measured well, we learned we had failed, we acted and got better results without killing the programme, just iterating. Celebrating these moments is part of how I try to depressurize measurement in the team (which is needed with someone like me in charge). It's an approach any digital marketer can, and should, take with their team.

GOAL, METRIC, TARGET

For about five or six years, we have run a campaign in analytics at Meta called 'better decisions'. The goal of this campaign is to improve the quality of our analytics as a way to lead to better decisions for the company. One key part of this work is to break down how to measure a team's success. We spent a lot of time working through this idea, and we have come up with a useful way of talking about success that helps analytics teams do their best work.

In general, every team has some big mission they are trying to achieve, such as connect the world online. Then they have a number of strategies to pursue to achieve that mission, like convincing everyone on the internet to use the service, and to get more people online in general. After that, they have a number of tactics lined up to achieve that strategy. In the case of this example, getting more people online could include using satellites for broadcast, placing WiFi terminals at train stations, running ads to tell people the internet is great or doing zero-rating deals with operators, in which internet service is provided free with conditions.

Those tactics then have goals, such as getting as many new people as possible to use our services with the zero-rating offering. Those goals then have metrics; maybe in this case it is the number of users on zero rating we haven't seen before. Finally, there will be a target, say, acquire 10 million more active users through zero rating than we would have had without it in the next six months.

This hierarchy can be broken down as follows:

1. **Mission** – What are you trying to achieve as a team, company or organization?
2. **Strategy** – How do you plan to achieve it?
3. **Tactic** – What are the actions you need to take to execute the strategy?
4. **Goal** – What is the outcome expected from the tactic?
5. **Metric** – How do you express that outcome as a number?
6. **Target** – How much do you want that number to move in a given timeframe?

I regularly see stages 3 through 6 conflated with one word: goal. This mostly causes problems when the metric doesn't accurately describe the goal, which can become a huge issue, as it leads you to think broadly, not precisely. For the example of a certain tactic driving more people to use your product, buy your item or sign up for your service, what I see most commonly is an attribution error and a lack of incremental measurement.

Specifically, let's say we create a zero-rating product with an operator where a user can use Facebook for free five days a month and then has to pay to upgrade to more days. A mistake I have seen in situations like this is teams measuring the number of people using this service, as compared to measuring the number of people using the service who wouldn't be using the product otherwise. The latter is clearly far harder to do. Precision in defining the metric so it matches the goal is important here. That then puts pressure on measurement teams to find creative ways to create that metric, which isn't trivial. I see this time and time again – executives just saying yes to a metric without fully considering whether it measures what they want. Metrics and goals need to be separate, and clear.

TARGETS, TELEMETRY AND GUARDRAILS

Another refrain I often hear from team members, colleagues and across the marketing industry is that we have too many goals. This even comes up in situations where I think we have a focused North Star and I have talked at length about the difference between metrics and goals. (This is worth noting, because it would be easy to read this book and think I have everything sorted and working the way I am describing – in no way is that true with a multi-thousand-person organization across marketing, design, analytics, internationalization and more.) I find that when people make this statement, they are confusing telemetry and guardrail metrics with goal metrics, and forgetting that the North Star metric that describes the goal is the only actual goal metric; everything else is just helping you to understand how the work is progressing.

Telemetry metrics are all the metrics around a metric target that describe how you did or did not achieve it. These include, for example, the number of people reached (an ad can't influence people without them seeing it), frequency of impressions per person (usually, repetition doesn't spoil the prayer, but there are diminishing returns), the budget spend, and dwell time (if people only watch three seconds of a thirty-second ad, then it's unlikely to convince them). Often these subsidiary metrics have targets we want to achieve in order to hit the big target overall. Any good measurement for a campaign should have a number of these metrics.

If you've ever been on the bridge of a ship, you'll know the captain has one goal, which is to deliver their cargo, whether passengers or freight, to their destination on time. The target metric is a simple 1 or 0 – did it happen or not? The bridge, however, has many dashboards. There are multiple sonar and radar screens, a complicated fuel readout, a fire detection system, waste and water systems (all with metrics on each tank and pipe), fuel metrics, engine performance and many more. A good marketer is like a good captain – they have all the dashboards and data necessary to see if their team will deliver on the overall target. Each dashboard has its own optimal operating window, and as a marketer you are trying to keep them in the window of optimal operation. That is the way it should be: you should have lots of metrics, often with their own targets around them. But you must remember they only exist in the service of the one big North Star goal, and the metric that describes it – if missing one of the other metrics gets you there, then go for it.

A separate class of metric is known as a guardrail metric. This metric is not your target, but a constraint. For me, the guardrail often tracks the brand strategy. A key example from my experience is Everyday Creativity for Instagram. All our social network brands have connection as a red thread in what their brand stands for. But each one has another value as well: privacy for WhatsApp, discovery for Facebook and Everyday Creativity for Instagram.

When I run campaigns to drive adoption of Instagram, it is critical that the team does so while expressing creativity, allowing Meta to maintain brand distinctiveness between products. This is true in other industries too. Hotel brands, for example, need to stand for premium or value, even if they come from the same company. I place guardrails on our Instagram growth campaigns in a way that I expect will force the 'creativity' survey metric upwards, or at least to remain neutral. Other guardrails might include cost per action (CPA) on direct response campaigns. The goal isn't to simply get as many registrations as possible, but to do so under a certain price.

So, though great results come from one clear North Star metric as your target, that doesn't mean you don't utilize and check other metrics. It's important the team is clear on the North Star metric, the telemetry metrics (including those that can be ignored if the campaign gets results) and the guardrails that must be adhered to in order to avoid mucking up some other part of the strategy. By following these metrics, you can steer your ship to give it the best chance of delivering your target and in the best way possible.

EXPERIMENTS

To validate if a strategy is the right one, you must execute it well enough, ideally perfectly, to know if it can work. If you execute poorly, then a question will always hang in the air about whether the strategy was good or not - its lacklustre results, or failure, could have been indicative of the execution, not the strategy itself. That's why my close colleague, and genius product leader, Naomi Gleit focuses Meta on perfect execution. Perfect execution allows us to validate whether a strategy is worth continuing to pursue. To know whether your execution was flawless, or flawed, you need a way to judge the actions you performed. I do this through a combination of experimental measurement, common sense and good judgement.

I cannot tell you how to have common sense and good judgement here – I'm not sure I'm the best coach on those anyway – but I can explain how to run good experiments. Fundamentally, there are three practical ways of running experiments I come back to again and again:

1. Randomized controlled (or A/B) testing.
2. Matched markets and cohorts testing.
3. Pre/post testing.

All three experiments have their place, but no matter which experiment you choose, you are trying to determine if the project you're measuring mattered incrementally to the company. Is it incrementally beneficial or would the company have been just as successful if you simply hadn't run the campaign? That's clearly critical information for the company, but personally I also want to show up to work knowing things are incrementally better because what I did actually mattered. Let's examine each of these three experiment types in more detail.

Randomized controlled (or A/B) testing

Randomized controlled testing (also known as A/B testing) is the gold standard of experiments. As defined earlier, this is when you test offerings or approaches using a randomly selected experiment group and a control group. What it means in digital marketing is taking a set of IDs (usually user IDs but it could be keyword IDs) and randomly assigning them to test and control groups. You then run a treatment in the test group, showing them an ad, and afterwards measure your key metrics to see if they changed in the test group who saw your treatment versus the control group who did not. This is an especially powerful tool in places where you have control over what you show to a given ID. For example, email, direct mail and in-product merchandising are excellent channels for A/B testing. I joined Meta because I believed we would revolutionize marketing through this kind of testing, showing the true incrementality of online display advertising, which Meta has achieved through lift studies (a product that does A/B testing as part of Meta's ad products). Over time, I believe more and more channels will have this capability (for example, connected TV), and it will help us be more accurate than ever about the effectiveness of our ads.

Matched markets/cohorts

Matched markets/cohorts is probably the most common testing in the history of advertising. It is where you run an ad to a market or cohort, then find a similar market or cohort but don't show them the ad. This is often location-based. You then compare the actions of those who did and those who did not see the ad. Matched markets is best in channels where you do not have a simple ID on which you can do A/B testing. For example, you could run a TV ad in Philadelphia but not in Pittsburgh and see what happens. This was the first incrementality measurement I ever worked on in my career – on eBay UK's first TV ad, while I was a junior analyst – and I still actively use it today. You can use this testing in any channel that lets you target cohorts in this way. Best of all, you can test multiple channels at the same time by, say, having a city with TV, radio, billboard and internet ads versus one with just a TV ad, or some other combination.

When you select matched markets or cohorts to test, they need to be matched by definition. We approach this by looking at our North Star goal metric and then ensuring that the cohorts or markets we are matching have similar per capita numbers for that metric and, importantly, similar trends. Imagine, for example, two states, both with 20 percent of people using WhatsApp, but one state has a growth rate of 20 percent month on month using the app and the other has only 1 percent. If you then run an ad to see how much you can increase the usage of WhatsApp in the state with 1 percent growth but use the state with 20 percent growth as a holdout, your test results would be useless because the markets weren't matched in a key metric, WhatsApp growth. Even if you grew WhatsApp in the 1 percent growth state by 5 percent, it would seem like growth was slower because the other state would continue growing at 20 percent month on month. You can run a similar thought experiment for one state with 90 percent of people using WhatsApp monthly and one state with 10 percent. An ad campaign to acquire users would have very different impacts in those two states, and so they wouldn't be matched.

Therefore, the most important aspect of this testing is to match both the absolute position and trend of the metric describing your North Star goal. We then tend to look at the metrics we are setting as telemetry metrics and guardrail metrics and make sure they are similar as well. We also look at utilization of the channels we are buying in. If you are matching India and Pakistan as similar markets but buying ads on TikTok, that would be an extreme mistake – as of 2025, TikTok was banned in India and available in Pakistan. Finally, we tend to evaluate demographic differences, like age, wealth and gender, to match markets, but this is lowest priority and often less important.

I use matched market/cohort testing when I back-test my randomized controlled test results (back testing here is to run another, different test to validate the results of the randomized controlled test). I might, for example, turn off paid search in, say, India but keep it on in the rest of the world as a control, then see what happens. Though this may be an old measurement method, it is a powerful one. For much of my career, I have had to quell both my own and others' arrogance about how great internet measurement is, by recalling the fact that long-term big-brand companies like Procter & Gamble and Unilever have mastered this approach to great success. They are good at knowing incrementally how many extra bars of soap will be sold based on an ad they run because they have to make them and stock them, and that's all thanks to how brilliant they are at this kind of testing. I feel this testing is the workhorse of all my advertising campaigns, and for giving your team air cover, nothing beats it, because seeing a change of results in a place you can visit versus some random set of users is visceral.

Pre/post testing

Pre/post testing is the bluntest tool of the lot. It's a straightforward before and after experiment: you weren't doing something, then you started doing something, and then you see what happened. Maybe there is zero awareness about a new product you're rolling out, but after a huge launch, everyone seems to be talking about it. Or maybe there is no direct response marketing, so you turn it on and test the results. The previous two methodologies work at any product stage but, generally, pre/post testing has to be implemented early on in a product you are marketing or a project you are working on.

It is also generally best used in a channel where you can't easily perform one of the other two methodologies, such as when you are early to market and running a test would be impractical. I have used this testing successfully but only in places – channels, conversion events and moments in time – where I was confident the results would be impossible to miss. When you can use this method, it proves to be the most impressive of them all, probably because it is so easy to grasp. If testing reveals a total step change in top line for some metric, everyone can see it themselves for the entire product. Pre/post testing is also a slam dunk as air cover for the team and inspiration for your colleagues about what marketing can do.

DON'T FORGET THE METRIC

Across all three of these experiments, you can test any metric, but the sensitivity varies dramatically depending on the metric itself. Generally, randomized controlled tests give you the most sensitivity and pre/post the least. Usually, behavioural metrics are easy to measure, and sentiment and survey metrics are harder to measure, but see uplift in an experiment.

For metrics that are harder to measure, go with bigger test and control groups. A 50:50 ratio – half in test and half in control – typically gives you the greatest power, but in many cases this isn't practical because you are supposed to get a result as well as run an experiment, and this would eliminate half your result by not marketing to half the audience. This is really where you come back to what *can* be measured should be measured well. But, as discussed, you should acknowledge some things just can't be measured easily. Even if there is a metric that will let you measure a certain goal or tactic, it may have so few data points that it is essentially unusable for experimentation. There is a lot more I could go into here on experimental practice around p-hacking, statistical tests and other new methods, but that would fill a whole book on its own. So, before I move on, I want to leave you with this: as I reiterate at the start of this chapter, if you need a data scientist and a microscope to figure out if you had impact, then you didn't. Too often I have seen results that are statistically significant but not actually significant being paraded around. Please, don't fall into that trap.

MODELS

Now I *love* experiments, but I hate modelled results, particularly media mix modelling (MMM). MMM is an analytical method for forecasting the impact of each marketing channel on an outcome. I find it upsetting whenever I see MMM used, because it means we don't have a real holdout and experimental design to see if a given channel worked. This opinion has been a source of tension between me and my measurement teams, including my mentor in marketing analytics from eBay, Dr Tom Tang. However, Dr Tang still works with me today, he loves MMM and he regularly uses it effectively, proving me wrong.

Of course, I am being somewhat tongue in cheek. You should indeed use models, but I believe you should only use them when you have run the experiment first, and then you must periodically back-test to make sure the result is still valid. Running experiments like those described determines the incrementality of a given channel. If it is practical, you should run those experiments for a long time to determine the long-term impact of the channel and to ensure the impact remains.

But the reality of the matter is that experiments are expensive. They take resources to run, both in terms of people and budget, and they can limit results. Consider effect size versus the size of campaign. You may need the holdout to be half the size of the campaign to be able to show a 10 percent lift in your

North Star goal metric with 95 percent statistical confidence in the result. But you would be taking half the set of potential customers and *not* marketing to them, therefore limiting the impact.

This is why models can be useful. After you run experiments, you get weights (essentially the incremental impact) for each channel. Then you continue to run the marketing campaign without the testing and use the weights to determine the media mix. You then estimate the impact using an MMM. Here, you are multiplying the reach and frequency of a given channel by the constant you gained from your experiment and summing across the channels. In other words, you are predicting the impact of the campaign using a model based on your existing results, stating that impact as your hypothesis of what will happen and measuring the result in a pre/post manner.

At Meta, we use models in multiple channels and campaigns, from direct response marketing paid search campaigns to brand marketing awareness- and consideration-driving campaigns. The key with models is that you must periodically back-test them. Models are always based on out-of-date data – your campaigns age, your creative goes stale and different channels fluctuate in their effectiveness, either because of diminishing returns or because changes you didn't even know about took place (like the deployment of a new ad-ranking algorithm). I have mentioned this before, but you can't take a result from five years ago and use it to determine how your marketing is working today.

So, yes, use models and trust them, but periodically *validate* they are still accurate and the world hasn't moved on. The canonical example in my experience is found in Meta's paid search work. I can't run A/B tests for paid search – it must be matched markets or pre/post tests. The costs of running these are big, because for many countries we need to turn their paid search campaign fully off for a month to see the impact. That would mean losing about 10 percent of our annual impact if we did this every year. None of my business partners are comfortable with this idea, so we run tests in different countries each year, then use models for the other countries and the rest of the year based on those results.

GOODHART'S LAW

In the end, measurements, metrics and models are only as good as your behaviours around them. British economist Charles Goodhart outlined his Goodhart's law as: 'Any observed statistical regularity will tend to collapse once pressure is placed upon it for control purposes.' I like to paraphrase this law as follows: any metric used as a target ceases to be a useful metric. Every metric can be gamed. Active users can be driven by clicks from users who bounce after one second. Revenue can be driven by high fraud users who cause credit card chargebacks sixty days later that never get attributed to marketing. To some extent, you can work around these types of issues with guardrail metrics. What matters most, however, is that you, as a leader, have the integrity to not game the metric deliberately, while searching for how it might be inflated accidentally. To do that, you can use a combination of the approaches outlined in the sections above:

- Fight for simplicity: it is harder to hide when your metrics are simple.
- Ensure your metric accurately describes your goal, and make sure you know where it is weak – ask your team to help you find that weakness.
- Put telemetry metrics around those weaknesses and the easy ways the metric could be gamed.

- Learn from experiments, and when the metric moves but you feel like something isn't quite right, dig in and figure out why.

- Listen to the anecdotes and user feedback – where they don't back your data, trust them and investigate them. Amazon executive chairman Jeff Bezos has said very publicly that when the metric and the anecdote don't match, generally the anecdote is true.

Above all, though, you must create a culture where people are rewarded for finding problems and sharing them with the team, bad news being communicated quickly to management and continual improvement of their work.

MEASUREMENT LEADS TO ALL GREAT THINGS

My boss, Javier Olivan, has bequeathed me some great sayings. 'In theory, theory and practice are the same; in practice, they are different' is possibly my favourite. Nowhere in my job is this maxim truer than in measurement. In theory, digital marketing solves all issues by uncovering the impact of our marketing. It delivers new tools to help us avoid wasting a lot of marketing dollars. Still, in practice, digital marketing is a huge step forward, but it is not perfect. Not everything that matters can be measured, even today.

For what can be measured, doing it well requires great measurement. This stems from a clear North Star goal and a metric to describe it. You also need to understand if you are executing well – again, measurement is key. Look at telemetry metrics, like the number of people who have seen your ads, and guardrail metrics, such as if a MAU you drove did anything more than just visit a site for a single page view.

Once you have this all in place, you must build great experimental infrastructure to measure if you had any incremental impact. The right form of experiment for the maturity of your product, size of expected impact and capabilities of the channel you are using is also necessary. You scale this whole process through models, which take experimental results and extrapolate them to large-scale campaigns. The final stage is periodically validating that your experimental results have continued to hold true, and the world hasn't changed so much that they are no longer valid.

Great measurement gives you space to achieve incredible things. It does this because results garner respect, trust and autonomy from your peers and management. Measurement also allows you to let your team run, if they are clear about what they need to achieve and how you will judge whether they achieved it. However, this can be a double-edged sword that kills creativity and experimentation if you punish failure instead of rewarding the attempt, where people experiment, measure results and change their campaigns based on that measurement to get better results in future. You can also create a far less impactful team if you only do things that can be perfectly measured. So don't form a tyranny of measurement – it is a tool, and one that has taken a huge step forward through digital marketing. Use it well and you will deliver great results.

8. MARGINAL AND INCREMENTAL RETURNS IN PAID CHANNELS

In many ways, I would argue this chapter is the most important one in the book. The premise here is simple. For many companies, especially the large ones I have worked at and with, there is a lot of pent-up demand for their product. People often end up visiting their websites and apps as a result of organic word of mouth, communications and brand marketing. At Meta, that means direct response marketing does not drive every conversion we track. So, we should *only* take credit for the incremental impact direct response marketing has on changing potential users' behaviour and converting them the whole way through the marketing funnel. This is imperative to understanding which methods, strategies and campaigns actually work – and which don't.

Take, as an example, buying your own brand name in paid search, a topic I touch upon in Chapter 5 and explore more intimately in Chapter 13. There is a great debate around the effectiveness of this approach. I, for the record, am generally against it, but I can always be convinced to do it with testing. Whether I believe you should or should not buy your own brand name, I, and the rest of my team, have to accept that the users we acquire after they click on an ad where we bought the word 'Facebook' in paid search are less likely to be incremental than if they came from a different marketing activity. After all, they were already searching for 'Facebook'. Of course, that principle extends to any other brand.

There are two key questions at the core of this chapter. First, what would have happened if you did nothing? You should know your incremental impact and not just take credit for every post-click conversion. Second, how much money do you make on the last dollar you spend? It's easier to spend your first hundred dollars effectively than your last. Both questions revolve around your ROI.

MAXIMIZE ROI

The point of paid online marketing is to, above everything else, maximize return on investment (ROI). When working with paid channels I believe there are two simple questions you need to ask: what is my marginal ROI, and what is my incremental impact? Marginal return is the return from your last dollar spent. Too often I see people measure average ROI only and not look at marginal ROI. But you can have great average ROI while you lose money on the margin. Incremental return is understanding what would happen if you weren't marketing at all, and its impact is the most important of the two. With incremental return, how much of what you track as marketing would have happened anyway? Sometimes the answer is that marketing has a bigger impact than you directly measure through simple post-click or impression measurement. But mostly, the impact is smaller. If you care about the outcome, then you need to know the incrementality for everything you do.

This work, focusing on incrementality and marginal returns, spoke to me in my early time at eBay and has returned dividends in my career ever since. (I have a lot to thank folks like Mike

Osborn, John Koryl and Tom Tang for; not just for their mentorship at that time, but also for my thinking in this section of the book. Both in my day job and in consulting and advising, their insight has been tremendously useful.) A huge part of the reason I became head of analytics at Meta is that I was trusted to do a bigger job based, in part, on developing a rigour for data in executing online marketing.

A focus on incremental ROI, overall and on the margin, is also valuable if you are a CMO or marketing manager working with finance. Finance folks intuitively understand marginal and incremental ROI, so if you can show them even basic technical understanding here, they'll better grasp your work and its importance.

In concept, maximizing ROI is simple:

1. There are diminishing returns in marketing, so your last dollar makes you less ROI than your first. Given the reality of a constrained budget, you should invest across your work so the last dollar in each channel or campaign makes you the same amount across them all.

2. Not all conversions you drive will be incremental, and the bigger and better-known your brand, the less incremental they will be. You should be disciplined about running experiments to figure out how many of your conversions are actually driven by you and only take credit for those.

3. In an ideal world, you should optimize to the marginal, incremental ROI of each campaign and channel.

You will get credit for trying. Having the finance department and C-suite recognize you are a marketer who cares how you are spending the company's money, and that you are spending it well, will go a long way.

Today most of the work to analyse and optimize marginal,

incremental ROI is done by the automated bidding systems and budget allocation systems that the majority of scaled campaigns use. But again, there is value in understanding what is going on under the hood in case anything goes wrong. There is also margin to be made from someone who goes beyond what the simple off-the-shelf technology provides, especially on incrementality.

LIFETIME VALUE (LTV)

To calculate ROI you have to know the value of the action you are driving. In my experience, you can typically drive three user behaviour changes:

1. Acquisition of a new user.
2. Reacquisition or resurrection of a user who was, but is not currently, active.
3. Increased activity from existing users.

Obviously, different channels are better and worse for each of these, and some new user acquisition is lead-generated, not from registration. To do any of the further calculations, however, we need to be able to convert these actions into dollar values. For most teams, their true goal isn't user acquisition or even MAU growth, but instead, revenue maximization. Figuring out how to calculate revenue earned from these three user behaviour changes is key to a lot of marketing teams, as it was for me at eBay, in my advertiser acquisition work at Meta, and in much of my startup advising and consulting.

For acquisitions and resurrections, look at an average user and calculate the revenue they generated on the first day they were registered, then the second day, then the third day and so on. I do this regardless of whether the person who registered three days ago is still active or not. This is because the probability of a person being active is just one factor in how much revenue a typical user generates on that day. This means you get fewer data points over time, because all people who use your service will have been registered for one day, but fewer will have been registered for two days, three days and so on. This causes the graph to typically get noisier the further out you go. The sum of all these values over the length of time you define as a 'lifetime' for a user becomes the lifetime value (LTV). I will show you an actual graph used to calculate this below. This approach also works if you just use resurrection instead of registration as the conversion.

Next, I measure this revenue only for conversions tagged through the given channel we are measuring. One fascinating thing I have found here is that clickers are gonna click. So, if you have a business based on people clicking on ads, you can get a higher LTV from someone who registers via an ad than someone who adopts your product from word of mouth. For other businesses I have found the reverse to be true – on average, an acquisition from pure word of mouth is more valuable than one from an ad, but it is clearly difficult, if not impossible, to deliver more word-of-mouth conversions through digital marketing.

After homing in on conversions tagged through the given channel we are measuring, we agree with finance on the duration of a 'lifetime' to use. Some companies swear by one year, though I have typically used three. This length is a source of great debate, and I don't believe there is a magic, accurate formula here, so taking a conservative approach (as in fewer years) is probably better.

Finally, you then sum the area under the curve for the

lifetime you have agreed upon with finance. You can see a real-world example of an LTV curve below. This curve is basically supposed to show the revenue generated over the lifetime of an average user on a service.

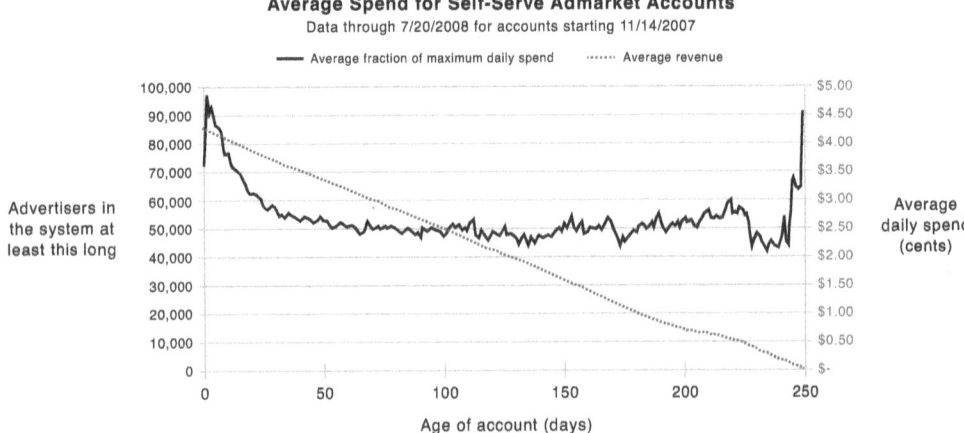

The lifetime value curve for advertisers acquired in the first year of Facebook ads

This curve is from 2008, looking at the 'lifetime' value of our advertisers for our self-serve ad product. There are three key takeaways to note:

1. The curve flattens quickly and stays flat, which is common.
2. There are fewer and fewer data points the further to the right you go (denoted by the dotted line) because not many advertisers have been using the new product for that long.
3. The graph jumps about (gets noisier) the fewer data points you have (as you move further to the right).

This graph was incredibly useful for us at Facebook for a few reasons. First, we could uncover the value of the advertisers we acquired. We asked finance to determine how many days we should take credit for them, and they decided on one year, though over time this went up to three years. Once we knew that, we could determine the revenue an average advertiser acquisition would give us. This gave us the R in ROI and let us set the CPA targets, with the action, in cost per action, being acquisition.

Second, given that the curve flattens, we only needed to wait sixty days to be able to predict the LTV of a cohort of users. In practice, this meant when we started a new campaign, like adding a new custom audience to target in buying Facebook ads, we could determine the lifetime value of those advertisers. That value showed us the ROI of that custom audience after sixty days of running the ads, as we were able to extrapolate the flat part of the curve out at day sixty for the remaining 305 days of the year.

I have used this approach as a consultant, employee, advisor, vendor and board member across pretty much every industry in some way. There are places where it isn't as valuable (like someone buying a car, which is a deeply infrequent purchase), but in most places this LTV work is core to the job, and the findings above and methodology are consistent.

For in-product marketing and direct mail, I typically run AB tests for a relatively long period (up to a year) and look at the uplift in revenue in the test vs control over that time. The result of the test exposes the value of the campaign. For offsite campaigns, where I can't set up as perfect an experiment, I regularly use short-term measurements, such as the revenue that has been generated in the actual session resulting from that paid ad offsite.

However, I personally believe this approach consistently undervalues offsite advertising. You could easily be taking a person and changing their state to be a more active user long term or even stopping them from churning so you don't need to resurrect them, through that paid marketing campaign. Clearly, if you define 'monthly' as active, then being active thirty days ago versus thirty-one days ago isn't, in reality, a big difference. But if you measure 'resurrections' as getting activity from someone who hasn't been active for thirty-one days, it most certainly becomes a big difference. That said, I have never successfully argued or investigated this theory; it remains a theory for me for offsite ads and a practice for onsite and direct mail campaigns. But if we, as an industry, were to solve this issue, it would be a game-changer.

Now that we have LTV for the events generated by our campaign, we can sum up the agreed LTV of all the events our campaign is driving to get the total revenue our campaign is driving. We can now use that total revenue to generate the ROI on our campaign. As a formula, this would appear as:

(revenue from campaign/spend on campaign – 1)*100 = ROI (as a %)

Next, we have to optimize to maximize that ROI.

MARGINAL ROI

Early in my career, I was lucky to work with a number of incredible people on the eBay paid search team. Mike Osborn, in particular, was a brilliant mentor and introduced me to allocating budgets based on marginal ROI. (There were lots of other awesome folks there, like Chris Howard, Chris Orton, Tom Tang, Matt Madrigal, John Koryl, Ramana Thumu and more I'm missing, who did really important work that remains influential on my approach to digital marketing.) With Mike's economics background, he treated buying paid search like a near-perfect marketplace. Since then, I have found buying online ads across all channels can mostly be considered through this lens.

To start, we looked at budgets on Yahoo!, Microsoft and Google and how we allocated across those channels using this methodology. Over time, people like Tom Tang (who I've been lucky to work with twice) created clusters of similar keywords. We could then cross-allocate budget at the keyword cluster level, not only the individual search engine or partner level.

So how does this work in practice? Let's run through a simple example. I have generated a fake marginal return curve here for a search engine we're allocating budget towards. It is an xy scatter plot, with daily spend on the x axis and daily return on the y axis, then a line of best fit, representing the trend shown, fitted to the data. In reality, the data is never this clean, and you will never have a data set this complete either, but it serves the purpose of how to think about this concept.

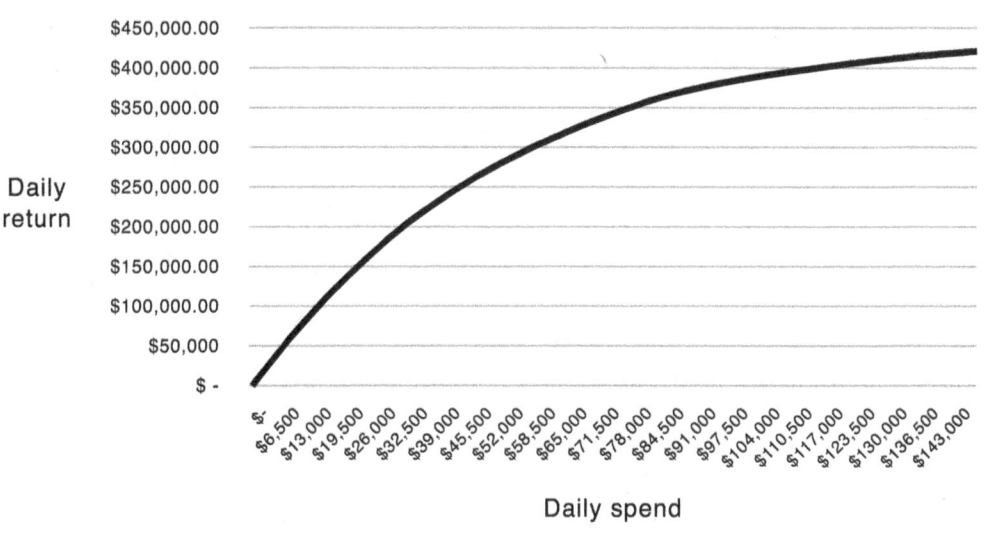

Daily spend versus daily return

The curve shown is fairly standard, and this generates an average ROI at each point of daily spend, represented in the following formula:

((daily return/daily spend) – 1)*100

With this average ROI at each point of daily spend, that looks like the following:

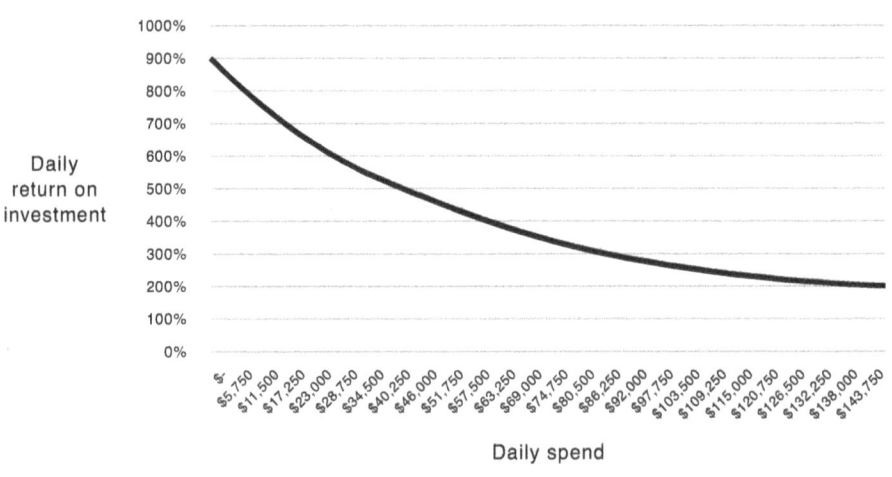

Daily spend versus daily ROI

Again, this is a totally reasonable curve. What's important to recognize, though, is what happens when you look at the marginal ROI at each point in the curve.

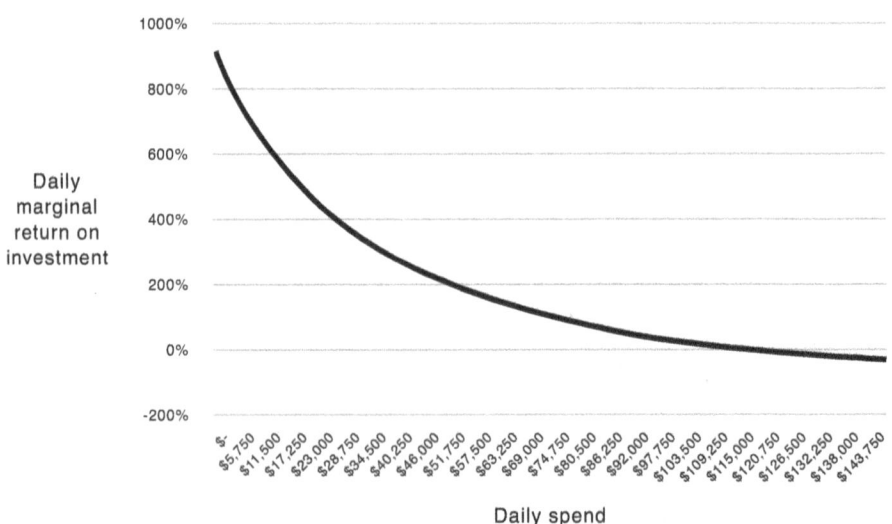

Daily spend versus daily marginal ROI

Daily marginal ROI totally changes the graph. Instead of having a healthy 200 percent ROI at the right-hand end of the graph, you actually start losing money on every dollar you spend over $115,000 daily. So, let's say you have a budget of $150,000 a day to spend on this particular channel. If you just gave back $35,000 a day, instead of spending it, you would move your overall ROI from 180 percent to 239 percent.

Looking at marginal ROI may feel simple or obvious, but twenty years after I had this revelation, I still talk to people for whom this is a surprise. So, check your numbers and check with your team. Ask them, and yourself, are you allocating based on marginal ROI or not? As mentioned, your data will not be as clean as the above, *but*, you should get some form of diminishing return curve in your scatter of daily spend levels. You will be able to fit a curve to that graph and create better returns than the simple average ROI gives you.

CROSS-CHANNEL BUDGET ALLOCATION

The second big revelation for me around ROI was how powerful cross-channel budget allocation could be, if done properly. Cross-channel budget allocation is how you allocate the budget you have to spend between your various channels, whether search vs social, social vs retail ad networks or any others. Here again I have generated data for two different search engines and asked the question, how do you allocate most efficiently between them? This graph doesn't look too dissimilar to the state of Yahoo! and Google in the US twenty years ago for many companies.

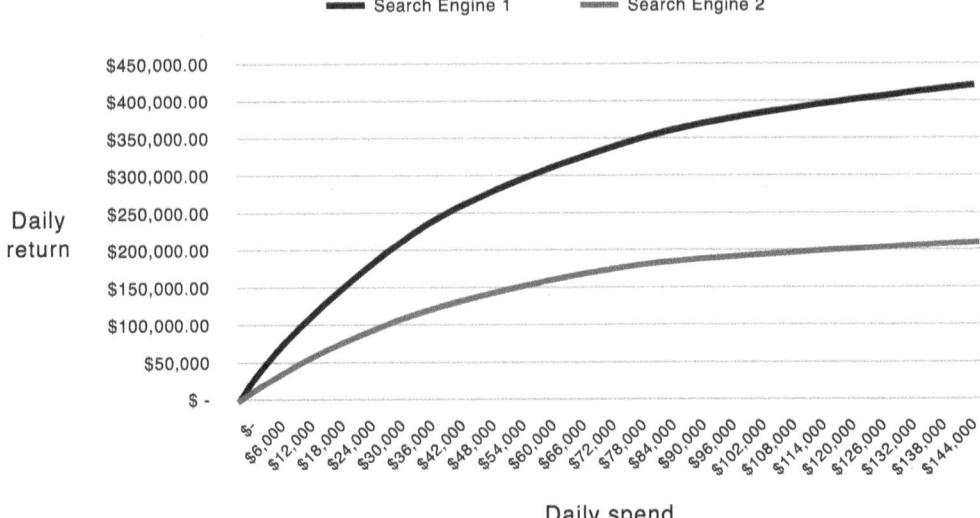

Daily spend versus daily return for two search engines

In this case, the assumption would be that search engine 1 (SE1) always has a greater ROI than search engine 2 (SE2). Following that line of thinking, you should invest almost all of your budget into SE1, while maybe keeping a test budget live in SE2 to track whether the returns changed over time; you would then revisit SE2 and allocate more budget to it if appropriate. This is how many decisions were made in the dawn of internet marketing, and there are still teams who allocate their budget that way today. This allocation would yield 180 percent ROI.

However, if you instead allocate based on marginal ROI being equal between the channels for a spend of $150,000 total, you would get an ROI of 343 percent, nearly doubling your ROI. In this case, you would allocate approximately $95,000 to SE1 and approximately $55k to SE2. You can see the shape of the curve here:

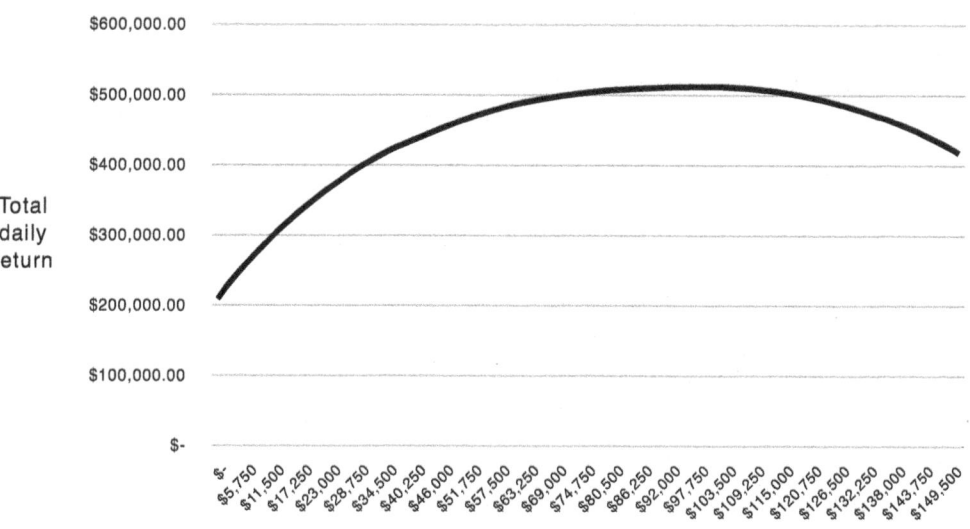

Total daily spend (of $150k) in search engine 1

Total daily spend SE1 versus total daily return

The teams I have been on and around have taken this methodology far further, enabled by the tools now available. This methodology can be used cross-channel, cross-company within each channel, and even at the cluster level of different keywords and campaigns within each channel and company you are buying from. As you can see, there is huge yield to simple budget allocation decisions based on marginal ROI, not just looking at the averages. (I also want to thank Jeremy Bulow from Stanford who, in my early time at Facebook, as it was then, really crystallized my understanding of this area.)

THE IMPERATIVE OF EXPERIMENTATION

In the last chapter, I discussed experimentation as part of measurement. In this section, I am going to practically apply it.

You cannot do incrementality without experimentation. As explained, the gold standard is randomized controlled (or A/B) tests. At Meta, we build these into our core platform with lift studies for those advertisers that have a big enough scale to run them.

Unlike the investment based on marginal ROI, I have seen less enthusiasm from teams to look hard at incrementality and track incremental ROI. I think this is because incremental ROI can be more threatening than marginal ROI as it raises the fundamental question: did my work matter? Marginal ROI is more a question of, how can I be better at doing what I already do?

I find the former question psychologically stressful, as I am sure others do too, but it is worth asking and answering, as it will allow your team to be the best team possible and ensure what you do makes a difference. So how do you go about uncovering and working towards incremental ROI? You want to do as much as you can with valid A/B tests. You should then scale the data you get from those tests with models to judge how your work is going overall. Finally, you must back-test A/B tests where you can, which I do by periodically switching off my marketing campaigns and ads.

For the A/B tests, a randomized controlled test is the holy grail. Your owned and operated surfaces are usually the best place to perform an A/B test to expose the incremental benefit of your marketing. Social is the second-best place to do incrementality testing. Social companies let you target individual users and usually run user-level holdouts for some time. To a lesser extent, display ads let you do this as well, but with lower-quality data and shorter durations over which you can trust the holdout. Usually, you can only do keyword-level A/B tests in paid search, which aren't great, and channels like affiliate marketing simply don't offer this option.

When you set up an A/B test, you must be clear on its hypothesis. In marketing, this is usually straightforward: the hypothesis is that the marketing drives the action you are tracking as the outcome of the marketing. Before you run the experiment, make sure it will be big enough to detect the uplift you want. These days, this setup is simple using an off-the shelf-stats package, and most vendors and agencies will even help you with it. But don't skimp on this step or you might find your test ends up telling you nothing.

When you run the A/B tests and see what number of conversions you get in your control and test groups, check that this is statistically significant via one of the above stats packages. Then use that data to show the incremental value of your campaign, *not* the full number of conversions you track as being attributed to the campaign, as that is almost always an overestimate.

When running the tests, have your team keep an eye out for contamination. The best way to do this is to look for attributed conversion events in your test group. I have seen this happen often in onsite merchandising across multiple companies. Say, a small engineering change takes place, and a measurement holdout is broken. So, we might, for example, show a promotion to install Messenger to someone in the control group, not just the test group. Or maybe a setting is misapplied in an ad server and banner ads go to our holdout users. When these users from our holdout or control appear as attributed conversions, we almost always have a big problem.

Contamination invalidates the entire test because test and control are getting the same treatment. This means you will see zero uplift because, as with all data, garbage in, garbage out. I often hear people bellyaching about the stats package they are using, but rarely about whether the test is fundamentally valid. At least once a year, though, I have a marketing campaign measurement materially damaged by a mistake in an experimental setup. Whereas I cannot remember a stats issue we haven't figured out how to fix.

When you get the test results, believe them and use them. You have to understand your test, recognizing its function and its limits, *but* if you get a result after all that work, whether you like it or not, please believe it. Again, across my career I have regularly had to deal with people throwing out test results because they didn't agree with them. Tests are informative, giving you insight into how close you are to achieving your North Star goal. If you don't use them, they are a waste of time, money and effort. Tests should influence you to change your behaviour based on the results. The most important way to do this is to take the test data and put it into models. (These models can be as simple as incremental percent change on a given channel to fully blown media mix modelling.) Then use that model to drive decisions and optimization in your campaign allocations and work.

Back testing

I personally add one more step into my testing protocols. As mentioned in Chapter 7, I find a back test useful to validate that the tests were correct. I learned this at eBay after a disagreement between Google and eBay leadership over Google payments, and a stunt Google did at eBay live Boston. In response, we turned off all our paid search Google advertising in the USA. When we did this, we were able to observe what happened to eBay registrations, confirmations, revenue and more in the US, then compare the results to the rest of the world where we hadn't turned off advertising. This pre/post test gave us lots of interesting data to validate our models of how valuable paid search was based on the limited keyword-level experiments we could run. Since then, I have made this a standard practice with all of the teams I have worked with.

To do this, we run the pre/post test in a given geographic

region or country. When selecting the region or country, we make sure it is big enough to affect the top line for the metric we are tracking, such as registrations, resurrections, active users or revenue. Then we agree ahead of time on a hypothesis for the test. Again, we usually hypothesize that we have measured marketing incrementality correctly; in turning off the marketing, we should see the top line of the metric we care about move by the amount we've predicted. We then determine an agreed duration for the test and go live. (Word to the wise: warn your colleagues you are running a test so they don't panic if their metric drops when it goes live.)

The proudest I've been of a result in this type of testing is one we found at Facebook when we ran a fully off test on paid direct response marketing for one of our products. We saw the MAU start shrinking in India, but as soon as we reversed the test, it started growing again. These results validated our methodology and helped us to defend our budget, while also influencing finance and product leaders to advocate for our budget as well. This was extremely important for us, as the company was facing a tight budget period at that time.

This method doesn't, however, need such a large-scale campaign to get results. Still, it does need to show a dramatic change. For example, if you are a third-party retailer on Amazon Marketplace, you have to decide whether to buy ads from their retail ad network or just go with ranking in search without ads. You could test the retail ads' effectiveness by turning them on for a year and then turning them off for two months to see how much your sales change. There are clearly costs to this method. In the first order, you might lose sales, and competitors may start ranking higher in the ads and seeing more value. But the value you get from knowing how many of your sales come from the ads versus organic traffic is supremely valuable for thinking through how you invest your dollars. This holds true for small hotels promoting on Booking.com through to Booking.com themselves buying massive ad buys on Google and Meta properties. It is a flexible, scalable methodology that can, and should, be used by everyone.

Limitations

In the end, you still have to know the limits of testing. The only truly valid multi-year tests I have seen have been those on owned and operated media, or a product someone controls themselves, like in-product promotions by Meta on Facebook. For example, we ran a multi-year holdout on our PYMK product, which suggests friends to people on Facebook, and both Meta and Google have run many-year holdouts on the ad product as a whole. You simply can't do this on your own ad campaigns, and as a practical matter, no company I know offers this as a feature in their ad platform. Performing such a test manually, by yourself, is impossible because users change machines, browsers and so on, which means that your ad-serving vendor will not be able to consistently track a substantial portion of users for a year or two. Because of this, users would shift between the test and control groups. That means any judgement of the incrementality ROI, the LTV of marketing to acquired users, and other considerations will always be a judgement call with technology existing as it does today.

At the same time, you may also not be recognizing the full value of marketing in your conversion action. I saw this at Meta when we only valued registrations as conversions and didn't value either resurrections or activity. We saw that when paid search was ramped up or turned off, the growth impact was larger than we expected. As we dug into this we realized we were driving resurrections as well as registrations. So we looked for and attributed resurrections as a net growth driver from paid ads and factored them in our value models going forward. To this day, we still don't value the activity of the users who come in and just do more than when they were already active, as we haven't found a good way to do so. Point being, limitations in measurement exist for all of us.

MARKETING RELIES ON ROI

Everything you do in marketing is based on how you measure ROI. Although you don't have to measure the return part of ROI in revenue (dollars), in my experience you generally should. Whatever your measurement unit, though, you should be able to calculate the LTV of each action you drive. Then use the sum of those actions to calculate overall ROI. Be clear that your marginal ROI is way lower than your average ROI and measure that carefully. From there, allocate budget so marginal ROI is equal across channels, companies and even sub campaigns. In my experience, that sort of rigour can give you massive uplift in your ROI – I've seen up to 100 percent.

Incrementality is a far harder question, but you should be asking it, since it is the most important question in marketing. Today, however, too many marketers rely on post-click conversions without asking, 'Is this marketing incremental or are we just tracking things that would have happened anyway?' The best way to do this is with an A/B test if you can run one in the channels you use. Paid social is an excellent choice here, such as the 'lift studies' Meta offers. I believe in periodically validating that my incrementality assumptions are accurate by running full on-off back tests regionally. The net of this rigour will make you, as a marketing team, more effective for the company and a better-trusted partner of finance, which will also make your life easier.

9. BUILDING THE TEAM

At most scales, you can't do digital marketing alone. Depending on the size of your business, you may not be able to hire a big team in-house, but unless you are among the smallest of businesses, you will need some agency support to help you scale. As you get larger, you will want a different set of agencies supporting while you also build out an in-house team. Once you are finally operating at scale, a fully built-out roster of teams and agencies will be needed to help deploy hundreds of millions, or even billions, of dollars. I have been lucky enough to work at every scale – from sole proprietors, to startups, to multi-hundred-person companies, to, finally, two of the largest advertisers on the internet during their peak – and the single most important factor to my success as I've climbed that scale has been the teams around me.

To hire great people, you need to look at their results. It is key that their skills really mattered at their previous job and their form of digital marketing was core to the business succeeding. For example, some of the best SEO marketers I know come from review sites like Tripadvisor. Tripadvisor's business model makes it harder to buy search traffic, so they had to become especially good at organic, free search results, and they consequently built one of the best SEO teams in the world. You ideally don't want to hire someone from a 'rocket ship' of a business that has never struggled because it is then impossible to see from the outside, and sometimes the inside, as to who made things happen and who just took a seat on the rocket ship and went along for the ride.

Finally, you want to be able to ask them what they did and what they are most proud of. You also want to hear them explain this accomplishment to a level that proves they truly did it. I look for people who worked on projects that made a difference to their company, who thrived through hard times, not just easy ones, and who can explain how to do the work they claimed to have driven.

You need great agencies to scale and provide access to skills that would make no sense for you to hire in-house, but that are imperative to your digital marketing programme. If you are a startup or small business, you will likely get some agency help from a small local web marketing firm or individual before you even have a full-time digital marketing person. When you get beyond just dabbling in ads and start looking at tens of thousands of dollars of spend, the next step is to hire a part-time consultant or consulting agency to help you, and then scale from there.

I would be nowhere without my agency partners. In my early days at eBay, Commission Junction and Mediaplex were both super-valuable, the former with building an affiliate programme from scratch and the latter with the tracking underpinning all our measurement work. Brilliant leaders at these agencies, like John Velcamp, Glenn Marr and Jonathan Forster, made it all possible. At the time of writing, at Meta, my longest-serving partners have been 3Q Digital (now rebranded as DEPT), who do online direct response marketing, and Kochava, who provide the technical platform. In addition, there are many other important agencies working with us today, not least Publicis Spark, on media buying, and Droga5, who helped us crush the rebrand to Meta as a creative agency. Agencies come and go with the work needed, and that is only natural, but done right, a brilliant agency can be a symbiotic relationship partner for a company for years, even decades.

Building the right team is a mix of having the right people in-house and the right agencies to support them and scale them.

'Not invented here' is a bad disease that sometimes prevents big firms from leveraging the brilliance of agencies – I strongly recommend that you fight this impulse whenever you see it rear its ugly head! Most of the time, you are not able to reinvent an entire industry or function, and the value of the decades of experience and specialty that exists outside your team – as a person, agency or tool – is often far harder to replicate than you think.

COMPOSING YOUR TEAM

Starting small

Your team depends on your scale (Captain Obvious here). As the leader of a small business or seed-stage startup, you mostly want to run digital marketing campaigns yourself or hire a single freelancer or small agency to do so. That means you'll still be closely involved at every step, which is good. It is extremely important to understand the channels that work for you, especially early on. Product and growth are all that matter in those early stages, and a lot of growth will be hands on and not scalable. Knowing what drives your growth from top to bottom will teach you where and how to change your product as needed and how it will interact with your best marketing channel.

Your best, and most important, marketing channel is generally tightly aligned with your product. An example would be a Boba tea shop optimizing to be Instagrammable, so they build a cute spot into the shop that gets people to take selfies, post them to social media and spread the word. Or a real-estate website or app startup, like Zillow or Trulia back when they began in the 2010s, could build listing and search pages to appear in the Google index, and then rank when people are shopping for homes, along with being the most valuable way to find homes they would like.

So, depending on your business, you want to hire people who have the right skills – an SEO expert won't help you create a cute Instagrammable spot, and an Instagram influencer isn't going to be the best at ranking for real-estate searches. Expertise matters.

Small to mid-sized businesses

As you grow, running digital marketing by yourself, or with a single freelancer or agency, gets less scalable. As a mid-sized company with, say, 50–200 employees, or a series A type company (a startup raising its first major funding), you want to start hiring in-house for marketing. Maybe you develop a team of two to four people when you have 200 employees. Typically, I find companies discover their superpowers early and get deeper and deeper on those over time. So, hire a specialist for what works best for you now – don't hire to speculate in other channels. If you hire to perfect what already has momentum, you can keep growing while deliberately experimenting on the side with other channels.

If you start to see signs of life or early results in those experiments, awesome – that's when you double down on that new channel and maybe hire someone to evaluate it in depth. It is at this point, when you are transitioning from a medium-sized company into a larger business, or series A into series B (a startup raising significant funding as they scale up with a proven track record), you should start to layer agencies into your team, as they are a scaled way to experiment.

Early on at Facebook, I focused on product-led growth, but I wanted to try other channels too. We experimented in-house with paid search and SEO and saw signs of life, as detailed in this book. As a result, we hired agencies for both of these channels. With the SEO agency's advice on scaling SEO, I was able to have the impact of a big team for just an agency fee; the search agency (who we've worked with ever since) both ran the search for us and scaled it. We also hired an analytics agency and an affiliate platform at that stage. Since we didn't have the resources to create a large analytics team in-house, or a full tracking solution with our software engineers, the analytics agency scaled our measurement sophistication. Similarly, the affiliate agency allowed us to experiment with that channel and gave us access to an affiliate network without us having to dedicate engineering to the project.

Knowing when to engage agencies is important, and you need to be big enough to use them. A rule of thumb would be that once you have a team of five to ten people in total on internet marketing, it's time to bring in agency assistance. If you pick the right agencies and tools at this stage, and manage them well, they will turbo charge your digital marketing. They certainly did for me.

As your business moves from small to mid-size, you should also start to specialize your online marketing team. A big decision here is whether you should give one of the people who scaled you to this point the job to manage that team. If that is possible, then I'd strongly encourage you to do so. The knowledge of your company – including people, processes and history – is incredibly valuable. Not having it makes the risk of hiring externally high. (Later in the chapter, I share how to maximize success if you do have to hire externally.)

From there, it is quite simple: build small teams against each specialty, layering in new teams as you test and learn more. Hire for real skills and experience in the space you are growing. And though experience and expertise matter, make sure you understand what space you are hiring for so you don't ignore people with super-valuable skills. For example, an email marketer and someone who does SMS marketing are both database marketers, but SEO and SEM marketers are not one and the same.

Larger businesses and enterprise

The transition into being a large business and, eventually, an enterprise requires layers in specialty cross-functional (XFN) teams. These may include data science (DS), data engineering (DE) and creative all working together to develop the best possible digital marketing. Though this is an exciting moment for a growing company, it is also a dangerous one. I manage some teams in my organization that grew from scratch and others that were reorganized under me, made up of members who already did similar work on direct response marketing.

The teams grown from scratch according to my philosophy require and desire far less XFN support in DS and DE. Instead, they do more of this work themselves, because we hired and trained people with those skills already. If you are too relaxed here, you can end up with a bloated DS and DE team. With such a large team, the speed of work can slow down to a trickle, as even relatively simple questions must pass back and forth between teams before being answered. Marketers in these teams also tend to generate far fewer ideas on how to use data to market better. To guard against this bloat for pure digital marketing channels, make it a requirement to hire digital marketers with the ability to analyse their own data, and build a culture where that is the expectation. If you don't, you will run into problems in spaces like paid search or social media direct response marketing, where data is such a major part of your success. However, as you grow into a bigger enterprise, the reverse is true for creative: you need to add more brand creative experience to the team and think bigger than just the direct response impact. Otherwise, you can harm the company brand long term.

More independence for your creative team is important so they can balance the needs of direct response marketing and the brand impact of their impressions. For example, direct response marketing can focus on price so much it causes people to consider a product cheap, not premium. If you're, say, a high-end fashion brand like Chanel, this is most definitely a brand impact you do not want. To protect against unwanted brand impacts, you can use a guardrail survey metric (such as, do users see Chanel as a premium brand?).

But that alone isn't enough – the guardrail at this point only shows when you have already caused harm. You need a team that thinks about this type of problem and prevents it from happening through the creative in the first place. Here, you need a creative person, team or agency to own the creative separate from the direct response marketing team. Again, you don't want a bloated team, but you do need creative folks who can balance brand and performance needs, finding creative solutions to both.

From here, growing further as an enterprise is a relatively straight line. Though, just as with the DS and DE, I would caution more generally about building massive teams. At Facebook, we have ten to twenty people working on direct response advertising for consumer. Even twenty years in, with hundreds of millions of dollars of spend a year, I believe we produce excellent work and get great results, without the bloat. Bigger teams don't necessarily mean better results, and a lot of these channels are almost fully leveraged. They don't require more people with more spend, especially if you also work with great agencies and tools.

With that in mind, as you grow into a large enterprise, you want more specialization and bigger, though not huge, departments to manage each specialization. You will also need to determine when some skills have become too important to do through an agency and you should bring them in-house. For example, eBay worked with Commission Junction until 2008 for affiliate marketing, but they then brought that platform in-house with the eBay Partner Network. Broadly, though, a mix of agencies, tools and in-house specialties is the best approach in modern internet marketing, just like in advertising during the heyday of ad agencies in the 1950s–60s. So, the question becomes, how do you pick the right agencies and hire the right people?

HIRING THE BEST PEOPLE

You may have an idea of what to hire for, but how do you actually hire the right people? Hiring people who help you scale is the only way to scale impact. I also deeply believe in expertise; I am not the best person on my team at managing any single channel, and that has been true for most of my career. (I like to think that at the start of my time at Facebook I was the best at managing a few channels, but soon after I began, that was no longer true because of the great people I hired.) As such, hiring the best people, retaining them and having them thrive is probably your most important job if you run an online marketing organization. This is my experience on how to do this successfully. Clearly, nothing here is a hard-and-fast rule, and I've had some great results outside of the parameters below. Generally, though, when I follow these guidelines, I get great results from hiring.

Were they on a rocket ship or did they go through a dip?

This has been one of the most important factors in hiring team members. There was a period at Facebook when we brought on lots of Google people and transformed large parts of the company with them. Many companies have also hired plenty of folks from Facebook in the past, before it became Meta, to help them do the same. But this strategy is incredibly high variance. It's difficult to tell the difference between those people who took a seat on the 'rocket ship' and held on to it tightly, and those who actually made things happen, changed the direction and helped deliver success. The latter are awesomely valuable, but I haven't found a good way to distinguish them from the former. This is especially true when looking in from outside those companies, but it's even true from the inside, because no one can have perfect insight across the entirety of a gigantic, successful enterprise.

When I joined eBay in mid-2004, it was at the end of its rocket ship period. It was the most valuable public internet company at the time, and it had been the public company that came through the dotcom crash most robustly. They had just completed the acquisition of PayPal, which was brilliantly done. They clearly articulated that in ten years PayPal would be worth more than the core eBay business. (They were right, and I don't think they get enough credit for that foresight or the execution on it.) Some of the people there were amongst the most brilliant and talented I have ever worked with. Following Q4 2004, however, the eBay stock price almost halved and we hit the buffers. The company went into self-protection mode and became far more disciplined.

The work got harder, and the compensation dropped. The company had been paying individual stock options (ISOs), which are stock grants at a given share price. If the price of the shares fell below your grant, you would lose money if you exercised them, causing them to become worthless, referred to as 'under water'. If they were above the grant you would make money. Unfortunately, with the sharp decline in eBay stock, many people's grant went under water on the stock part of compensation. This happened to many folks in the dotcom bust, too.

The upshot of that period was a lot of people left. Why was this an upshot? Though, as I mentioned, some of the people there were amongst the most brilliant and talented I have ever worked with – some were, well, not. I'd argue that more of the latter left than the former. The people who stuck it out weren't just loyal or unable to move but were better at their job. I don't really know why. Perhaps performance management got stricter? Perhaps they just understood what was going on better and knew we could work through the setback? Time and again when hiring, I have found that someone who has been at a company that went through a tough period, made it to the other side and was part of the turnaround team is more likely to be good at their job. People whose work is not consistently as good have often just been at a company during the easy sailing.

Was online marketing critical for that company?

This question is a big deal. Almost every large company now has an online marketing team, but some are incredibly competent, while others are not. How do you tell if you are hiring from one of the good ones? The rule that has worked for me is to just ask how critical online marketing, and the specific channel I'm hiring for, was for the companies they have worked for. This is not to say there aren't brilliant teams at companies where online marketing or a given online marketing channel isn't crucial.

My point is that if online marketing, or one specific channel, is truly make or break for a company, that team will be under high scrutiny. Their work will be reviewed and judged continually at the most senior levels, which means there is no way the team can coast, get away with shoddy work or outright fail. The following examples illustrate this point in the extreme:

- In the early-to-mid-2000s, affiliate marketing was by far the most important channel for eBay. Our affiliates spent more than us, and more effectively, on paid search. Around 2004, I argued that the affiliate programme at eBay was the most talented team. By the late 2000s, we moved paid search in-house and it was the most critical channel for us, so the team had to be incredible, and it was.

- If you look at Zynga, the video game developer, around 2012, two channels drove their business: cross-promotion of games to existing clients and buying social media ads. If I were to have hired former Zynga employees at the time, I wouldn't have focused on hiring from their search engine optimization team, I would have been looking at their social media and onsite merchandising teams, who were killer.

- Tripadvisor is an SEO company through and through. Yes, they had paid search too, but their entire business model wouldn't work without free search traffic, so hiring from their stellar SEO team in the early 2010s would have been brilliant.

- Candy Crush from the social games company King would never have been what it was without incredible mobile ad buying, especially social media. When Candy Crush was released in 2012, originally for Facebook, I would have looked at the talent on King's paid social media team above any other.

- At their peak, Groupon's email marketing was the entire business: send emails and get them delivered, opened and clicked. They must have had incredible people working on their email marketing.

Again, I do not intend to denigrate the teams that were not crucial for those companies at those times. I just know that the crucial team will have had their work held to a high bar, and if I were to hire someone who thrived at those teams at the time, the question of whether someone was good at that work will have had a higher probability of a yes response. Of course, it's not a certainty – we all make mistakes and can get worse over time or in a different environment, but on the whole this is a helpful way to consider potential hires.

Do they jump around a lot?

I find better hires when I bring someone on who has generally stayed over three years, or ideally longer, at all the companies they've worked for, and who has had at least one long stint somewhere, close to ten years. When coupled with the point above about working on a crucial channel for the company, this shows they need to have survived and thrived on that high-calibre team. Being on it just briefly and moving on is a counter signal. I also like to build for the long run. If someone believes their best career option is to get promoted by jumping from job to job, or who gets bored once they've gained mastery of their role and company, they are simply not who I am looking for.

Be consistent with questions and look for correct answers

I try to ask the same questions over and over for the same roles. Though this leads to hearing the same answer in many cases over and over, it creates a type of calibration that can help me compare potential hires. My favourite question is 'What is most important for growth?' I strongly believe there is a correct answer – customer retention. As the world of social has evolved,

I've gotten new answers to the question over time. But the fact remains, without retention you will never have growth, no matter how good any acquisition or other tool you have might be. The logical next question is, what matters most for customer retention? There are a range of right answers here depending on the industry, but in social media it is connecting people with content they care about, through friending, following or, increasingly, AI. You want to hire people that have a good gut feel for the business. An understanding of such core concepts is necessary if the person you're hiring will run a chunk of marketing for your business. Correct answers exist, and matter, and you want to look for them with every hire.

PICKING AN AGENCY AND BUYING TOOLS

What sort of agencies do you need?

You typically need three or four agencies, starting with a small generalist agency and building up the others over time:

- A technical agency or platform that will help you with all the difficult tech stack integrations with the major ad providers and with some form of ad bidding engine. (In this case the tech stacks are the collection of technologies your company uses to create, track and run digital marketing campaigns.)

- An actual marketing agency that will traffic your ads, use the technical tools and scale your team.

- A creative agency that will pump out the direct response creative you need, providing direct response experience while sticking to the company brand guidelines and keeping the brand guardians satisfied that the brand is being respected.

- An SEO agency, potentially, to help you with organic search.

If possible, you should do SEO in-house because an internal person has a better chance of making good SEO happen than an external. At the same time, I have had valuable help from SEO agencies in the past (and have been a consultant for SEO myself). Perhaps it is best to say you need the internal talent to make use of any advice from an SEO agency. With the right internal talent, however, you should not need an SEO agency. I don't think that's true for the others – technical, marketing, creative; they are not optional. Even working for a massive tech company like Meta, I still buy those services instead of build them.

There are a lot of commonalities in selecting an agency. Here are a few basics to consider:

1. Competitively bid to get the best result.
2. Get references both from the agencies and through any backchannel, such as colleagues or other people in your industry.
3. Ask them for case studies of when and where their work got results.
4. Have key internal teams (including finance and procurement) interview and vet potential agencies, as they will need to respect them.

This fourth suggestion is the most make or break factor. You can't go it alone on any of these agencies, and if you can make your internal partners feel responsible for the success of integrating the agency, you are more likely to succeed. This step is missed far too often. Since marketing is not the number one stakeholder – it is typically finance or the owner of the P&L (profit and loss) – for marketing to get what it needs we have to internalize this idea. Fundamentally, hiring an agency isn't complicated, but it is hard work to do it right.

Selecting a technical platform

Oftentimes people use the same company for both the technical platform and the marketing agency to manage campaigns. More and more commonly, the best of each is being acquired by big agency holding companies or developed in-house. At the same time, Google and Meta are both handling bidding engines increasingly better with their automated optimization campaigns. There's a good chance that over time the value in the bidding engine part of the stack continues to decline. That said, most marketing teams never get the full technical support they need, even at a company like Meta, eBay or the other firms I have advised or worked with. So having an agency that can manage all the integrations with the tech stacks of the various players, especially as they get more complicated, is key. With that in mind, prioritize those integration specialists because rebuilding the integration expertise and technology in-house is likely wasteful (and you won't do it as well).

In order to select the best agency in this case, you need to look for whether or not they have delivered results for their other clients and what they are most proud of in their marketing materials. Closely examine if the clients they are proud of find this sort of marketing critical to their success, and make sure there is more than one such client. I've hired an agency in the past that was dominated by one big partner, and, not surprisingly, the reference check with that one partner was excellent. After the fact, I found lots of people they worked with who had the same experience as me – they couldn't integrate with someone other than their long-term, main partner. The agency was simply unable to adapt to other companies. As you can see, the usual reference-checking techniques matter here.

The most important test for selecting an agency for the technical platform is whether the engineering or tech team would like to work with this agency. Part of making this collaboration successful comes from working with agencies that are experts in your tech stack. (For example, if you use a platform like Shopify, you need to hire an agency with expertise in that platform.) Look for positive feedback when you introduce the agency to the engineering team. You want your people in-house to feel that the agency will be a real value-add. It is also critical that the engineering team feel they are part of the decision to hire this partner and are excited about working with them. In other words, you want engineering to feel invested in the success of this partnership, not resentful of it.

Nothing can make a technical agency succeed more than an engineering team that is excited to work with them. For example, when we were technically implementing all our third-party tracking, having such a team was undeniably important. That's because this is generally boring engineering work, in which you are just implementing someone else's specifications, not innovating. It also has lots of downside: if you do it wrong, the marketing won't work; you can implement it in a way that slows down the site, eliciting criticism from your colleagues; and you can introduce security holes by adding third-party code into the site.

You therefore must have a group of engineers who are passionate about this work. We were lucky to find them in Tel Aviv and create a team of people with lots of experience in digital marketing who have a passion for this area. Up until then, it was a super-hard slog.

So, for this one you need:

1. A track record of success.
2. Great reference checks from multiple clients.
3. Proven experience with the platform you use.
4. Excited engineering teams who feel ownership over the choice of agency.

Selecting a marketing agency

The marketing agency you choose to work with is truly a critical partner. Sometimes you can combine it with the technical platform, as mentioned, but at other times you cannot. What I look for in a partner here is an agency that knows more about the platforms that we are buying from than my teams do. That allows them to teach us about what we should be looking for and doing, especially as we discuss with them what we don't know, and to push us to do better.

When you talk to them, the agency needs to be proud of their results, not their industry awards, and their references (both from people they recommend and your own backchannel) need to be great. Companies don't typically like to share proprietary data on their results, so most of the effective digital direct response campaigns don't even submit for industry awards. If they do, they only share high-level results, which makes it hard to tell how much impact their campaigns had. As such, marketing awards don't tend to correlate closely with the most effective work.

Pricing here is also important, as the work is typically less value-add than the other agencies. Still, you can be penny-wise and pound-foolish by going for the cheapest option and then harming performance on huge media budgets. The biggest consideration though is a clear sign that they are ahead of you on understanding how to get a channel's best results. So keep the following in mind as to what you will want to get out of a marketing agency:

1. They teach you ways of getting the best results that you don't already know.
2. They have excellent references.
3. They are competitive on pricing.

Selecting a creative agency

I was advising a charity on their online marketing recently and they were excited to show me the agency running their digital direct response marketing creative work. The agency's home page featured rotating images celebrating the creative awards the agency had won. Nowhere on the home page was a mention of the ROI. I showed them the equivalent homepage for the team working on my digital direct response marketing creative. This one mentioned no awards, but highlighted case study after case study on ROI.

My number one sign to look for in a creative agency is that they focus on their results over their awards. They need to be able to walk you through several examples of where their creative has made the difference on sales. As with the other agencies, you then need to check their references through the backchannel, speaking with their clients to make sure you get feedback that proves they can do what they say can. Beyond that, for a large company you must vet the agency with the brand marketing team to make sure they are comfortable with their craft and approach. The checklist here:

1. They focus on results and can share great case studies.
2. They reference-check well.
3. Your brand marketing team is excited to have them and is invested in their success.

Selecting an SEO agency

The number one question for an SEO agency is if they can get results for their client's company – this is the hardest thing for an SEO agency to do. In interviewing them, you should look at three factors to judge whether they will be able to generate the results you want. First, get their case studies. Second, when you check their references, ask specifically about their ability to deliver the desired outcomes. Finally, have the team that would need to implement their advice (most likely engineering) interview them and ensure they are bought in to the agency.

The number two question is if they are above board in the actions they take for you. Is their link-building clean, as in are the websites they end up linking to yours legitimate? Or are they taking risks that you end up paying for after they are no longer your agency? For example, link buying is broadly banned by search engines, especially Google. This is a practice in which you, or your agency, buy links to your site to promote it for crawlers. Crawlers are the programs search engines use to index the web. When you promote your site to crawlers, they will find it, index it and judge it to be important, ranking it high in the search results. (I cover this topic in more detail in Chapter 13, on search, but the right links are important for ranking high in search results.) If a search engine finds you have bought links, however, it typically penalizes you for violating its terms. When an agency takes risks like this then moves on, you're left holding the bag. This is where references from previous clients are crucial, as is understanding their reputation around the SEO industry.

So, best practices for hiring an SEO agency would be the following:

1. Get their case studies to prove whether they had a true impact for their client.
2. Ensure the team who'll implement their recommendations is excited.
3. Check references to uncover any shady tactics and understand their reputation throughout the industry.

When to bring it in-house?

Though working with agencies can be incredibly valuable, there comes a point when you should build a skill in-house too. So how do you decide the time is right? Consider companies like eBay and Amazon. They built huge in-house paid search marketing engines and affiliate networks, even if they seem to have rolled back on these somewhat in recent years. If you have a huge scale, it can be ROI-positive to move in-house. But recognize you will lose access to cross-company learning and best practices, because you will no longer use agencies and third-party tools that have to support multiple partners. Instead, your in-house team only supports you and only learns from you.

That's fine in a slow-moving channel because little changes. In a fast-moving one, this can be a huge detriment, and without some massive benefit from a deep in-house integration, the in-house approach ends up being a net negative. (An in-house integration is when you can leverage data or integration with the product in a way no third party ever could; for example, when Amazon affiliates browse Amazon, every page has a special toolbar integrated through which you can immediately build a custom promotion for that page, including a tracking link – no third-party affiliate programme could do the same.)

Let's take a step back and look at Amazon and eBay in more detail. They both developed famously impressive in-house SEM tools and affiliate platforms, but how did they decide to do that? The answer for Amazon is straightforward: they built affiliates in-house from *day one*, at a time when few affiliate agencies existed. But eBay began its 'eBay partner network' in 2008, prominently moving away from their affiliate marketing agency at the time, the aforementioned Commission Junction. I have advised a lot of CMOs and growth teams who have thought about doing an affiliate programme in-house and I think you need three fronts to justify doing it in-house:

- Is affiliates a big channel or is it likely to be one, and therefore a large amount of your spend? It was for eBay and Amazon.
- If you are already running one, are you dealing with huge fraud cases where the agencies are not successfully protecting you?
- Is there a proof point with a competitor running a successful in-house affiliate programme (showing a competitor successfully doing the same thing always helps an argument)? I believe for both eBay and Amazon there were proof points at the times they launched.

Moving in-house would allow eBay to save on agency fees that would be material at that size of programme and would enable them to more tightly manage fraud, which was a major issue at the time. That combination was certainly enough. This choice seems to have been the correct one as both Amazon and eBay continue to manage their affiliate programmes in-house in the mid-2020s, even if they are less important channels for them today.

When it comes to paid search, Amazon, eBay and other companies that built incredible in-house paid search tools have moved to more of a hybrid model in this channel. Some functionality is in-house, but a lot is through agencies as well. At Meta, we certainly use an agency in paid search, despite being a tech company with a large budget and the skills to build bidding systems. The reasoning for this decision is four fold:

1. The scale of team to build the tools exceeds the agency fees.
2. The learning that takes place through cross-client work is valuable for building better tools.
3. The pace of change of the search market is fast.
4. There is little value to deep in-house integration.

Let's take a closer look at each point in detail.

The scale of team point is simple. Sometimes agency fees set as a percentage of spend are so large that it is worth building a full in-house team because you will save so much money. This point should be discussed at the beginning of any conversation around in-house work.

On the learning point, experience across many clients helps build better tools and services. A myopic focus on your industry, or just your company, will cause you to miss opportunities to make better tools, systems and best practices.

On the pace of change, the industry isn't mature, search keeps evolving and, as I write this, it looks like it will continue to dramatically do so through AI. That constant state of flux means you need to be nimble. A large enterprise building employee tools is just slower than a tech company fully dedicated to building tools for one vertical with lots of competitors. If the agency doesn't move to match the pace of industry change, you can switch agencies. But if you don't move to match the pace of industry change with an internal team, it will be hard to tell until you have fallen a long way behind.

Finally, the level of integration with the core business can play a major role in determining whether you should move in-house. In some fields, like SEO, there is a huge need for internal integration. You need to change the actual website, products and so on to appear high up in organic search. In that case, all an agency can do is give advice. In a space like SEM, however, you only need lightweight in-house integrations to track conversions and send data. In that case, the SEM agency can act independently. That makes the value of moving the tool in-house far lower because there is less co-ordination cost between agency and company.

Of course, there is always an exception to the rule, and in-house integration is no different. If you use, say, the open source content management system WordPress as your platform, you can actually have an agency build and operate a lot of your pages and perform SEO work for you. That leaves you with two approaches to fields that require deep integration with the core business, and you should trade them off depending on your particular situation. The first is bringing them in-house. The second is finding a way to make it easier for an agency to operate without needing to work with too many internal teams, as with using a platform like WordPress for your content management system.

A summary of selecting the right agencies

There are many other agencies and tools you might want to consider. It is useful, for example, to hire a conversion rate optimization agency from time to time, but I haven't found an ongoing relationship with one necessary. (Here, I have worked with Stephen Pavlovich – an absolute legend of the space – at his various companies and in his various roles.) You will often need affiliate and email marketing platforms, rather than building them in-house, and the right kind of technical agency can help you here. With that in mind, I'd focus first on having a great technical integration partner.

Above all, though, you have to take the decision of in-house versus outside agency seriously. That may sound obvious, but it's an important point. When I've been involved in a project where we have taken this seriously, we have never regretted it – when we haven't been as careful, we have. To make sure you are taking the decision seriously, remember to do the following:

1. Determine your requirements.
2. Ensure the key internal stakeholders feel invested in success.
3. Run a good selection process with competitive bidding and reference checks.

This is a simple set of rules to state and put into action, but sometimes the pressures of business force us to rush them or not even fully consider them. I strongly encourage you to take the time to make agency choices well. Unwinding such a relationship is hard and costly. Clarify that with your stakeholders up front and don't let yourself be rushed – if you do, you'll regret it.

HOW TO GET HIRED

Even if you have incredible skills that align with the section above, you might still be frustrated by your search for a great job in this field and wonder how to get hired. I have hired, or managed the hiring of, thousands of people in my career, and there are two factors that matter the most:

1. Skills – do you have provable skills that will make people want to hire you?
2. Access – do you have the network to even get considered for the job?

Before digging into these, there is one caveat to note: if you want a successful career, you should not be getting hired often. In other words, moving from company to company is over-rated. A lot of the current wisdom is that you can advance your career faster by switching often. But, in my experience, the most senior and influential members of any company or agency have been there a long time. They have grown in the company, built trust, and understand how the company works and how to get things done.

The vast majority of the absolute pinnacle of talent at the top tech companies today are long-term employees. Look at the folks who took over as CEO of Google (Sundar Pichai), Apple (Tim Cook) and Microsoft (Satya Nadella) in the last twenty years. They were all long-term company veterans pulled from an executive group of long-term company veterans. This doesn't mean everyone's goal is to be in the top executive tier – it comes with a lot of tradeoffs in life – and long tenure isn't the only way to get there, but if you want to be senior and actually get things done, tenure is strongly correlated, so don't job-hop too much.

When it comes down to being hired in this field, few things matter more than competence and the ability to prove it. You need to actively demonstrate that you have the necessary skills. In online marketing, that means you need to be somewhat technical and able to describe how you would measure statistical significance, implement conversion tracking, design and run experiments, traffic ads at scale to get results and so on and so forth. Nothing is more frustrating in an interview than hearing someone describe a great project they were part of, only for them to be unable to answer questions on how they achieved those results. This inability to describe the actual work proves they don't know enough to have driven the project. When pressed in an interview, you must know enough to explain the work you supposedly drove.

You must also be able to provide real examples of where you drove a project that had an impact that mattered in your career. Of course, first you need to have actually driven them, which means you can convincingly describe your role in getting the results. Second, those results must have mattered for your team and, ideally, the whole company. A lot of people stumble here – they describe a cool project (or multiple) they drove, but it didn't make much of a difference when all was said and done. If the best projects you highlight in an interview didn't move the needle, that isn't a good sign of your judgement on what matters most or the work entrusted to you in your previous job. A corollary to this idea in how you shape your career is working where your skill matters (online marketing writ large, for example, but, within this industry, SEO, affiliates, social or otherwise as your specialty).

To find the best jobs, a robust network, and stellar reputation with the members of that network, helps. Nothing is as powerful as a warm introduction from a respected intermediary. When you build your network, it is most powerful if people within it are truly familiar with your work, and if you have helped them succeed in some way using your skills. Every full-time job I have got has come through directly applying, so I don't think building your network is as critical as the advice above, but most of the best people I have hired have come through my network, not through blind trawling of LinkedIn or career website applications.

A strong network doesn't just get your foot in the door with a referral; it can also play a major role in regard to your references. No matter how you apply or who recommended you in the first place, you need excellent references to land a great job in online marketing. Before you go job hunting, make sure you have a list of credible people who will act as your references. Note that, in addition to their credibility, you want to include people who will have seen your work first-hand, and ideally they will be at a similar or more senior level to where you are in your career.

Keep in mind, finding a great job and developing a successful career in this industry isn't simply about who will hire you. If you want to build your skills and have a real impact at work, go where your skills matter. That may not be essential for a happy life – it's of course totally fine to have a job that just pays the bills – but if your skills aren't appreciated and you don't get the chance to make an impact, it will be harder to get other people in the industry, or folks outside the company, to listen to you.

Marketing isn't crucial at every company. You can still have a wonderful career as a solid marketer without ever feeling too much pressure because, even though the department is necessary to the company, it is not completely critical. The issue with those roles is that you, mostly, won't drive results that really matter to that company, and it will be harder to get the industry or other folks outside the company to listen to you because they will know the role of marketing where you work. I personally find that frustrating, as I want to be somewhere my work is important, not just to me and my team, but to the company overall. As such, I believe the magic happens when you are in a company where marketing matters, and you are good at it. In those environments, you can drive amazing results, shape the direction of the company and go home from work satisfied that the time you put in was worth it.

SUCCESS DEPENDS ON YOUR TEAM

It is rare that you are so special and your business so small that you can go it alone. Your success will depend on the team you draw around you. As you grow – which is the ultimate goal – that team should be a mix of in-house teams and agency teams. As you start small, look for generalists, usually an agency or consultant, that can help you even before your first hires. Then as you scale up, you can pull more marketing in-house and become more specialized. When hiring people and agencies, look at their track records. Did the work they performed matter? Did they have real impact and can they prove it with details, references and ideally examples of pushing through hard times to better days?

Most capabilities should not be brought in-house fully, and you should be thoughtful of the pitfalls of losing nimbleness and industry best-practice sharing if you do. That said, there are some places, like SEO, where deep technical integration matters and, when you are large enough, bringing the skill fully in-house, as compared to using agencies, is the right move.

If you want to be hired, you will increase your chances through having deep, provable skills, a great network and a great reputation, but if you want to climb to the top levels, do not jump around too much. And if you follow that advice, you will find yourself on a great team – and there's nothing better. A great team is a wonderful thing, and I am lucky to have one and be part of one. The majority of my direct reports have worked with me for over a decade, I have worked for my manager for over a decade, and most of my agencies have been with me for as long as I have been CMO, if not longer. I count myself lucky, as it makes the work fun and builds a rapport where we can move fast because we know and trust each other.

10. WORKING WITH OTHER INTERNAL BUSINESS GROUPS

Successful marketers do not operate in a vacuum, and this is especially true in a medium-sized or large company. For this chapter, I am going to assume you are an expert in digital direct response channels. Typically, by nature, you do not own the products you market; that's the product group owner or business group owner. You also have budget management and allocation from finance, so you regularly work with that department.

In recent years, the procurement function in finance has also taken a larger role in marketing contracts, which has been reflected in industry media with some consternation. In fact, one industry commentator has called procurement one of the 'four horsemen of the dullpocalypse', describing procurement as just caring strictly about costs, unable to see the value in unquantifiable creativity. In some companies, communications is part of marketing; in others, like Meta, it is housed in a different division. In addition, a partner organization, and of course direct response marketing as covered in this book, also has to partner with brand marketing. These are the main partners you have to care about working with: comms, brand marketing, the product or business owner and, of course, finance. Building great relationships with these functions is vital to smooth operations.

WORKING WITH FINANCE

Working with finance is the single most important functional relationship. If the CFO and finance department are independently telling the CEO that your digital marketing division is a good place to invest, in the long term the credibility that comes with that endorsement overpowers everything else. If, however, they are consistently complaining to the CEO about the investment in your organization being an unjustifiable waste of money, you will have a drag on your ability to operate. You may never be able to pin down where this drag is originating, but it will make progress so slow you'll feel like you're running through treacle. Worse yet, in crisis moments, your work will be cut first and hardest.

So how do you win finance over? I suggest the following:

1. Deliver results that matter.
2. Measure what can be measured well.
3. Logically explain the rest.
4. Treat procurement as an asset and ally.

Delivering results that matter to the company is fundamental to gaining favour with finance. Let's dig in there to better understand why.

Deliver results that matter

There are three points buried within this goal. First, you have to actually do work that is of consequence: it matters if it succeeds. There are many projects that, even if they succeeded tremendously, no one cares. You need to spend enough time truly scrutinizing your work, and ask yourself, 'Does it matter if I succeed?'

Second, your results must be big enough to matter. Teams regularly move a number by a level that might be statistically significant in a test, and celebrate this result tremendously, without asking, 'Is it actually significant?' Would a dispassionate finance person care if this win went away? Often the answer is that your results are too small. As I'm fond of saying, if you need a data scientist and a microscope to determine if you had impact, then you didn't.

Finally, you need to explain your impact well enough that it can be understood. A good example here is thinking about something like impact on net growth versus gross acquisition, as discussed in the earlier conversation about growth accounting in Chapter 3:

+ Acquisitions
- Churn
+ Resurrections
———————————
= Net Growth

Let's say you work for a mature, large social media business where your net growth is a million users a month. This growth might be driven by acquisitions of 15 million users a month, churn of 30 million a month, and resurrections of 16 million a month. Say your team is actually responsible for 10 percent of acquisitions and 10 percent of resurrections via paid media. If you were to explain this impact to finance, what do you think their response would be? It sounds good, but does it sound business-critical? Hardly – it sounds optional when described like that.

However, your business is actually creating 1.5 million acquisitions and 1.6 million resurrections a month from paid media – that's net 3.1 million to the positive, when the business is only growing by a million users a month. If you were to turn off paid marketing on that business, it would start shrinking by

2 million users a month. This explanation completely changes the narrative. A smart finance partner should work this out for themselves, but why make it hard for them (or, in the end, harder on you)? They are busy answering lots of questions and shouldn't have to be experts in your area, as well as every other one. Explain your work the right way and your value to the business will be understood.

Measure what can be measured well

In almost all fields, not everything can be measured, and that is OK. What matters is to distinguish what can be measured and to measure it in a way that your partner – whether finance, business owners, the CEO or anyone in between – can respect. Gaining respect for your methodology here buys you space elsewhere, meaning they will have more trust in your decisions and approach. The goal, then, is to measure what can be measured well – and make sure finance believes it. A top-level goal of mine for the past twenty years across Meta and eBay has been that the CFO of my area (or, if appropriate, the company) believes the measurement I perform.

I've mostly done this by booking regular proactive reviews of our results and methodology with the CFO. Historically, we had these meetings every two years, but they have become more frequent. In this review, my team and I bring a full breakdown of experimental methodology and test results, and we bare the problems we're experiencing.

We are also open about what we don't explicitly know. After all, there will always be limitations to measurements. For example, in a big country like India, we can run tests that show the full impact of marketing with tight error bars, but in medium-sized countries, like France, or smaller countries, say Chile, that's impossible. In those cases, we have to extrapolate or bundle the tests. Another example of such limitations relates to incrementality. We can explain to the CFO we are incremental for a year, but we can't tell them how incremental we are over multiple years – and we don't claim to be able to do that either.

During these reviews, we ask for suggestions and ideas of how we might do better at measuring and explaining our results. This is helpful because the finance team is experienced and smart, and they often come up with good ideas that make us better. It is also valuable, because if they can't think of a way to fix a problem we're experiencing either, they accept the limitations and where judgement must be applied.

Logically explain the rest

As discussed in Chapter 7, on measurement, once you have shown finance true measurements of your success, then you gain the trust to explain your logic on programmes that can't be measured as easily. I have experienced a lot of debate, and sometimes great disagreement, over whether the cost of doing measurement is not worth the measurement's benefit.

For example, pulling out of a major conference could lose us a prime spot, force us to renegotiate a good contract early or even signal to the market we are an unreliable partner. Measuring the effects may be impossible, but logically, there are a number of issues that could arise and end up hurting our brand and business. I have often had quite heated disagreements in this area, and I feel I have only won out because of the basis of strong measurement in the places possible and respect for, and partnership with, finance.

Treat procurement as an asset and ally

The final element in working with finance is procurement. If you want to avoid the CFO whispering in the CEO's ear that marketing is a waste of money, you want to avoid procurement whispering in the CFO's ear that marketing is sloppy and wasteful in contracting. An advisor or an employee procurement has always been a key operational arm for the CFO to implement policy. The CFO then hears back on how and whether teams are appropriately and efficiently spending the company's money. In short, procurement is hugely influential on whether finance thinks you are a competent team player shepherding resources well, or not.

Working well with procurement is pretty simple: respect your procurement partners and consider them part of the team. Maybe I am lucky and Meta just has great procurement, but I've always found that this team makes our work better (I found this at eBay too). They are an awesome asset in negotiating with vendors to represent the constraints of corporate interests (the proverbial bad cop in good cop, bad cop) and freeing me and my team to focus on value creation and opportunity.

Include them up front, discuss what you want to achieve and what they want to achieve, and then plan negotiations together. Share with them the results you are driving and celebrate their work with their management. Just be a good colleague and you are 90 percent of the way to victory here in gaining a tremendous asset. Every time I hear of folks having huge issues with procurement, it usually breaks down to not including them early enough and not ensuring they have the business context they need.

GETTING SUPPORT DURING LAYOFFS

Don't get me wrong – there is a *lot* more to finance than what I'm describing above. If you are just operationally shoddy and don't spend your budget when you say you will, or you are late filing accruals, or you make any other manner of operational faux pas in a way that causes them compliance, accounting or risk headaches, you will justifiably have a frustrated finance team. But fundamentally, if they believe in your ROI, the CFO will usually back you over those hurdles and argue that you just need to be more operationally competent. The real danger arises when, even if you are operationally smooth like butter, you're a bad investment in the eyes of the CFO, and finance in general. The real benefit is when they think you are a great investment and the best place to spend the next incremental dollar available.

The rubber really hits the road with finance on budget decisions, and no budget decisions are more consequential than dealing with major cuts and layoffs. When I became CMO, my predecessors and other CMOs told me that you hadn't really led a marketing team unless you'd gone through cuts. When business turns bad, marketing is often seen as optional and ends up first on the chopping block. During Meta's layoffs in 2022–23, I experienced this a bit earlier in my role than I had hoped.

In the consumer and public affairs marketing side of my organization, we saw around 20 percent cuts in the overall budget, whereas in business marketing we saw cuts of around 50 percent. The difference between these two groups boiled down to the relationship with finance and the business owners inside the company. At that stage, I had been running consumer marketing for two years. During that period, we had worked with finance to cut, optimize or repurpose programmes that didn't have great metrics supporting their effectiveness. This meant we had already cut a large chunk of the media budget and restructured the team. We had also proven to our business partners that we delivered the type of value they cared about. On the business marketing side, we hadn't done this work yet. We had large programmes with few success metrics against them, and our business partners were questioning the value of our teams. This wasn't a great situation.

The layoffs then came down to two questions. First, what is the stack rank of projects in order of the value they deliver to the company with cost against them? Second, how much are we expected to cut based on evaluating the value of the projects on that list? We considered these questions with the senior leadership across finance, legal, HR and the business owners, which mostly entails product leaders at Meta but also included sales for business marketing.

Those meetings were super-instructive. In consumer and public affairs marketing, finance agreed with our stack ranking and value estimations. The business leaders said they were willing to cut their budgets to protect ours because of the value the work delivered. We still cut some programmes that were clearly optional and strategic, recognizing they were not appropriate in the constrained budget environment we found ourselves in. But fundamentally, we had a room full of cross-functional team partners making our arguments for us. As a result, the job cuts were simply the average for the company, and below average for non-tech functions. This stark difference between these teams showed the value of having done the work in the good times so that when tough times came, as they always do, your partners believe in your value and stand up for you. That support is necessary because you will never win if you are standing alone.

I was deeply impressed with how the marketing leaders responded. They were mature and executed the unpleasant programme of cuts with the most compassion and professionalism I saw in my organization. When I talked to them about it, it turned out they had more experience than any of my other teams in dealing with cuts and layoffs. As mentioned, it is so common that marketing gets cut first, and that then gets reflected through the whole industry from in-house teams to agencies, that these leaders were prepared.

If you are a marketer, and especially in a leadership role, this story is far from theoretical. Unless you are abnormally lucky, there will come a time in your career where you will have to make some cuts. It's extremely difficult, but by developing those relationships of mutual respect and trust with finance and business owners earlier on, it will hopefully be a bit easier for everyone, and you can mitigate losses to your teams.

WORKING WITH BUSINESS OWNERS

In general, marketing doesn't own the P&L. Given, this isn't true in every case – for example, Procter & Gamble are one of the best training grounds for marketers to this day, and they often own a P&L for a company or region. (This ownership is partly what trains them so well, as they truly take responsibility for the marketing's outcome and are reviewed on delivering results.) Typically, however, you have either a centralized marketing team under the CEO, COO or CRO, or you have a decentralized marketing team sitting within individual business groups. In either structure, though, you will have peers. If you are centralized, these will be full business groups or other functional leaders; if you are decentralized, these will be subdivisions of business groups you partner with and need to work with. For all intents and purposes, I see these business, functional or sub-business groups as fairly interchangeable, since they all have people leading them who need partnership and support.

The most important aspect of working with business owners is having empathy for them. Their jobs are hard, and if you are working with them, and not *for* them, you are probably one of multiple functions they need to do their jobs, but that they do not control. That's a tough place to be, whether you own the whole business group or just a subdivision. So broadly, as a marketer, you need to hold this context in your head as you consider their behaviours, stresses and actions.

You must also understand their goals, metrics and targets. Are they in a place where the CEO is telling them to drive growth or to get expenses under control? Do they need a new product to be an absolute slam dunk or to squeeze more results out of an existing legacy business? Having that empathy puts you in a place where you can be a force multiplier for them – not another headache. You want to go to them with proposals fully aligned to their needs, deliver results when you execute them and in doing so be drawn into the core of the team.

This is how my career took off in growth. I brought the marketing channels from this book to the table to help accelerate user and advertiser growth for Facebook. As business groups worked with me and executed my recommendations, my team and I gained trust and were seen as a driver of results. In turn, that reputation gave me a seat at the table for digital marketing when we created the growth team, which was critical to the business's success, the success of our function (such that growth marketing became an industry term) and my personal career success. All of this success stemmed from understanding the needs of the business group, making sure our marketing projects aligned with their needs and delivering results that they believed.

MAXIMIZING WHATSAPP GROWTH IN THE USA

Now that I've discussed one of the more painful experiences of my career as a CMO – handling the Meta cuts in 2022–23 – I'm happy to share one of the best. As discussed, in 2022, we were asked to market the privacy of WhatsApp around the world in an effort to make it known as the most private messaging app out there. We built small campaigns with limited budget for such a global remit. We were asked as a secondary, guardrail metric to avoid hurting WhatsApp's usage – a campaign that emphasizes privacy in such a way could have the reverse effect, terrifying people and causing them to run away. We understood the most important goal for the WhatsApp leadership was growth in the USA, so we evaluated what the limiting factors were there, realizing awareness was key.

As a result, we scoped this campaign to focus on moving people's perception of privacy and maintaining, or improving, our guardrail metric by testing that it did not scare people away globally, while working to boost awareness in the USA. The results of the campaign were excellent and tightly aligned to the WhatsApp leadership's goals at that time. In fact, they were so successful that, in the year-end budget ask, the leader of WhatsApp (Will Cathcart) requested more headcount and dollars for our team. This has now happened multiple times across multiple business groups, but this was the first major ask of the kind after I had become CMO.

This is the ideal outcome of working with a business group well and the best way to ask for budget. When respected leaders say you should invest in marketing because they believe the impact is critical to their results, everyone listens. And by being deeply aligned with the business group here, everyone won.

GETTING BRAND AND DIRECT RESPONSE MARKETING TO WORK TOGETHER

At both an industry and company level, a tension exists between direct response marketing and brand marketing. This was true even back when David Ogilvy was writing about marketing over forty years ago. There is no trivial simple solution to overcoming that tension, and I don't claim to have solved the problem completely myself. That said, I believe there is real magic when you can get these teams operating as a single unit.

The marketing funnel doesn't have a big line in the middle of it, and individual customers and prospects will move up and down the funnel. That means the best marketing is full-funnel thinking, considering every level from awareness to action as a single system, not as siloed teams. At awareness, you need more brand, and at action, you need more direct response. Overall, though, you need to get results no matter what, and you need to build a long-term brand, not destroy and cheapen it for a few short-term conversions. Clearly, then, it all matters.

You must breed a culture of respect among your teams. There is a term that tends to hurt this possibility, and remains one of my biggest pet peeves: performance marketing. There is no such thing as 'performance marketing', which is one of the terms that has historically been used to describe the marketing I write about in this book. I am trying to kill that term (even if I sometimes slip into using it, and I used to love it) because *all* marketing performs.

If you are a direct response marketer working with brand teams and you call yourself performance marketing but call them brand marketing, you are setting yourself up for an antagonistic relationship. You should also be good enough to know it isn't true. Start from a place of respect when working with brand marketing as a direct response marketer and everyone will get along much better.

Next, you should help find out what the brand marketers are worried about. For example, most brand teams have some struggles with measurement, and in this case, direct response marketing tends to skew to practitioners who are more comfortable with numbers. That means you have something useful you can bring to the table to help them. Further, when you measure how brand and direct response drive actions together, they consistently amplify each other. A great awareness campaign makes more people move down the funnel and get picked up by great direct response marketing. Propose how you can work together to prove your combined value, help show that value, and directly provide support with any questions they have in the process. This is how I believe I built a great relationship with my predecessor, Antonio Lucio, an acclaimed rockstar marketer, who recommended I take over from him as CMO. It is also how I believe we've got results in my new role, having these teams operate as one. Showing up to help and partner as a direct response marketer, rather than criticize, is important to building great working relationships but sadly, it is not the default setting in my experience.

Finally, you have to care about the brand. As already stated, a great digital direct response marketer must be invested in the long term and shouldn't be willing to sell off the company brand for a few short-term conversions. This isn't always easy, but you will find great brand marketers have empathy for this situation. In addition to caring about the brand, be vulnerable, ask for help and be humble enough to take it. Make sure your direct response campaigns align with the brand marketing team, and don't frustrate them or harm their goals. Yes, do this with guardrail metrics of the kind I have described above, but above all, do it in conversation and partnership. If you both help and seek help in this way, you are a great partner, and if brand and direct response act as one, the results are incredible.

WORKING TOGETHER

My entire career has been based on influence. Generally, I had very little control of the most important and effective marketing channels, of my budget allocation and of the results I was supposed to drive. I have explained how I built my career and the influence of the growth marketing team. This happened by giving advice that produced results, but it required engineering to implement that advice: promoting advertiser growth tools in product, adopting SEO best practices to rank in Google and helping drive contact-importer conversions. None of that would have been possible without great working relationships with my XFN partners at Meta. Your team need to be great partners with other teams to get great results.

The best way to be great partners is to understand and respect what your counterparts have as their priorities. Finance, business groups and brand marketers are the three most critical partners for digital direct response marketers. And as you can see, these three groups have different objectives. Your job, then, is to understand them, make it easy for them to work with you and help them succeed in achieving their objectives. If you do this right, momentum will flow to you. In hard times, you will get support, and in the good times, you will get fuelled to do your best, most impactful work. To be a great marketer, you need to be a great partner.

3

THE CHANNELS

In each chapter so far, we have looked at tools and principles cutting across all channels. As I begin a deep dive on channels in this part, the lessons from Part I are particularly pertinent, so let's quickly recap them:

- You need a clear North Star goal, and a metric that describes it. Nothing mucks up a marketing programme more than being unclear on what success is and how you determine if you have achieved it.
- You must have a good handle on where you, as a company, are in the marketing funnel.
- Although these channels can work throughout the funnel, they are best at the demand and action stages.
- Which conversion action you want will strongly influence the channel you use. For example, you can't normally use product-led channels to promote registration because someone has to already be registered to see them.
- The creative varies by channel – you can't, for example, run a banner ad in a paid search, text-only placement.
- Targeting also varies by channel. For example, in social media, you can advertise to someone behaviourally, but in paid search you can only advertise based on their current search behaviour.

As you will see, the basics critically interplay with all these channels, but as you dig into the depths here, I hope the channels really come to life in a way that allows you to move beyond the basics.

The infrastructure, as explored in Part II, underpins every lesson in these chapters: You need great measurement in place to understand how your marketing is working. You need, in the paid channels, to care about marginal return, not just average returns. And you need the right teams in place to get all that done.

Above all, as you work through this part, looking at these channels in detail, I hope you will remember the two guiding principles:

1. **Tools evolve – but principles are timeless.** Every channel has a parallel in the history of marketing and those parallels provide insight into marketing's timeless principles. This is useful to not just understand the current channels but also future-proof you for adapting to how they evolve. Digital will be changed by AI in more ways than can be imagined today; understanding the related timeless principles will help you react better.

2. **Incremental results are everything**. Experimentation lets you understand your incremental impact. Each channel has different nuances for how to do this, and I cover them throughout this part. But please remember post-click tracking with no experimentation on incrementality is likely to be a waste of your marketing dollars.

Each channel that is covered in the part that follows has wonderful capability for impact.

- **Product-led channels** – These are great for upselling and cross-selling existing users, much like merchandising units at the end of aisles and the choice of which shelf to stock items for sale in a supermarket. They require technical skill and creativity, and they have the advantage of being mostly free.

- **Partner-led channels** – These have waxed and waned, but they are on the rise today with retail advertising networks from the likes of Amazon, DoorDash and their global equivalents. Partner-led channels have been my first love in digital marketing ever since I cut my teeth on affiliate marketing. There are risks of fraud, but they let you try a lot of approaches quickly, making them super-valuable.

- **Search** – Both organic and paid placement in search rely on the right topics and keywords. Many failures start from not researching what you want to rank for before jumping into the weeds of technical SEO and keyword bidding. (I will explore this concept in depth in Chapter 13.) It can also be hard to do incrementality testing with search. Search suffers from the tyranny of post-click tracking, which search companies promote to their benefit.

- **Social** – Organic social's success comes down to being interesting and giving the user what they want. Much is made of 'the algorithm', as if it almost has a mind of its own. In fact, the algorithm tries to increasingly serve the user's interests. Paid social is the culmination of the field of digital marketing, featuring the best targeting, the best auto-optimizing AI and the closest to incrementality measurement of any channel. Surely, more channels will come, but as the most recent and largest channel, social is the most advanced today. I am super-proud to have been part of building social media marketing into the giant channel it is today – it remains the leading channel in capabilities and measurement.

What happens next is anyone's guess, but it seems certain that AI will dominate, rearranging every channel in its wake. Search is already transforming into answer engines, with fully AI social interactions and other advancements. So this ride isn't over, and that's what makes it fun for me, closing in on three decades into this journey. I hope that the principles and advice described in these chapters will help you find that same enjoyment in riding the next waves of digital marketing innovation.

11. PRODUCT-LED CHANNELS

Product-led channels are as old as sales and marketing themselves. If a shopper is walking through the aisles of your supermarket, you market discounts and new products to them throughout the store. If a patron is in your bar, you promote specials and other options to them on chalkboards and menus, enticing them to spend more. Shop windows have displays to tempt potential buyers inside, and loyalty programmes send coupons through the mail to their loyal customers. All these classic in-product promotions exist in some form on the internet today, and they are all powerful channels for digital marketing.

There are two large types of product-led channels: in-product merchandising, where you promote your product or service to someone currently using it; and direct mail, where you reach out when someone is off it, or not currently using it. These channels work brilliantly throughout the marketing funnel. Say, you are an online clothing retailer and you have added a new line to your collection. At this stage of the funnel – awareness – you could email your loyal customers, especially those who have bought similar clothes in the past, inviting them to come check out the new line. When they visit your website, you could have prominent merchandising that guides them to the item page, moving them down the funnel from awareness through to decision. And if you get the promotion right, you can move them right along to action. If your North Star goal is adoption of a new product, product-led channels are brilliant for getting an existing customer the whole way through the marketing funnel for that new product. The drawback, of course, is these channels are not the best to acquire new customers overall.

In-product merchandising can leverage the best of the principles of great merchandising and personalized service. It must, however, interpret those principles in today's context. You need to think about who you show what merchandising. This decision is driven by targeting at its basic level, but it is important to also consider the value of different possible products for different people, and the number of times you have shown them that promotion and they have ignored it. This process starts at the top of the funnel, making people aware that your offering exists and tempting them to interact.

Personalization is expected in a modern app or website. You must use the context you know about both the individual and the page they are on to customize your marketing to get the best result. The better you do that, the better the outcome you generate. The final step is the actual creative you show them, and the conversion flow you deliver them into. Once your marketing has moved them from not being aware to actually deciding to click and take action, the conversion experience must be optimized to take advantage of all the work you have done to get them there.

For direct mail channels, nothing matters more than the data on which you base the marketing. Generic direct mail is basically useless on the internet, but targeted, personalized mailings are invaluable. To get great targeting and personalization depends on great data. The saying 'garbage in garbage out' rings true. Once you have a great data set to send the notifications out, they have to actually arrive, which is not a trivial consideration. Then you need to get those notifications opened, which requires custom creative. Finally, once again, when you have moved them through the whole marketing funnel to take action, the conversion flow must work well.

With these steps and uses in mind, let's dive in to these two incredibly powerful product-led channels, beginning with in-product merchandising, one of the most important and underused forms of marketing today.

IN-PRODUCT MERCHANDISING

In-product merchandising, also known as onsite merchandising, is a special case of in-product marketing, in which you are merchandising one of many particular items within a store, whereas in-product marketing refers to marketing anything in the product. The basic concept of in-product merchandising in modern internet products is nothing new, and there's much to learn about this channel through standard marketing theory and practice. The main difference today is just that product placement and promotion are in a new venue: the app or website versus the physical store. As internet products have evolved, the line between what is product and technology and what is marketing has become more and more blurred. This is why the growth team at Facebook, and now Meta, was and is so successful. Within that, 'product growth', or 'growth marketing', is the team I started, which blends product, analytics and marketing expertise, operating at the boundary between those disciplines to get the outcomes the company needs.

When you think about recommendation engines, like PYMK on Facebook or the similar items unit on Amazon when you browse a product, what are they but merchandising units? Even navigation is just an extreme form of onsite merchandising – you make editorial decisions about what features of your product or categories you are selling and then you put in the navigation in a particular order. Just like the layout of a supermarket, the navigation of an e-commerce site is a product placement decision drawing on the classic four Ps of marketing (Product, Placement, Pricing, Promotion).

As with the physical world, a large, generic chain of bars or pubs is totally efficient and effective, but if the bartender remembers you and you get the personalized touch, the experience is even better. On the internet, code is all that is needed to create that personalized touch. Just as a bartender who knows your name and favourite drink is more likely to get you to buy another round, a product that welcomes you in the same way will get more sales and conversions. In the physical world, we lament the loss of the personalized touch of the little local store, but we love the convenience of the big supermarket. On the internet, you can give a customer both, and this will only get better as technology, especially AI, advances.

Targeting can be more detailed

A huge advantage for product-led channels is the ability to use first-party data. In general, it is clear that there is a consensus that a distinction exists between first-party and third-party data. First-party data is data you generate while using a product, which is then used by that product to improve your experience. Third-party data is data generated outside a product and then used to improve your experience in that product by, for example, giving you more relevant ads. In some cases the law itself allows companies to do more with first-party data, which means you can do more to personalize your ads and promotions onsite or in your app than you can offsite or outside your app.

All onsite targeting can be seen as a form of a recommendation engine. Examples cut across different internet industries: ranking links in any navigation menu, choosing which users to show in PYMK-type units, promoting items a shopper might want to buy in a shopping system, promoting videos a visitor may want to watch or recommending news stories to a reader on a site like the BBC. None of these actions is purely marketing, but none is purely product either. This is why I believe magic happens when you have technical marketers working closely with technologists.

My first experience that blended marketing and the product itself was with a cocktail recommendation engine on my old cocktail recipes website. This concept is basic today, and large language models (LLMs) have taken graph data and how to explore it to a whole other level. That said, I found the principles I learned through that experience extended to recommending accounts on social media, rooms on a travel site, and items for sale on an e-commerce platform. They were also pretty useful for understanding how to use machine learning (ML) at Meta. The same principles hold.

To create the recommendation engine, what I wanted to understand was how related any two cocktails on my website were. As mentioned, they were mostly user-generated, and though I moderated them, I couldn't just do a mapping of them myself, showing how they connected to each other across hundreds of cocktails. The way I chose to relate these cocktails was to see if someone had visited cocktail A during their session on the site, did they also visit cocktail B? I logged all user journeys and extracted all the cocktails they visited in a given day. Then, for every cocktail, I counted how many times that pair appeared in a day and the order they appeared, so either A then B or B then A. I then added that information to a database. I would then aggregate this database monthly, trim the data down to only ten cocktails, to save space and drive performance, and for each cocktail, generate a list of the other most visited cocktails if the user visited that cocktail in a given day.

The results of adding this as a link unit at the bottom of the cocktail page was a double-digit percentage increase in page views on my cocktail site and an increase in depth of sessions.

There was also, I believe, an increase in SEO traffic because I dropped the bounce rate signal for Google, which is how quickly users go back to Google after visiting your website – if they return right away and search for the same phrase or keywords again, Google seems to think, fairly, that your site wasn't a good result to give. I did, of course, exclude any clicks on the link unit for future calculations of cocktail relationships.

The results were awesome, but the most interesting insights I found were through exploring the big database as a graph. Lots of clusters of data emerged: all cocktails were clustered together on ingredient (e.g., all vodka cocktails were close together in the graph); all cocktails with ruder names (e.g., sex on the beach) were clustered; and all cocktails were clustered by glass type and so on. This was my first experience with recommendation engines and the power of defining the relationship you want to explore between two nodes in a graph and how every cluster I could think of was expressed when I queried the data, and presumably many more I didn't think of. (This has some similarities to how LLMs work: they have tokens as nodes in a graph, and between those tokens are weights to indicate how closely they are related. The result is a network of nodes and edges that appear like neurons and synapses in the brain, known as a neural network.) Purely algorithmic recommendation units – ads that show the output of the recommendation engine for users to click on – are a hugely important form of onsite merchandising and in-product promotion. Thinking hard about how you define the features you use to do the learning for those channels is extremely important.

Value models

When it comes to rec ommendation units, CTR isn't necessarily the most valuable goal for your company or product – your North

Star is rarely just getting a click. Actual conversions are what count the most. Often, these conversions are sales in service of the very simple North Star goal of revenue. Conversions vary in value too, so selling a more expensive product is better than selling a less expensive one. A hotel would rather book out their most expensive, highest-margin room over their least expensive, and a clothes store would rather sell a pair of expensive shoes over a cheap accessory. As such, you have to understand the value those clicks will deliver, both on conversion rate and the value of those conversions.

The pioneers on this value model were Google and their approach to the search channel. In the early 2000s, a company or individual could bid on paid search with Yahoo! by keyword, but Yahoo! ranked the ads by how much you bid. Google created a simple, revolutionary change to this process. They ranked the ads on estimated or expected CPM (eCPM) instead of cost per click (CPC) bid. To do this, they started by predicting the click through rate (CTR) of the ads they had available by serving the ads in their search results. They could see how many clicks they received per impression shown, and then they used that information to predict their CTR in future. (Google, and the whole industry, have since become far smarter, creating algorithms that cluster keywords and analyse ad content to predict CTR before an ad is even shown.) Then they looked at the CPC they would charge for that ad. They took that CPC and multiplied it by the CTR they expected. This told Google how much money each ad would make them, and they ranked them based on that value, the eCPM.

This early ranking system meant you could bid, say, $100 a click, but have a CTR of zero and still appear first in a search, without making the early search engines, like Yahoo!, any money. Though that's an extreme example, you could have regularly bid twice as much on CPC as another advertiser, and, even if the other advertiser had three times the CTR, you would rank above them in paid search. The new system Google invented fixed this issue, ranking the ad with the highest revenue per impression first (in this case, half the CPC but three times the CTR gives a 50 percent higher CPM). It all came down to your competitor's marketing funnel. They may have had a brand with great awareness, so customers would already be far down the marketing funnel with intent to buy. With precisely the same ad, but a different brand, you might end up with triple the CTR and 50 percent higher CPM, as in this theoretical example, or more.

By maximizing revenue per impression, Google revolutionized the industry. The expected CPM is the bid in the ranking system for all the major ad systems today. Every recommendation engine should think hard about this approach. Just as it was revolutionary for search – and, indeed, all ads on the internet – it should be so for your recommendation model too, whether you are recommending bunches of flowers at a local florist or merchandising millions of products at an online commerce giant.

IMPRESSION DISCOUNTING AND PERSISTENCE

One important factor in predicting the CTR of an ad is how many times someone has seen it. When someone has seen your ad fifty times and not taken action, they probably won't take action the fifty-first time. So, the more you show an ad to a user, the more you should discount the likelihood they will respond to it. This idea is known as impression discounting. You should be persistent in your creative, but you shouldn't be irrational about it. Similar to the above section on value, this concept is important to in-product merchandising, but it applies to more areas. Impression discounting and persistence should be considered relevant to mobile versus desktop search, or feed versus right-hand column social or above the fold versus below the fold banner ads and so on.

I've already noted that an ad performs worse the more you show it to the same person, with a decline in CTR with each impression (as discussed in Chapter 6), and you should factor that result into your advertising plan. For example, you could sequence in other ads with higher CTR as their predicted CTR exceeds that of the first ad. You also need to think about *where* the ads appear, especially with recommendation systems (the actual unit that shows the recommendation and what the recommendation engine shows within the unit). I learned this fact first-hand with Facebook's PYMK.

With PYMK, the same recommendation of a person a user should add as a friend could appear in lots of places: the right-hand column of the desktop website, the feed as a unit midway down on mobile, as a suggestion right after the user has sent a friend request, and many others. (If you think back to the point made about prominence in Chapter 6, this consideration becomes obvious.) When the recommendation pops up as a suggestion after sending a friend request, it is going to be quite prominent, and the impression really counts. The right-hand-column impression on desktop, however, is low prominence, so it should probably not be counted as being as much of an impression as the pop-up. The feed placement lies somewhere in between. Similarly, sometimes a user sees the whole impression when a merchandising unit loads, or an ad is shown, but at other times they may only see the first ten pixels of the recommendation within their window or above the fold. Clearly, if someone sees only ten pixels, it is unlikely they internalized the recommendation the same as if they saw all the pixels.

The key lesson here is, don't make all impression discounting the same. When you sequence ads or discount a merchandising impression as having been shown to a user who didn't respond, make sure you are thinking about where you showed that ad and how much of it you showed them.

Though I discuss persistence a lot in Chapter 6, it remains relevant here too. As it relates to in-product merchandising and marketing, there is no better example than the Hotmail email footer. (My favourite recounting of this example is in *Viral Loop: From Facebook to Twitter, How Today's Smartest Businesses Grow Themselves* by journalist Adam Penenberg.) With Hotmail, you could send and receive email for free and access it from any internet service provider (ISP). At the time, in the late 1990s, no other company provided the same offering.

But Hotmail had an issue getting the word out about this fantastic offer. Since it was free, they didn't have any ad budget. So, they added a link at the bottom of every email sent by someone in their system. It worked like a charm, generating exponential growth through what would prove to be probably the most viral marketing campaign of all time. It is worth noting that the product – free email with access from any ISP – wasn't fundamentally viral. They had to actually insert this unnatural link (which would now be called a growth hack) to make it viral.

Once that was done, however, Hotmail took the lead in email, and Microsoft is still reaping the benefits from Outlook.com about thirty years later. I doubt it could have been this successful if it wasn't persistently appearing in every email users sent out. I realize this approach is at odds with the idea of ad sequencing and impression discounting, but the persistence here was *so* high, and the promotion itself was so inoffensive, that it really worked. That combination meant the consistent pressure was the right call.

I have had many examples of persistence paying off on my team, creating and placing ads that were presented in the right context and at the right level of prominence to be noticed, but not overwhelming. Two, in particular, relate directly to the power of contextual promotion in in-product merchandising.

CONTEXTUAL PROMOTION

For many years, my team at Facebook and I would run promotions for Facebook Messenger to get potential users to install the app. (I was very lucky to work on this project with the brilliant Mike Winters, who invented many of these promotions.) The promotions often took the form of big banner ads at the top of the Facebook newsfeed or even interstitials when users opened the message notification surface. Interstitials are ads that fully take over the screen, either when users start using a product or app or between two actions on a product or app. For example, many news sites have interstitials telling users to log in or subscribe when they start to browse down an article. The most successful

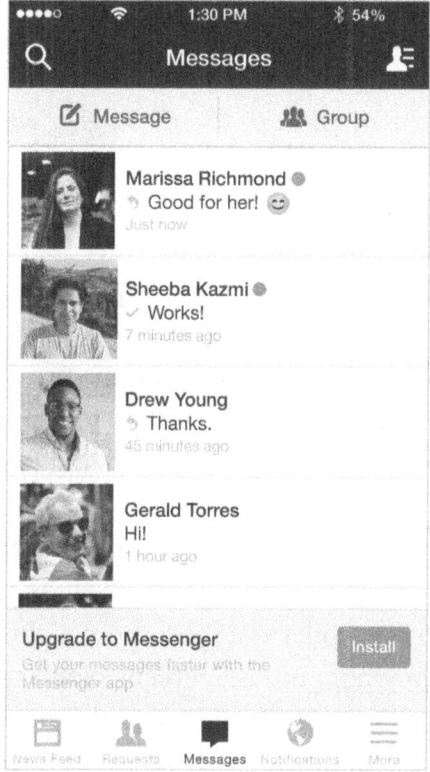

Persistent install promotion for Messenger

ad in terms of total installs of the Messenger app, driving around a third of all installs, was a persistent promotion inside the Messenger notification screen. This promotion can be seen in the screenshot above (see the grey bar at the bottom with the green button saying 'Install', pictured here in grayscale). The ad was completely persistent and contextually relevant.

It worked in regard to persistence, because the ad was small, so the design and product teams were fine with letting us run this promotion all the time. Even with a low conversion rate, this huge number of impressions would drive installs. It also beat another persistent entry point, where we had put the install link into the navigation menu. The reason for this was twofold. First, although the navigation had higher reach, the Messenger notification surface had massively higher impressions as people used it more frequently than navigation. Second, the notification surface also had a higher conversion and impression rate. This is because people were in the mindset to use messaging when on that surface, and the idea of trying a separate app was reasonable for them.

A second super-powerful example of persistence in contextual promotion was my first project at Facebook, in which I was tasked with driving advertiser growth. As mentioned, we quickly realized that onsite merchandising was the most powerful channel we had. Within that channel, the most powerful links were those users saw when looking at their page admin dashboard. On the dashboard, we featured a link to the ad product. Further, every ad unit on Facebook (at the time these were all the rail of ads in the right-hand column of Facebook, shown in the figure above) had an 'Advertise' link at the bottom of it. We decided to move that link from the bottom of the unit to the top. The result was a whopping 30 percent increase in advertisers acquired from that link. That moved the top-line advertiser acquisition for the company and, at a constant LTV for those advertisers, clearly drove incremental revenue.

Ads in the early Facebook web product showing
promotions to advertise

A further advertiser growth link, added in 2008, was more powerful still. This was a link within the user's admin dashboard that featured a big green button (as discussed, a defining part of my career) placed at the top right corner of the page, pictured in greyscale in the screenshot below. The link and its presentation were so hugely powerful because of the context; when users were looking for the performance of our page, we presented them with an option to get more out of it by creating

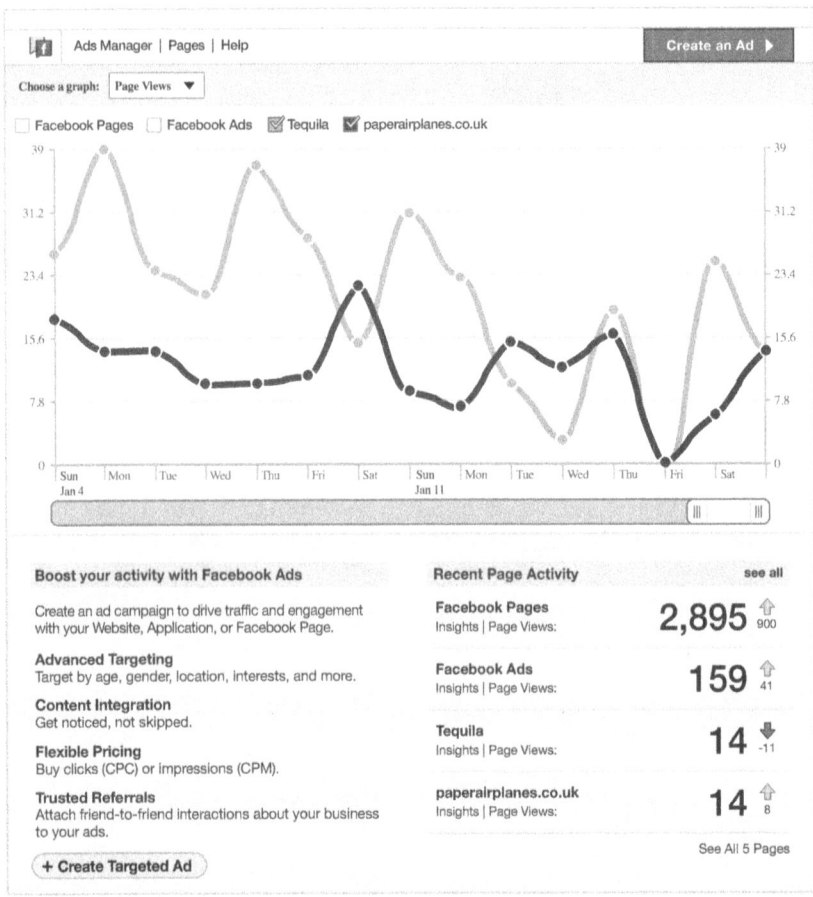

The power of the big green button placement

an ad. (You will notice the link says, 'Create an Ad'.) This was a major result that we came across by accident.

We were running a test with an analytics vendor who found that in France the 'Advertise' link on all the ad units on Facebook. com was converting around 40 percent higher than the global average. We evaluated this data and realized the language of the link was translated into French not as 'Advertise' – which was what we were using at the time – but 'Create an Ad' or 'Créer une ad' in French. As a result, we moved from the more passive 'Advertise' to 'Create an Ad' everywhere, and we increased the global conversions from online merchandising by around the same 40 percent France was experiencing from just that one change. This is still one of my favourite wins of all time. As this example shows, testing copy in an ad or on a button is truly important, and the basics, like testing button wording, matter. (With wins like this and others, Brian Hale went on to take advertiser growth at Facebook to new heights, especially with the advent of mobile ads.)

A final superpower in context marketing is chaining, in which when users take one action, we suggest they take another action. Broadly, marketers use this technique with tremendous success all the time. At Meta, the most successful advertiser acquisition link was when we promoted advertisers' ability to boost a post as a sponsored story, right on the post and right after they posted it. The most successful contact-importer promotion was immediately after users contact-imported, prompting them to import their other email accounts. And the most successful upsells in e-commerce are merchandising that states, 'You bought this item, have you considered these similar items?' There are many more examples, but all of them prove the point that, wherever you can, you should promote people to take an action in context of the place they are and the actions they are taking at the time.

IN-PRODUCT MERCHANDISING PERSONALIZATION

Personalization for in-product merchandising is more powerful than for any other channel, so it is a special case. Just as with other channels, when it comes to in-product personalization, and product-led channels generally, you should always personalize a product or service to an individual when you can. As discussed, personalization gives users a better experience, resulting in better outcomes from your onsite marketing. There is also an expectation that you at least use first-party data to improve the user experience with in-product merchandising, while also collecting better and more data than you would have access to if the user logged out of your site or app. Remember, behavioural data beats all other data, so the goal is to try and personalize on behaviour if you can, but don't ignore basics like name and demographic in that personalization.

Social proof is a big benefit here. This works in a hierarchy. Think about your use of online shopping or travel sites. Multi-star ratings and positive reviews from people you don't know – sometimes people who are completely anonymous – increase your likelihood to take action; fewer stars and negative reviews will decrease that likelihood. Social proof is even more powerful, though, when your friends, family or acquaintances have taken an action. This is why across all of social media you see lists of friends, or groups of friends' profile pictures, who have taken an action. (I believe Facebook was the first to do this at scale with social ads launching in 2007, then attaching this information to our onsite merchandising for features like the contact importer, giving us double-digit uplifts in performance.) Social proof works. Personalized social proof is even better, and when done right, it helps people find actions to take that make their lives better, all based on the wisdom of crowds.

Another simple form of personalization, as mentioned in Chapter 6 and recurring throughout this book because it is so core, is just acknowledging someone by name. This polite gesture works online just as it does in real life. Throughout my career, this small detail has ended in double-digit uplifts in email marketing opens and click through rates. We applied it to onsite merchandising for the contact importer shortly into my tenure at Meta, and it did the same.

Note that personalization can go too far, tipping over into territory that may feel like it is too much or is overwhelming for users. When you show them suggested friends on a social media platform or suggest products, services or sites, all based on what they have done online, and what your systems predict they will do next, acknowledging explaining how you might predict someone's behaviour and make a recommendation based on it is a very powerful approach, in two ways.

First, it improves conversions by reducing friction and increasing the relevance of an ad. An example here, which is not relevant today but was impactful twenty years ago, was when social networks promoted contact importers. We obviously all wanted to increase conversion. At Meta, we showed users the logo of the email provider they used to sign up to Meta in the promotion. This provided a double-digit percentage uplift on conversion on one of the most important funnel elements for our growth at that time.

Second, it makes a promotion far more acceptable to people to explain why they are seeing something. Amazon, for example, regularly includes a note stating something along the lines of 'because you bought this item, we are showing you these items'. This allows them to give highly relevant promotions based on purchase behaviour and explain them in a way that makes people feel comfortable, even if there are other factors at play. This is a real win-win on transparency and conversion rate.

So where's the line between good marketing and marketing that has gone too far? I would say use your gut here as a first pass. If you don't feel comfortable with it yourself, and you understand the system, your users likely won't either. Then take what you do to user research. As a small company, this can be informal, such as asking friends, and as a large company, you can run actual studies that are quick and lightweight, taking a few days not weeks. There are diminishing returns in personalization which, when you go too far, likely tip into turning people off and hurting conversions. I have never reached that point in my work through common sense and user testing. If you do the same, you should stay on the right side of that line too.

Conversion in the ad

Hopefully it is clear throughout this book that the conversion flow matters. In optimizing that flow, the best thing to do is reduce the steps to conversion. For example, I remember my close colleague Naomi Gleit and me giving a presentation at our F8 conference on how reducing the registration form for Facebook from a multi-page flow to an embedded one-page form on the Facebook homepage completely changed our conversion rate. Amazon optimized buy with one-click, and even tried to defend it against all new comers with a patent. Shopify uses shop pay and stored credential to increase conversion for all its customers by removing the payments step across multiple sites and storing users' credential as a service. Pretty much every company that doesn't use Shopify but does e-commerce tries to do the same. All of these examples are standard, good approaches to conversion rate optimization.

In the extreme, though, an inline conversion in an ad is as good as it gets. An inline conversion is one in which the user can complete the entire conversion flow within the ad before click-ing through to a website – or even without clicking through at all. Three excellent examples come to mind:

- Microsoft put the login button inline for the Microsoft single sign-on in the actual ad to contact-import from Hotmail. (When users sign on, they authenticate who they are so Microsoft can share their contacts with an app.) This resulted in a double-digit percent increase in conversion.
- Google and Apple launched one-click app install ads in their app stores where users had an option to just

click the install button instead of being taken to the app store page before installing. This change made these ads substantially more effective.

- Facebook created lead-generating ads where users could submit as a lead to a marketer (for example, an auto salesperson) by just clicking 'Submit' in an ad, sending their phone number to the salesperson.

So just remember, when it comes to removing steps in a conversion flow with in-product marketing, the answer may be that you can put the entire conversion flow *in the ad* itself, reducing steps in an ad conversion to their logical limit.

DESIGN AND PROMINENCE OF IN-PRODUCT ADS MATTER

This is a tale as old as the advertising industry itself. In newspaper ads at least half a century ago, advertisers paid more for above the fold than below the fold, where the newspaper literally folded in half; more for the right-hand page than the left-hand page, since readers would first see the right-hand page as they flipped through the paper; and more for colour than for greyscale, as it was more likely to catch the reader's eye. Making sure you place an ad where people will see it remains extremely important today.

This practice, however, has been the main source of tension with designers throughout my marketing career, and across all the companies I have helped or worked for. Design aesthetics tend to call for more subtle treatments – like grey links on white backgrounds, for example – and often I find designers asking for iconography over words. There are two issues here. First, subtle links do not drive potential customers to take action. They may, for example, overlook the link. Some people have poor eyesight, others are moving fast and scroll past the link entirely, and others may just be distracted, and the product being advertised isn't their highest priority at that moment. Second, people usually don't understand what a clever icon means, no matter how well designed.

To overcome these issues, create a strong contrast for your call to action and, wherever possible, provide words not icons to drive actions. A usual pushback on this latter point is a concern over character expansion in translation. For example, words in German typically take more characters than their English equivalents do, affecting the design of the button or icon when translated. I have found this issue surmountable. My teams have made Meta products work in countries around the world, doing translations and customizations for specific locales, like Arabic script reading from right to left. This process is known as internationalization and localization, and, at least with Meta, for over a decade we've always found a solution.

Sometimes, though, it is just hard to cut through and have designers acknowledge how much prominence matters for conversion. That's where the 'big green button' comes back into play, in the form of what I call 'the big green button test'. This is when I propose a small test in which the design makes the call to action so prominent it can't be missed, so much so that it is taken off the table as a variable. After that's done, we check the conversion volume in that scenario and determine what we want to leave on the table for aesthetics. Time and again this test has been incredibly effective for winning arguments with my design teams. This has led to another joke about my career: in brand marketing, my job is just asking for a bigger logo, and in direct response marketing, it is asking for a bigger, greener button. There's a lot of truth in this. I find when I have my brand hat on (higher up the marketing funnel) I always care about the prominence of the brand, and when I have my direct response hat on (lower in the marketing funnel) I always want a bigger, more obvious call to action, and generally I ask for it to be green.

As you can see, in-product merchandising is a tremendously powerful tool throughout the marketing funnel when you are merchandizing new products to existing users. The targeting, personalization and persistence you can achieve are second to no other channel. You can certainly go too far on persistence and prominence or move into overpersonalization, so pay due respect to the channel and the people you are merchandising towards. If you do that well, this overlooked channel will become one of your most impactful and serve your North Star goal time and again.

DIRECT MAIL

What's old is new again! Direct mail (DM) is a product-led channel that reaches beyond the people engaged with your product at that moment. If you have the right data, with user consent, in your database, you can connect with the right user with the right message at the right time. This channel is also useful at every stage of the marketing funnel – all the way from awareness to action – when promoting new products or services to your current customers. But, as discussed in Chapter 5, you can only do this if your message is delivered and people are enticed to open it.

This is another space that proves how much the basics matter and how nothing is truly new in online marketing – the guiding principle that *tools evolve, but principles are timeless* rings true once again. For example, Tony Fu, one of the best digital marketers I have worked with, started his career fully offline in direct mail with letters sent by the post office. After we had worked together for a decade, he was working on SMS and push notifications. All three tools required incredibly similar thought patterns and solutions. Getting into the specifics of data, delivery, creative and conversion is rewarding in direct mail. I have found that learning the details for one DM channel transfers smoothly to all other DM channels, even if the specific names and measurement tools – like deliverability, open rate and conversion rate – vary.

Database marketing depends on the database

In the movie *Glengarry Glen Ross*, there is a truly epic scene in which Alec Baldwin's character lectures the salespeople on how to sell starting. 'You've got the leads. Mitch and Murray paid good money. Get their names to sell them.' Your database contains your leads, and as the character reminds us all, you must 'always be closing' those leads to 'sign on the line, which is dotted'. This is the oldest form of database marketing – salespeople getting lists of people to visit, call or otherwise contact to sell them products. The whole process starts here. If you are going to market or sell based on email addresses, phone numbers, house addresses or some similar contact method, you must know which leads in your database are the 'good' ones. These are the leads that have the quality data, obtained with the appropriate consent, attached to them and are most prequalified to drive a conversion.

The 'garbage in, garbage out' cliché in the data analytics and computer science world holds true in database marketing. In fact, in database marketing, it can be even worse. If you have garbage coming in, you might send irrelevant messages that get relegated to spam, have users turn off your notifications or opt out of your emails, or even report your emails as spam and get your entire system shut down. So, garbage in, nothing out, ever again! That is all far worse and longer-lasting than a poor-performing email campaign, and it is also something I consistently find a company has done when they ask me for help. It is often hard to recover.

That said, the upside of database marketing is amazing. Starting as just letters stuffed in envelopes, direct mail, as a direct response marketing channel, blossomed with many great practitioners. Capital One may well have been the company that perfected this approach, but the Sears catalogue in the US deserves a special mention for revolutionizing marketing with this channel. For me, though, *Scoring Points: How Tesco Continues to Win Customer Loyalty* by Clive Humby, Terry Hunt and Tim Phillips – a story of classic, stuffed-envelope direct mail – was the book that inspired me to start a career in marketing.

Tesco, the UK supermarket chain, has a loyalty programme featuring a Clubcard, a loyalty card, which provides discounts and perks. Core to Tesco's success is how the Clubcard ensured the company had up-to-date home addresses for their customers. This differentiated them from all other loyalty cards at the time. While every other loyalty card gave you cash off or coupons in the checkout line, Clubcard mailed you money off coupons periodically, based on your spending in store. This meant that, in order to receive your earned discounts, you had to keep your postal address up to date.

This tiny detail was critical in many ways to the success of the programme, but one particular example is worth highlighting. If a competitor opened near an existing Tesco, Tesco would historically blanket the surrounding area with money-off vouchers to try and stop customers from even entering the new store. This was expensive and wasteful, because loyal customers who would not have defected anyhow took these coupons to get money off. Using the Clubcard data, however, Tesco could know who shopped at the store, whose spend was dropping and where they lived. They could then target money-off vouchers for those specific customers to incentivize them from defecting to the new competitor store at the individual level, all based on their actual behaviour and the items they liked to buy. Humby, Hunt and Phillips suggest this approach was quite successful, and I wonder if part of why Tesco has lost momentum at the time of writing, in 2025, is because the internet has dramatically changed how people shop, including having their groceries delivered directly to their door by all their traditional competitors in the UK, which requires home addresses, causing the Clubcard to be far less of an advantage.

Still, Tesco created a unique way to develop and maintain a database of valid addresses and tokens to which they could send direct mail. This database had excellent data appended to it for marketing, even down to shoppers' geographical location. They created a programme that caused customers to fight to make sure they received mail from Tesco because it contained actual monetary value for them. This can be seen over and over again – the single most important thing in database marketing, and DM overall, is the quality of the database you are mailing to and the quality of the data appended to that list for targeting and personalization. If you are going to run a large-scale direct mail campaign, no matter the medium, you have to care about the quality of your database, because without a good database, there is little point even trying to do database marketing.

Deliverability matters

In Part I, I explain how you need to log the entire email path from generation to conversion on your email marketing, measuring the drop-offs at every point in your conversion flow. The drop-offs can happen at any point, but the biggest typical drop-offs are when you try to send the mail – be it SMS, push, email, offline or whatever form it takes – and have it delivered. If it is delivering, you are then relying on the content to be compelling enough to make the recipient take action.

Once you have a great database, featuring up-to-date, correct addresses and other related data, your next job is to actually deliver messages to those addresses. Clearly, making sure your mail gets delivered to the right person is a huge challenge in all direct mail, starting with the post. As direct mail evolved and email came along, a whole new set of challenges and opportunities emerged. The postal system wouldn't tell you if you were sending a mailer to the wrong person at the wrong address. With email, however, you could now receive an error code (such as 4xx and 5xx series) that told you what happened to your message. You could also now track open rates, using data on when images in the email loaded from your server, and click-through rates. This data could publish a whole funnel of how successful you were at sending and delivering email and whether it was intriguing enough for recipients to open and take that next step to click on what you'd sent them.

But those were the easy, early days of email. Sadly, all this logging was abused by spammers. This caused the tools to be obfuscated. For example, loading images by default stopped, making open rates hard to understand. This was all done for good purpose, protecting people from spam and, although spammers were the worst, sometimes large companies' email campaigns look little different to spam. As a result, these changes in how email is delivered and tracked have led to many legitimate marketers making mistakes that harm them in ways that take a long time to turn around, if they are able to do so at all. The good news is there are ways to protect yourself up front as you get started here, and there are now vendors who can handle a lot of these potential issues for you. The bad news is the vendors are not all equally good – their tools are powerful, but they all make mistakes using them, and so can you.

To keep yourself from running into deliverability issues early on that could hamstring you nearly forever, consider the four following steps you must take when sending direct mail emails:

1. **Make sure your mail transfer agent is in good shape.** This is normally fairly easy, but when I joined Facebook, we were still using Zuckmail 1.0, which wasn't industry standard. Today, it's best to use a reputable, large-scale vendor to provide this service.

2. **Acquire email addresses in a clean way (i.e., with someone's consent to use them).** Then validate those addresses by sending them an email to confirm the user gave you their address. There are vigilantes surfing the web who add email addresses they don't own that belong to spam honeypots, everywhere they can, and you will almost certainly be no exception. These addresses are like mystery shoppers who have snuck onto your mailing list and are trying to catch you if you make a mistake. As a result, you need to follow the rules. For example, only subscribe someone to a mailing list if they click on a notification email from you and confirm their address, which these honeypot addresses will never do. Make sure you unsubscribe users when they click 'unsubscribe'. Some of these honeypot addresses will report you if you send a single email to them, even if it is 'confirm your email address'. As such, you need to be disciplined about how you accept and confirm email addresses and only send email marketing to people after they have confirmed they want it.

3. **Prepare email vendors when they are going to get a new, large campaign from you.** Register your email template

before you start to send a new type of email at significant scale. This allows you to pre-warn email providers that a new email is coming. You should also warm up new IP addresses slowly, as compared to suddenly going from sending no emails a day to multiple per hour. If you go straight from zero to a hundred you will undoubtedly end up in spam, so warm up by gradually ramping up volume. Registering your email template and ramping up that new campaign is relatively specialized and here is where having a great team matters. Whether you have someone on your team, or a third-party vendor, focused on email delivery, they will know the current best practices here. Get a real rundown from them ahead of starting any new campaign.

4. **Look at the errors you are receiving from emails you send, then check that they are reasonable**. You can get data directly from mail providers on whether you are being marked as spam. There are also services that will track the health of your domains and IPs, then report back on how often you are ending up in the spam or other folders by email template. They can then provide best practices on how to avoid this issue.

This rough checklist is true across all types of notifications, including SMS, push and messaging app deliverability, so if DM is critical for your company, get help from an expert agency or hire a great person with experience in this work. Ask them for a deep dive on this area, and make sure you are satisfied with what they share. This is one of those places where a little technical experience goes a long way, and building a great team around you will help you get the details right.

There are countless companies that fail before they even start by getting stuck in the spam folder, forcing them to burn a domain or a set of IP addresses. There are other companies I have helped that have unknowingly bought IP ranges, or even entire web properties, that already had spam penalties on them, and they didn't understand what was going wrong until we checked. Once you have done the basics to make sure you can send email, aren't spamming people and are responding appropriately to errors and unsubscribe requests, you can start going further down the marketing funnel and increase your open rates (covered further in the creative section later in this chapter).

Though I have mostly covered email and postal mail here, SMS and push notifications have some special points to highlight. I want to emphasize again that everything in this section is valid for these channels too. Simply swap the address you are sending to from a mailing address to an email address. Swap to a phone number for SMS and most messaging apps, and to a push token for push notifications. You have data associated with each of those IDs that will allow you to check if your message was actually delivered and acted upon, and that can make your direct mail more effective.

SMS

Being flagged as spam is a major concern for SMS, as is the potential to waste a lot of money. In general, measuring and understanding why you were blocked as spam in SMS is super-similar to how you'd approach the issue with email. Some users game the system to maliciously make money from the company sending the SMS, or simply to cost the company money. At Meta, we have also seen this done out of user error and confusion, where, for example, users ask to have an SMS resent multiple times in just a few seconds instead of waiting for it to arrive. Either way, you end up sending a lot of SMSes and that can be costly. Rate limits – only sending one SMS to a given number in a time period, say, five minutes – are important here. Using them ensures you don't resend the same text message to the same user multiple times in a short period, unnecessarily spending your money and unnecessarily annoying users in the process.

Otherwise, end-to-end measurement usually gives you the answers you need on the effectiveness of DM for SMS. Any major issue you are likely to encounter here usually happens at the carrier level, so it is useful to look up the carrier of a phone number. If you are sending SMSes at any scale, you can usually find someone at the carrier to help you fix potential errors. It is also worth considering if you can send messages via WhatsApp or other free messaging services, thereby saving money. For example, consider authenticating a phone number. I have used multiple internet services where I can select to get the authentication over WhatsApp and, in fact, we now successfully use this approach for account recovery ourselves for Facebook and Instagram.

Push notifications

Push notifications are easy for users to turn off, so 'pushability' is the number one consideration for deliverability. For example, is your push token still valid? What is it valid for? Can you buzz the phone, or only light up a jewel notification on the app icon? Tracking this information tightly is super-important, as some surprising trends may occur. For example, sending fewer notifications will sometimes drive total conversions up, not down. A big driver is if your app always has an unread notification count on it. People learn to tune those out, so you have to get the balance right here. Similarly, if you send a lot of low-quality notifications, users will turn them off and you will have a hard time winning them back.

For both these reasons, you should be more selective in the content you send via push notifications. These should only include the best content and be of higher signal than you might be used to in other direct mail channels. Further, if you are carefully tracking whether your token is valid, and what for, you can then prompt users in the app to turn push notifications back on, using the techniques discussed in the in-product promotions section above. You can even be persistent in this pursuit in logical locations, like your notification or messaging section for your app, where you could have a permanent banner warning users that if notifications are off the product won't work.

All channels

Across all channels, you want to measure your bottom of the funnel outcome – the action you want someone to take – and the other telemetry metrics as much as you can, continually and longitudinally, over time. You need to set up alerts so that if there is a sudden shift in a channel's performance, you will see it fast. Usually measuring the bottom of the funnel gives you that information. If anything goes wrong further up the funnel (from generation to conversion), investigate it immediately, using your detailed logging of the whole conversion flow. Typically, the changes that happen are sudden, but unless you have an alert or continual monitoring system, they often get missed. And they can remain overlooked for a long period because usually direct mail isn't your whole business – one channel degrading takes time to notice. The worst issues, though, are pernicious and creep in more slowly. With that in mind, check your DM channels periodically, monthly or quarterly, and perform deep dives into the health of the system, tracking how results are trending year on year, then investigating any reductions in performance.

Creative dos and don'ts

When I think about direct mail marketing, I have a lot more suggestions on what *not to do*, whereas, for any other channel, I tend to lean towards what you should do. The truth is mistakes have cost me more in the direct mail space than I have made from optimizations. Still, there are plenty of 'dos'. For one, you should move as much as you can towards trigger-based notification marketing, in which the direct mail is triggered by an action the user has taken or a major change in your service relevant to the user.

When I started at Facebook, our email marketing was based on sending inactive users a copy of their newsfeed. Inactive users had few friends, who generally themselves were low activity and didn't post much either. That meant their newsfeed was basically empty and uninteresting. So, we showed them the product wasn't good for them as a way of trying to get them to use it more. Hardly shockingly, this didn't work. We suggested a change of approach, instead informing the user of their pending notifications. During ramp-up, users generally have more of these notifications since they are accepting friend requests and responding to the odd new message. The performance of this campaign was way better because it gave the user a reason to visit and something constructive to do.

Similarly, while I was at eBay, campaigns like 'renew, replace, replenish' - which reminded users to buy razor blades and other products they tend to purchase frequently, say, every thirty days - were way more successful than just plain merchandising newsletters. The tradeoff here is that they were lower reach than a generic email newsletter. So even though each campaign would be way more efficient, it would produce fewer total conversions. In an ideal world, you should create a large number of these personalized, tailored, triggered campaigns, and fill in the rest with remnant newsletters. That way, you don't miss out on the reach, and you maximize total return. How much you invest here depends on how valuable this channel is for you, and for many companies it doesn't make sense to do this much work. For example, if someone books a holiday with you once a year or buys a kitchen appliance from you once every five years, sending them weekly email newsletters is unlikely to be truly engaging. You need to be thoughtful here about your business and what makes sense.

You can get to an advanced place with these campaigns, where you can even optimize to have in-product actions generate notifications that bring inactive users back. In social media, for example, PYMK does this with friend requests and follow requests, generating notifications. Amazon is doing clever work here as well, getting folks to subscribe to notifications, such as following an author. This lets them notify a user for updates, like when that author adds a new book or other publication. These are both win-wins, where the user gets notified about something they want, and the service is able to send them a message that encourages them to visit.

As you use more notifications in your direct mail strategy, defaults matter. For example, early on at Instagram, the default for notifications when someone liked one of your posts was to be off. This made a lot of sense for power users. If you are a power user and make a post that gets 200k likes that day, you'd be getting more than two notifications a second on average, making your phone unusable. Most of our employees were some form of power user, so these notifications were just not useful for us. They also felt spammy and annoying, and gave users a reason to turn off notifications, or even invalidate our whole push token at the operating system level by turning it off in the operating system settings.

At the same time, as discussed in Chapter 1, for a new user, that first ever like on their first post is a meaningful experience. Having the like notification off by default would rob them of a great experience, and it robbed us at Instagram of an extra visit or login and ramp-up opportunity for the user. Although it was hard, we convinced the team to switch the default for new users and got great results. Thinking through your defaults for when to notify people is important, as is understanding that power users are *not* the same as marginal users. You must therefore put yourself in the place of the marginal user of your product when considering your options.

Another creative 'do' in this channel is to work within the constraints of the space. In email, you need your subject line to be short, pithy and readable. The only job of the subject line is to get your email opened. Do an A/B test on these subject lines, get to the best one, personalize it and use their name (by now you know the drill!). In SMS, you need your creative to fit in the character length of the SMS. This is often broken by tracking URLs, and also, if you translate your product, the previously mentioned character expansion. Not fitting into the length of an SMS has two issues. First, it costs you more because you will have to send twice the SMS segments per message, doubling your price (operators charge by segment sent for SMS). Second, it will harm performance. At a minimum, your message will be broken over two text messages, but at worst, you'll actually put a message break in the middle of the URL to be clicked on, causing it to be unusable. I have been responsible for both these mistakes.

Inside email, make sure the email works with the main email providers you are sending to. Over time, there have been a lot of changes with these providers and how they operate. Sometimes providers have image load on by default, sometimes off by default. Sometimes they'll load images as long as they clearly aren't a tracking image, which has a URL personalized to that email and is used to log user behaviour, not to provide utility. It is not simple. You need to put in the time and effort to see how your image will render and make sure it will always work well if the images don't load.

In the vast majority of direct mail marketing cases, the email body only has *one* job to do: make the user click. So don't put too much in the email, confusing the situation. Market the hook to the user, point them at an obviously clickable button, and then get out of their way. Make sure the landing page to that button is right, though. The upside here is you can, and should, use all the tools the provider gives you. For example, I love Asana notifications in Gmail because they let me respond to a comment inline, within the email in the Gmail interface.

Space constraints matter in push notifications too, but with subtle differences. Too often, the interesting content is cut off on many devices, so they don't grab users' attention and make them want to click. The advantages of modern push notification systems are also regularly overlooked and not used. For example, the Windows desktop push allows users to reply inline on their WhatsApp notifications without opening the app, and on Android, there are extra actions that now appear when users expand a notification, providing more options and making it easier for them to use the product.

Look at the actual devices of the people using your products and observe how your notifications look on those devices. You can clearly send different notifications to different phones, so don't be afraid to change the text for phones with different screen sizes. Again, this comes down to having clean data at the user level tagged to the user ID and push token in your direct mail database. This allows your technology to vary the message based on information about the user.

All that being said, the general principles of the earlier creative section hold true in this channel:

- Make the call to action prominent.
- Personalize: for example, use people's names.
- Be careful in your persistence and consider what you send DMs about; ideally make it more about notifying the user. Once you've decided, however, you should be persistent. Use the advanced functions of the email or notification provider.
- Performance really matters here – we've all seen an email where the images don't render and there's no way to interpret it. Don't do that.

The four Ps of creative – prominent, personalized, persistent and performant – are represented throughout these steps, and they are just as useful here as in any other channel's creative. Keep them in mind every step of the way, and you'll find yourself performing more 'dos' than 'don'ts'.

Conversion rate drops off with time

My final note on direct mail is that if you want to do great notification-style marketing – the most effective approach in this channel – then data freshness is important. If the action you are triggering on happened three days ago, your conversion rate will be exponentially lower than if it's a good trigger. I learned this early on in my career at eBay, and it speaks to how online marketing teams and product teams should be tightly integrated. The eBay direct mail team and product notification teams were organized separately when I was there, and there was a lot of tension between them for some reason. As a result, the email marketing team would send all their emails to users through a third-party email platform and not built into the product.

Any email created by them had data that needed to be

extracted daily from the data warehouse, which itself was extracted daily from the production databases. Then this email had to be transferred and loaded into the email vendor's data warehouse. Next, the email vendor's system ran the queries on that database to send the triggered email marketing, such as the previously mentioned 'renew, replace, replenish'. Most of the time, that entire process took anywhere between forty-eight to seventy-two hours. Data pipelines fail, moving large bits of data takes time and data infrastructure certainly wasn't self-healing then (and still isn't to a large extent today). That meant a human was needed to notice if a job failed and to restart it. This situation caused us to always send emails a long lag time after the action that was relevant had passed, making the email not timely and less helpful than it could have been.

When I was asked to work on email marketing for consumers at Facebook, I swore we wouldn't make the same mistake. My team worked closely with the growth engineering team to do all our consumer email notification marketing inline. I wanted to bring together the magic and creativity of marketers coming up with ideas for what kind of notifications we might use, and what kind of triggered campaigns we might produce, with the technological brilliance of engineering to natively make those happen in production with delays of just minutes or less, not hours or days. I feel we achieved that, but only thanks to the great people on both sides – marketers technical enough that the engineers respected them, and engineers willing to be inspired by marketing to build their ideas. If nothing else, that is the core of great digital marketing – engineering and marketing acting as a single unified organization to get results.

THE STRENGTH OF PRODUCT-LED CHANNELS

Product-led channels can be both in-product with merchandising and out of the product with direct mail. They allow you to cover the entire marketing funnel for new products you want to market to your existing customer base, but they are not great at acquiring new customers. For the right North Star, though, they can be incredibly powerful. These channels benefit from well-structured data and their creative needs to stick to the four Ps: prominent, personalized, persistent and performant. How that shows up differs between DM and in-product merchandising. In direct mail, you need to worry about delivery and being marked as spam, so you can only be as persistent as the channel allows. With in-product merchandising, the more persistent you are, the more you have to dial back prominence.

Broadly, though, these two product-led channels have a lot in common with each other and perfectly illustrate the guiding principle that tools evolve but principles are timeless. Someone doing merchandising in store for John Wanamaker in the nineteenth century or in the Sears catalogue in the twentieth century would recognize the techniques of Amazon today in the twenty-first century as classic, great, in-store merchandising. They would surely be jealous that personalization can be so much better than store location- and section-level personalization, that letters can be delivered instantaneously and that we can take the principles so much further with today's tools. I am sure we, too, will be jealous of how future AI-enabled marketers and augmented reality interfaces will be able to take the principles further. Still, the echoes of nineteenth-century department store merchandising, twentieth-century catalogues and twenty-first-century websites will continue to resonate for marketing's future generations.

12. PARTNER-LED CHANNELS

Partner-led channels are a series of channels that follow more of a partnership or affiliate model and that behave similarly to each other, but differently to search and social. These channels feature an interesting combination of unpaid and paid results. In digital marketing, they began with banner ads, pop-ups and affiliate marketers in the 1990s, and they are another canonical example of how the tools evolve but the principles are timeless. Definitions related to these channels get blurred too. For example, retail advertising networks and app store ads are somewhere between typical partner-led channels and search.

When digital marketing first appeared, these channels were the same as buying ad space in a magazine. You could buy an ad in, say, *Gardeners' World* if you wanted to target gardeners, one that would run in the magazine and on their website. Those online ads started out by looking very much like ads in a print magazine or newspaper. As discussed, over time these channels evolved. Advertisers could now get more advanced types of ads. Some, such as homepage takeovers, were more interruptive than others. In print, these were like a full right-hand page take-over in a magazine, where the reader is stopped as they are paging through by an ad that interrupts their browsing. Other ads were more subtle, like the now-classic banner ad.

Over time, the interruptive formats lost out, and the more native ads won, because of people's preferences and good incrementality measurement that showed marketers what drives incremental conversions. Netflix was the last major holdout on pop-unders, where they would load a browser window in the background, and often load the full website in the window they wanted to send people to. (As you'll read, the brilliant Kelly Bennett at Netflix decided to do away with these.)

New, advanced forms of targeting also let you reach those people who were, say, gardeners, but not just in gardening magazines or on gardening websites. This gave websites higher revenue, provided users with more relevant ads and delivered higher conversions. As discussed, sometimes targeting went too far, but most marketers have now settled into a better place in which they can get the balance right.

Programmes were also created in the mid-to-late 1990s that allowed companies to farm out decisions on where they showed their ad, paying a commission to the intermediaries. These are the previously mentioned affiliate and banner advertising networks. Both are amazing tools that let you scale into multiple channels, sample them and learn. As you know, I got my start in affiliate marketing and absolutely love the channel, but it does have its drawbacks regarding fraud, as do banner advertising networks.

The newest form of partner-led channels is once again an approach that has existed for a long time in the offline world but is just now starting to grow on the internet: retail advertising networks. Benedict Evans, a wonderful tech analyst and newsletter author, says that Amazon is taking the Sears playbook from the twentieth century and gradually implementing it for the web, and I believe he's right. Meanwhile, for a long time, supermarkets have had manufacturers pay for placement, promotion and more. But only in the last decade has this idea started to come along online. The principle that retailers will make manufacturers pay for placement and promotion is timeless, but the specific tool now has changed with ads in and around an e-commerce or app store search result.

These partner-led channels will continue to evolve but looking at them through the lens of history and how they have evolved already will help you choose how to use whatever comes next. Making sure you measure their incremental impact will help you pay the right amount for the value they truly provide and keep you from the many pitfalls of pure post-click tracking discussed throughout this chapter.

DISPLAY ADS

It's well documented that *HotWired* – the first online magazine and precursor to *Wired* – created the banner ad in 1994. The idea was both simple and brilliant: you could now have an image on your webpage that enabled you to carry a sponsor's message just like in a print magazine. This marked the beginning of internet advertising in general and display advertising specifically. Within five years after *HotWired* premiered the first banner ad, this kind of advertising powered the internet and the dotcom boom. Everyone was copying the idea and innovating on the concept.

The early days of display advertising went fast. A simple static image banner ad was all the rage for the first few years, but by the end of the 1990s banner ads featuring animated flashing GIFs took over. Next came Adobe Flash, where the ads became fully interactive. At that time, the ad I considered the most successful was 'punch the monkey'. This was indicative of banner ads of the day where users were encouraged to punch a moving monkey and win a prize, like at a carnival stall. When they successfully clicked on a slow-moving monkey in the ad, they clicked through to the target website.

Unfortunately, this ad approach was badly abused by a small set of affiliate marketers. Users would land on a website that would immediately ask them to fill out their contact information, resulting in a lot of spammy emails with just enough information to make them personalized and more performant. Then, to qualify for, say, a free piece of consumer electronics, users would have to complete a set of offers usually including one like signing up for an online subscription. All these ads typically came through affiliate programmes, and the conversion form for getting the free consumer electronics was so negatively optimized that few people got to the end and converted. But the person running the banner ad got a good payout and someone they could spam for years to come. This was the sort of low-quality bad ad that prevailed on the web then, and it is a good reminder of how far we've come today. (It was always fun to catch the moving monkey, though, and I could rarely resist it when I saw the ad!)

Ads just got more and more disruptive from there, until by the time I started my career, most web portals, as they were known – like the AOL homepage, Yahoo! homepage or MSN.com – were, in my opinion, just covered with rapidly moving ads. There was nowhere for viewers to rest their eyes. The next natural innovation of this descent into eye-bleedingly negative user experiences was pop-overs. These were ads that popped up all over the website in a full browser window or a JavaScript layer, interrupting users' browsing in order to get them to see an ad. (Recall the MySpace ad discussed in Chapter 1 featuring the Incredible Hulk smashing through the screen.) Sometimes they were hard, or even impossible, to dismiss until the user had taken an action, like signing up to a newsletter. Unfortunately, some of these still exist in today's apps and websites, but in many ways the simplicity and personalization of Facebook's and Google's ads at this time was a response to that sort of annoying experience.

Over time, this type of disruption really annoyed people. Don't forget, the internet was super-slow then in comparison to today, and users were paying by the minute. The pop-overs' net impact for sites was so bad, and drove so many users away, that they were shown less and less. Instead, pop-*unders* became all the rage. The idea was that as, say, Netflix or eBay users got to the end of their session and closed down the windows, they found a fully loaded site that had earlier been opened in a browser window underneath the window they were using. They would then, in theory, suddenly realize they wanted to sign up for DVD delivery or buy a collectible online. This idea did not always, if ever, work as planned. These actions frustrated users so much that pop-up, and pop-under, blocker software started to appear. The pop-up blockers themselves were often co-opted by affiliates; this free software would rewrite the HTML of any site a user visited and insert their own affiliate ads into any page that user looked at. Finally, the browsers themselves built in the technology and turned it on by default, blocking pop-up and pop-under windows.

The last big company I remember running pop-unders was Netflix, right into the mid- to late 2000s, long after we'd walked away from them at eBay. Kelly Bennett, the new CMO at the time, smartly, and brutally, cut these techniques. His team then measured what happened to Netflix's results – the answer was nothing. The Netflix team had been scattering cookies around the web by popping under the website and using post-click measurement. They had incorrectly attributed all these conversions to their marketing. This is one of many reasons that post-click measurement without lift studies or incrementality measures is so dangerous. To my understanding, these cuts freed up budget that helped Netflix create and market their first Netflix originals. Bennett and the team thought that would be better marketing and, clearly, they were massively right. From being a lagging marketer behind the times, still using pop-unders, they went on to redefine the game for everyone in streaming.

Measuring the impact and recognizing fraud

Bennett's approach was the key to the future of display advertising: measurement. These ads were initially bought and treated like a sponsorship or a traditional ad in a newspaper. You paid for the placement based on the Nielsen-rated size of the audience or service you were buying, but you got no stats back in return. However, companies quickly realized that, on the internet, they could log impressions to figure out how many times their ad was viewed. The cost for these impressions was handled in CPMs. So, initially, if you were running a marketing campaign, you would pay for your ad based on how many times it was actually seen. This felt like a huge jump forward from TV or print media where you had to trust the Nielsen score, Comscore or a similar survey method that estimated your reach and frequency.

Over time, this approach advanced to targeting, as described in Chapter 4, with advertisers dropping cookies and tracking conversions subsequent to a click on their display ads, known as post-click conversion, and conversions subsequent to impressions, known as view-through conversion. They could also now access tracking survey-based metrics for people who had seen their ads.

But, as Goodhart's Law shows, a metric ceases to be useful when used as a target. And here is where issues started to arise. As with other channels, partner-led channels began experiencing fraud: some intentional, some accidental, and it was, and is, often hard to know the difference. The fact of the matter, though, is that not all impressions were created equal, and they could be miscounted. This happened for a number of reasons. Broadly, though, they all boiled down to impressions not being seen by the users who were being attributed as seeing them, or not showing up as intended, which could apply to the ad itself or to where it appeared, such as on a site where you may not have wanted it to. So though the impression may have been counted, no one would have actually seen the ad, hurting both your data and results; or the impression may have been seen but in a place you really didn't want it to be seen. There were four particular ways in which this could take place that are worth highlighting:

1. The impression was served on the site in good faith but appeared below the fold, and even though the ad loaded, no user could scroll down far enough to see it.

2. The space where the ad should have appeared, called the unit space, was seen, and the tracking pixel fired, but the ad was too big to download, so users only saw the blank white space there, instead of the ad.

3. The ad was deliberately shown so that it wouldn't appear properly, or at all. Either the ad itself was shown in a 1x1 iframe or pixel *or* the entire site on which the ad was shown was loaded within an invisible 1x1 iframe on another site, which would then show up in the tracking data as the site from which the ad was served. Sometimes, even a full click on the ad was forced using code – usually JavaScript – if you were paying CPC (cost per click), not CPM.

4. The ad would be shown, but on a site where you explicitly didn't want it to be. For example, your ad might pop up next to inappropriate content. This could be done by loading an iframe, where the iframe loaded the ad inside a page on a reputable site. So, to the tracking, it looked like the ad was being served on a reputable site, but the user would see it elsewhere.

Most often, I saw the third way happen when a company had its own affiliate programme who were being paid for the impressions they generated. That meant they wanted as many impressions as possible and didn't care whether anyone saw the ads. As a result, the company itself was being defrauded as well, not just the client.

When ads showed up in the wrong place, such on unexpected websites, it was, and is still, a frustrating experience. For example, let's say you buy ads from a vendor on a wonderful parenting site for your parent-relevant creative. This may perhaps be part of a run of network buy with an aggregator who purchases ads across many sites. (In a network buy like this, you purchase any inventory across the whole network that the aggregator has access to.) Without looking at the referring URLs, you find you are hitting all your impression goals. Then, subsequently, it's brought to your attention that an image of your ad is showing up in a pornographic website.

Early on in partner-led marketing, you could find this information by looking at the URLs where your ad loaded. Over time, however, clever advertisers from which you could buy ad space began hiding the referrer and protecting their iframe from being broken by code running in them. In other words, you could no longer see where exactly your ads were being served and appearing. I have only seen malicious examples here, and they happen a lot. When an unscrupulous site or network is not hitting its goals, it just feathers in a percentage of porn site impressions to juice its numbers and make its revenue. Sometimes the ad network itself doesn't know this is happening, and it is one of the sites they are subcontracting with that is defrauding both the ad network and the client of the ad network. Unfortunately, this problem persists today.

Fundamentally, though, the right question to ask has always been and will always be: 'Did anything happen because I ran my ad?' Even though it is frustrating when ads are run in the wrong place, I haven't, yet, seen massive brand damage come from a business having their ads shown in the wrong place against their will. Don't get me wrong – it sometimes causes large press cycles, lots of thrash inside a company and can even lead to marketers losing their jobs for letting it happen. But the true impact has not, to my knowledge, caused a brand to experience meaningful amounts of harm.

You may think of these stories of fraud and ineffective post-click tracked, non-incremental advertising as old tales of the Wild West of early internet advertising, but that couldn't be further from the truth. Large companies today still need to keep an eye out for fraud, and smaller companies should try their best to work with the more reputable players. In the well-documented Uber case discussed in the Introduction, CMO Kevin Frisch's on/off test of their marketing with the Fetch ad network found that there was no incrementality. This had been a huge spend, making up a very large percentage of their total sign-ups. It was obvious that fraud was afoot. Uber alleged the network was using everything from forced clicks (auto-redirects) to showing real ads on porn sites against their contract, which stated Uber's advertising would not appear on such sites, in the 2020s. (This proceeded to a court case that Uber won in January 2021.)

All these issues are still alive and well today, and fraud and ineffective advertising continues to affect companies as advanced as Meta and Uber. Understanding how it can happen is useful, and knowing the best way to find fraud using true incrementality measurement, not post-click attribution, is a critical tool in partner-led marketing and display advertising in general. Luckily, however, there have been some advances across the industry to help prevent this type of fraud, including a focus on standardization.

Standardization

The impact of well-meaning partners serving your ads poorly, or bad actors committing straight-up fraud, led to the establishment of the Interactive Advertising Bureau (IAB) and other important groups that have developed standards on how to serve and place ads online. When I started in the industry 'IAB standards' were treated like a religion. They offered both technical standards and solutions that enabled a level playing field across sites showing ads. When companies that served ads were certified independently as adhering to those standards, companies that bought ads could be confident they would get what they paid for and be more effective in using design resources. The need for standardization was twofold, affecting both measurement and creative design.

Not every team can have as advanced marketing measurement as big players like Uber, Meta or Netflix. Since that's the case, the industry recognized a need for standardized measurement that could be easily audited by third parties that could be employed to find fraud or low-quality work for smaller companies, as compared to them having to handle it in-house. These audits were necessary due to bad behaviour that took place in the 1990s and beyond; the type of behaviour that the IAB was established to protect advertisers from. This led to specific tracking and measurements with definitions, like how many pixels of an ad needed to be visible to a viewer, and for how long, for it to be considered an impression. This thinking remains the basis of all impression tracking today. Whenever you see a new format that has no standards yet, it's a good idea to recall these protections and why they came about.

On creative design, IAB standardization set specifications for ad placements. When I got started, the most common was the basic banner ad, 468x60 pixels, but the IAB added other ad types, like standard leaderboard, an ad of 728x90 pixels, and skyscraper, an ad of 160x600 pixels. This meant an advertiser could commission a set of standard ads for a company, resting assured that they could run in most places. Meanwhile, a site owner would know that if they produced a certain set of sizes of placement, they would get ads to run in those spaces. This made our work as internet marketers easier in the early 2000s, and we take it somewhat for granted today. But a lot of gratitude is owed to the IAB and other industry bodies for this work, which helped companies big and – especially – small to get results, create assets efficiently and not be defrauded.

DSPs get advanced on targeting

As discussed in Chapter 4, in the 2000s, companies would work directly with all the sites they wanted to buy advertising from, drop a cookie and target users on those sites. Over time, this process became unwieldy as they worked with so many sites and needed growing technical skills to target in a way that didn't cause their website to slow down, harming people's experience. A solution had to be found, and the market answered: in the 2010s, demand-side platforms (DSPs) came into their own. These platforms simplified implementation of tracking code on websites and handled ad purchasing for companies based on their instructions. Now, they could apply one set of code and one bid that would cover thousands of advertising partners. The DSP's technology allowed companies to bid, in real time, on a given impression, based on the targeting data they had for that impression and how much they valued it.

During this time, the quality and relevance of internet advertising stepped up significantly. Re-targeting, as covered in Chapter 4, was a huge part of this evolution. Multiple companies would now bid to show a person an ad that was relevant to them; and those bids would be higher based on the companies' opinion of how likely that person was to convert. This process incorporated a lot of proprietary data: What section of the site was the person on? How recently? How deep in the conversion flow did they go? Did they even have an item in their checkout basket? How likely were they to click on an ad? Of course, the list of questions and data points went on and on.

Though there were great benefits here, this new process was harmful for brand marketing online. Ads bought on a CPM basis were served to people who were not necessarily predicted to click. Some of these folks were the right targets, who would notice the ads and hopefully click, but many others were not and were even prone to ignoring advertising completely. There are lots of reasons for this, including lack of interest, ad blindness, undetected ad blockers and more. Obviously, though, they were unlikely to notice the ad served.

The ads bought on a CPC basis were, naturally, shown to people who seemed likely to click, and were therefore not completely ignoring the ads. This meant the value of display advertising online was, and still is, undervalued for brand outcomes, and hence awareness at the top of the marketing funnel. At some point, though, this opportunity will be seized and fixed. One attempt underway is called 'reach block' buying, in which you make sure your ad is seen by everyone in the group you are targeting who use a product in a given timeframe. As a result, the people who would normally be served a CPC ad would see an ad that wasn't optimized for, or bought, on a click basis. For this reason, if you want top-of-the-funnel brand impact, reach block buying is sometimes more effective. Still, most brand ads are not bought this way today. There simply isn't enough inventory and a lot of those impressions in the reach block can be sold far more lucratively on a click basis.

The other reason this new system wasn't great is that it simply went too far. As explored in Chapter 4, targeting caused users to be chased around the whole internet by a pair of shoes they chose not to buy from Zappos. People find this type of targeting irritating. Hence the backlash against targeted advertising, which resulted in new privacy laws. These have been particularly prevalent in Europe, where they're seeing a cookie banner or platform policy changes like cookie deprecation in Safari. But something is lost here.

People prefer relevant ads, and I'm not sure the downside is that huge to being shown ads based on items I've considered buying compared to the upside of more commerce, growth, transactions and jobs. But the backlash is here, and as internet marketers, we have to respond to it. This means that we should work hard to remove people from our targeting when they have bought from us, and we should frequency-cap so potential, or current, customers don't see the ad too many times. This is better for the person seeing the ads and saves us money as advertisers. At the same time, it's important that advertisers speak up for the value of this targeting, or we could face legislation and platform changes that harm something good.

Whence the future of display advertising?

Display advertising has always been a balance between interrupting, and potentially annoying, users, and driving effectiveness. Go too far and you hurt your site or app's performance. This has been the case throughout the history of marketing. For example, the more striking a newspaper ad or billboard location, the more you pay for it. Internet display advertising has learned the same lessons as analogue media. Finding the right balance will be the core of how display advertising evolves.

What I find most exciting is the evolution of television advertising. Live sports coverage is finally transferring online which, for many, was the last reason to keep watching analogue live TV. A new, large ad audience of online television viewers is emerging. In response, the major streaming services are creating ad-supported tiers, and the large offline TV companies are creating more streaming services, even for entertainment like live sports, as seen with ESPN in the USA. This combination of factors will not just lead to exciting growth in TV display ads on the internet; they will also be layered in with high-quality targeting that doesn't exist in analogue TV now.

These ads will be disruptive, just like modern analogue TV ads made up of non-skippable ad breaks in live sports or your favourite programmes, unless you pay extra for ad-free TV. But the ads will be more relevant than current TV ads because of targeting and ranking. This innovation will bring new life and opportunities to top-of-the-funnel brand marketing, combining the best of modern direct response techniques and traditional ad formats, and giving consumers far better ad experiences than previous TV audiences. With AI tools promising the ability for ordinary people to direct the creation of professional-quality video, this is an idea whose time is coming.

For example, consider what it could be like in the not-too-distant future, when someone is watching a football game on a Sunday afternoon on ESPN. They reach half-time, and as the game cuts to a commercial break, instead of seeing the same generic nationwide ads that many travel companies currently show, viewers might see an ad for a specific destination their targeting profile suggests they would be interested in. I might get an ad for a historical destination like Rome, someone else might see one for a beach holiday in the Bahamas, and yet another could get one for a sporty adventure holiday in Peru. This would make the holiday company more effective and make the ad experience better for the people seeing it.

Of course, this potential depends on whether marketers can create good targeting post platform and regulatory changes. Again, I am hopeful. We are creating privacy-protected methods of targeting where smaller amounts of data on a user's browser history – for example, creating maybe ten buckets within a site of users – combined with their ad-interaction history, and context of the pages they have viewed ads on in the past few minutes, will make it possible to provide a personalized, relevant set of ads using modern AI. This can get better still as time goes by. People can then have an explainable set of ads, but one that also gives them the highly relevant experience they want.

I believe that, over time, we will realize we've gone too far with regulation in Europe, and that it is harming growth and innovation in a way that hurts Europe's economy. I am a passionate European – my dad is German and I grew up feeling both British and German. When the EU commissioned Mario Draghi, the former head of the European Central Bank, to write a report on EU growth, he found that the US was 16 percent larger than the EU in 1990; in 2023 it was 30 percent larger. The US is ahead and pulling ahead further.

There is a lot of ground covered in the report, so I am just referring to a subset here. No EU company has been founded in the last fifty years that broke $100 billion in market cap – the US has multiple. The majority of those are pure tech and significantly funded by either ads or purchases from companies that sell ads. The EU has passed regulations that, as I see in my everyday work, make people in tech reticent to invest. I travel extensively in Europe, talking to top marketers, and the conversations in Europe are just different from the rest of the world. In the rest of the world, I have conversations about growth; in Europe, I have conversations about how those marketers can adhere to regulations. These regulations are all well-meaning, but they are also stifling growth. I find in senior-level meetings European companies spend huge amounts of time with us on factors that will drive no growth and, in my opinion, mostly just stop consumers having better, more personalized experiences that they like, such as receiving more relevant ads. It is true that a small subset of people do really care about this issue, but my opinion is that the broader population of Europe has been hurt by over-pandering to that subset, without any politicians willing to stand up for the benefits of growth.

The tone, however, is changing, thanks in part to the Draghi report, which stated there is too much regulation and it is stifling growth. Companies I meet with are frustrated now at the reality of the regulations imposed and the delays on them getting the latest technology from the US because tech giants are sceptical about rolling out in Europe. Hopefully we will see change and the rest of the world will take note that Europe may have led the world on regulation, but they lag the world on growth and innovation. To follow the European regulatory route is likely a path to the European outcomes, and that would be a shame since economic growth helps everyone, and I see no sign of issues that European laws have supposedly stopped being a big issue elsewhere. We will have more regulation around the world, but I hope, because of the European example, it won't be as extreme. That will allow us to spend more time on real problems, as compared to focusing on stopping companies from showing people slightly more relevant ads.

Finally, the battle against ineffective and even fraudulent ads will have to continue too. Measurement methods will evolve, standards will evolve, certification and audits will evolve, and bodies like the IAB will continue to be crucial. In the end, though, the only true way to know if your display is working is to have a test plan, ideally high-quality A/B testing on an ongoing basis, supplemented with periodic on/off tests to validate the A/B test results. No matter the display channel, targeting technology or placement, this type of experimental plan works.

AFFILIATE MARKETING

As discussed in Chapter 4, the affiliate channel can be amazing, as it allows you to explore lots of different online marketing tools and see what works well for you. It can even keep all these channels live, when you either can't afford to on your own or don't want to build a full online marketing team at scale in-house. Working with affiliates also allows you to ramp up quickly if you get the compensation right for the affiliate and you have the ability to expand your business rapidly. That said, in many ways this channel is also the riskiest due to its issues with fraud. Even worse, you get exactly what you pay for, meaning that, even without fraud, you really don't have aligned incentives with affiliates on incrementality.

I haven't seen any great examples of affiliate compensation that fully measures or optimizes for incrementality well. If you are a small business, this is less of a problem because incrementality is usually obvious. But if you are a large player in your country or field, this can be a big issue, as the affiliate channel will probably be just one small part of your mix – the headache of worrying about fraud and managing so many partners may be more than the channel is worth. Certainly, over the past twenty years, affiliates have gone from being core to the biggest players on the internet – both in general and in e-commerce specifically, such as with companies like eBay and Amazon – to being much less prominent in their channel mix. For the larger players today, like Meta and Google, there aren't any large affiliate programmes to work with. That's probably worth keeping an eye on – if the big internet players start broadly re-entering affiliates, that will be a sign the channel is regaining relevance.

There are two rules of thumb for running an affiliate channel that have served me well throughout my career: first, be careful what you pay for, but second, pay enough for it – the outcome is binary. Let's look at both in more detail.

Be careful what you pay for

I have already mentioned, in Chapter 3, how big the shift from confirmed registered users (CRUs) to activated confirmed registered users (ACRUs) was for eBay. One amusing episode in that process stands out as a perfect illustration of being careful what you pay for. When we moved from paying for CRUs to ACRUs, the trust and safety teams at eBay saw a spike in accounts not paying for auctions they had won. They tracked these accounts and found that the spike came from accounts that had been acquired through affiliate marketing. When we got on top of this, we found it boiled down to a set of incentive affiliates.

Incentive affiliates are affiliate marketers who run websites where their users get points for completing actions the site asks them to complete. These points can be cashed in for purchases on some such sites or entries into a competition or sweepstakes. Since we were now asking users to activate their accounts, these affiliates were asking their users to not just register, but to activate as well, and they explained ways to do this that did not always have the best end results. Some great bids came in from users, but so did many low-quality bids, including a lot of accounts who would bid on an item and then not pay, or who would complete a chargeback with their credit card, which was net negative for both eBay and the seller impacted. This was totally allowed by our terms, and I think neither we nor the affiliates had any idea of the negative consequences that were possible.

As a result, we changed the terms of our affiliate programme and banned this behaviour, specifically offering incentives to perform actions without talking to us first to see if we could mitigate unintended consequences. We also publicly communicated that while we appreciated these affiliates, this behaviour was more harmful than helpful, and they would need to stop using that approach unless we worked together to mitigate the issues. (I gave some public speeches about this at Commission Junction University – which was a conference run by the major affiliate marketing platform Commission Junction – where, generally, the affiliates understood our changes and were supportive of them.) The experience also made us realize that the historic conversions these folks delivered as CRUs were actually low value because, at that time, many of those users only did the actions the incentive programme told them to do – it didn't create any great long-term behaviour shifts. The issue was on us, though, because they were doing exactly what we paid them to do, and acting completely within the terms of our programme.

There are plenty of other examples of how these affiliate programmes can lead to unintended results. I've experienced some of these myself, and others have been relayed to me by friends and colleagues who have been affiliates or who ran affiliate programmes. A few of those include:

1. A gaming site that gave people extra lives for taking an affiliate action.

2. A browser extension that replaced existing links (affiliate or not) with their own affiliate links when someone used it and then gave them cash back for using the toolbar.

3. Sites that ask users to complete three affiliate actions to be entered into a prize draw.

These examples concerned companies big and small, while creating some real impact, and some less real conversions. They are funny, generally well-meaning and within the affiliate terms of service, but they are also low value because of the misaligned incentives between affiliates and businesses. With that in mind, think carefully about what you want out of working with your affiliates. Talk to your affiliate platform partner and get their advice on how to set yourself up for success.

The worst-case scenario here is, of course, fraud. In the end, you are just tracking for a conversion to be attributed to a given affiliate, and bad-acting affiliates can game this system. In the past, a lot of this came down to getting a cookie on someone's machine and taking credit for a conversion using that cookie. This resulted in a huge form of fraud called cookie stuffing, where bad actors would get your cookie on as many browsers as possible so they could take advantage of any action subsequently taken by that person, despite not causing that action. (We'll go through the most famous example of this fraud later in this chapter.)

Cookies have become less effective over time. Some browsers, such as Safari, are now blocking them, and other forms of tracking are being used instead. For example, some advertisers are moving purely to session-based tracking, in which a user clicks and converts inside that session, instead of being tracked across multiple sessions on a site. If this trend continues, cookie stuffing specifically will become less of an issue, even though other forms of fraud in this space will surely come about.

One of the last potential issues to consider here with affiliate programmes is how to handle your payment timelines. Since chargebacks can become a real issue, your payment timelines have to allow for time for all the chargebacks to come in. Someone, for example, may use a stolen credit card to make purchases online, then get paid out the affiliate revenue share on those purchases. When the owner of the credit card realizes they have had their credit card stolen, however, they initiate a chargeback. This takes weeks to process – maybe forty-five to sixty days, though it's getting faster – and in that time, the payout to the affiliate completes and they take that money away into a happy future.

So, affiliates do *exactly* what you pay them for, for better or worse, so you must be careful what you pay for.

But pay enough for it . . . the outcome is binary

This second rule of thumb is key. Affiliate marketers run on a tight margin, and they are flexible in most of their business models. This setup can lead to seemingly bizarre behaviours, such as doing quite little with a programme until it reaches an ROI threshold, at which point they might increase their activity by ten- or even a hundredfold in a month or less.

You will need to recruit affiliates to your affiliate programme. To do so, the affiliate network you work with must want to recruit those affiliates to try your new programme. I would advise starting slow and testing with users the affiliate network recommends. Get feedback on how your programme is performing for the people tested and spend time with them, and your affiliate network partner, to understand what you need to improve. It is unlikely you will get everything right straight out of the gate.

In my experience, there are usually three main questions to ask yourself that really matter:

1. Does your product have a reasonable conversion rate for its category?
2. Do you pay enough for those conversions so your affiliate partner can make a margin?
3. Can your programme scale to large volumes of transactions?

The first two are obviously connected. You can have low conversion rates – like a credit card sign-up, for example – but provide a high payout so that the partner can make a margin with low conversion rates. As mentioned, this can create a bizarre situation if you get this balance right.

Since affiliates are typically liquid, fast moving, flexible and motivated by profit, they may scale incredibly quickly if you get to their magic number – or shut down completely for just a 5 percent drop in what you pay out. This is another reason why you need to have serious conversations with affiliates and your affiliate manager about what's working, and what isn't, in your programme when you start. Maybe you are miles away from this point, or maybe you are 10 percent away in your payout.

Knowing this status is important as it will give you the best chance of succeeding and not giving up right on the cusp of success. Often, you have to look at special incentive programmes to get affiliates to try proactive approaches too, like bonus rates just for the first month and hidden tiers for super-affiliates. Having scale incentives also matters – you should pay affiliates more if they get to higher volumes of results for you to encourage scaling.

All of these considerations lead to question 3: can your programme scale? To attract the largest affiliates to your programme, you don't just have to make the payout per conversion worth their while. You need to be able to take a large volume of conversions to interest the big affiliates. These can be big businesses. Remember, affiliates used to be the number one marketing channel for eBay and Amazon. That also means truly huge volumes of conversions are possible when this channel works.

Channel conflict can be very real

If you are a big company and you develop one of these mega-affiliate programmes, it is pretty easy to run into large-scale channel conflict with your partner-led channels, when you and your partners are unintentionally vying for the same ad space, creating direct competition between two channels. For example, a search channel run internally can end up competing with search run by someone in the affiliate channel, so you end up in a position where an affiliate you're working with is bidding on the same search term as you in other channels. They are buying on the same social network as you, for the same people, and even posting the same organic social content about the same event. This situation is bad in plenty of ways, but there are two major issues: first, this is one way in which the affiliate channel becomes less incremental, as already discussed, and second, it pushes up prices. Though channel conflict is primarily a concern for larger companies, this can happen at any scale, no matter the size of your business, so it's worth taking note.

Within all your other channels, you can choose whether you bid against yourself or not for ad space. Some companies are smart at this method, which allows them the chance to get a higher share of voice in any given channel. The sports merchandise and memorabilia company Fanatics, for example, had official online league stores, a Fanatics website and online team tores for their merchandise partners, including major sports leagues in the USA such as Major League Baseball (MLB). They managed to own multiple ad slots everywhere a business could market online, especially search. Say someone searched for a baseball team like the San Francisco Giants. Fanatics would bid for a position with a single team (the Giants), then with the MLB store and finally with the Fanatics store. The strategy could lead to the top three paid search listings and the top three SEO listings all being stores run by Fanatics, maximizing their share of voice on the search results page. But if not done intentionally, or correctly, channel conflict can wreak havoc.

For eBay, channel conflict with affiliates became a particularly big deal in paid search in the mid to late 2000s. Our affiliates were better at paid search than we were internally. They had developed clever and effective keyword lists that we couldn't equal. In the early days of paid search, this advantage was more than OK. In fact, it showed the value of an affiliate programme: a new channel came along, the slow-moving big company couldn't figure it out quickly, the affiliates swooped in and filled the gap, and eBay benefitted from that partnership. A few years on, though, eBay figured out how to create a better keyword list internally, value it better, bid it better and so on. Having affiliates bidding too broke this clever optimization. As affiliates bid on the same keyword as eBay, for example, prices were driven up – in effect, we were competing for ad space with ourselves.

As such, eBay, very publicly, banned affiliates from paid search as a business model in their programme. This caused a lot of frustration in the affiliate community, especially with large search affiliates. This was the right move, but the team at eBay who made these changes had to be willing to be quite unpopular with people they had worked with for a long time. This included me, as I had to talk at conferences and in small groups with people impacted by this change. In general, though, we took too long to mandate this change and, at least in part, this relationship management ended up slowing us down and wasting money.

A cautionary tale from eBay

In May 2014, one of eBay's top affiliate marketers of all time, Shawn Hogan, was convicted of fraud and sent to jail for five months; a second, smaller affiliate we worked with, Brian Dunning, was jailed for fifteen months. As far as I know, this is the only affiliate-marketing case where someone has ended up in prison. They were convicted of wire fraud, which they had performed through cookie stuffing. The basics of this approach were explained earlier in this section, but this case was specific and indicative of a broader problem. (There are numerous accounts of this overall issue on the internet today.) For me, the experience cemented the fact that fraud can happen, even at the scale of tens of millions of dollars, in one of the largest internet online advertisers in the world. If that was the case, then it seemed to me it could happen with any business working with affiliates.

The story starts in the 1990s, when link-sharing ad networks would serve a banner ad on your site in return for impressions on someone else's site of your banner ad. These were initially successful, until forum owners decided to put the banner they were serving at the bottom of popular forum pages, leading to loads of impressions but no clicks. This meant people were getting less and less value from these link-sharing ad networks, causing them to die out in the late 1990s and early 2000s, along with a lot of other businesses in the dotcom bust.

Shawn Hogan, an affiliate marketer, was running a forum in the mid-2000s called Digital Point Solutions, which a large number of webmasters used, so he was well known in the digital marketing world. He decided to try link-sharing ad networks again, despite their earlier failures. The fundamental difference with his approach was that instead of being client-side Java-Script code, he offered a server-side package with code snippets in various computer 'languages', such as Perl or PHP. These would render a link and a small tracking pixel when a page loaded. The upshot was Google would crawl the links served by this code as if they were organic and, in turn, use them to rank the sites higher in search (we will cover this in Chapter 13). Links to one website from another website were, and remain, the key to ranking in search, so people started to rank higher with his revamped approach.

Hogan paid for running this network by taking a small share of the links and serving them for himself. Using these, he ran an interesting stunt where he created two URLS on his website, one being something like 'expedia.htm' and the other 'ebay. htm'. He would then use his share of links from the ad network to link to those two URLs, and he ranked highly in search engines for those terms, like Expedia and eBay. This stunt won him a lot of fame in the SEO and affiliate communities, and his ad network took off even further.

There were other tools used in this ploy by other affiliates, including Brian Dunning, mentioned above. One tool I remember was a world map you could put on your MySpace page that would show where your visitors had come from around the world using their IP addresses. There were lots of other techniques to get widgets installed on pages all over the internet. I had a cocktail of the day widget that got loads of installs, and I used it to generate backlinks to my cocktail site and drive ranking. It was tiny, but it still got a lot of traffic. Combined, these widgets were highly effective if someone wanted to create one and use it for cookie stuffing.

Hogan's network started to make money through the eBay affiliate programme, and eBay believed this was through a proportion of links that were served around the web as affiliate links to eBay. That certainly may have been true at first, and over time, for some of the traffic. However, a second form of traffic was being generated where that tracking pixel would call a script that would redirect to the eBay homepage through an affiliate link. This process would drop an affiliate tracking cookie. This was par for the course for cookie stuffing, which eBay was well protected against, so why were we tricked here?

Typically, cookie stuffing can be detected through huge volumes of clicks with low volumes of conversions. This didn't happen here to the same extent as usual because the affiliate link wasn't called on every visit. In other words, it appears the traffic was sculpted. For example, rather than redirecting a person to eBay through their pixel every time they served the pixel to that user, the affiliates did this only once a month or similar. Rather than dropping the tracking cookie on every user, they dropped it on those with higher likelihood to convert, such as EarthLink or AOL ISP users. This meant it took eBay longer than normal to find the fraud, causing the company to lose out on $10m (officially $28m was judged in the trial).

Even though there are surely more Hogans out there today, affiliates remain a viable option. They can be amazing, entrepreneurial and a brilliant way to try new channels. They respond to being paid enough, and when paid enough they can scale wildly. You have to be careful what you pay them for, though, because they will do *exactly* what you pay them for, and if that's getting a cookie on someone's machine who later converts, at least some will do that in non-incremental, nefarious ways. A great affiliate platform partner will help you avoid those issues and guide you to making the best of this incredible channel.

RETAIL ADVERTISING NETWORKS AND APP STORE ADS

The latest brilliant addition to the field of partner-led channels is retail advertising networks, in which a retailer like Amazon or Walmart stocks your product for sale on their website and sells you ads to promote that product on their site, and in some cases off it. This is a booming online marketing channel at the time of writing in 2025, but it harkens back to principles that supermarkets have been using for a century or more.

As mentioned at the start of this chapter, Benedict Evans, the brilliant tech analyst and newsletter author, posits that Amazon is doing everything Sears Roebuck did as a retailer, without pride, and online. A listing of items for sale, free delivery and returns, a robust offering of almost every product imaginable – this all fits with the Sears catalogue and mailers of yore. The latest example is Amazon ads.

At first glance this idea may seem non-intuitive. When you go to your favourite retailer, for example, you may not think of seeing ads in the aisles, but you'd be wrong. Fast-moving consumer goods (FMCG) companies care a lot about driving in-store decision making. Retailers figured out long ago that there was a business opportunity here: 'slotting fees'. Slotting fees are a payment you make to a retailer to guarantee that your products will be shown on their shelves in a store. In some cases, you can pay to have your product on a certain shelf at eye level. You can pay to have an extra end-of-aisle display in the grocery store or a poster in a bookstore. How you pay is murky – sometimes it is just a direct-payment slotting fee, and in other cases it is part of a complicated stocking contract with discounts, priority stocking, speed and other factors thrown in as part of the deal. Clearly, this is complicated, because a store that doesn't stock any Procter & Gamble products will struggle, so the exact details of how these promotion and placement options come together is a complex negotiation.

For the first twenty years or so of online retail, no one tried to apply this concept. You had ads, and you had product listings. But as online retail matures, and we enter the later stages of this economic cycle, companies are pursuing more ways to make money. In the process, they are dusting off that old Sears playbook to get inspired and open up new business models. Taking a cue from the past led to today's retail advertising networks.

In the US, Amazon.com and Walmart.com both have retail advertising networks. You can choose to pay them in much the same way as either search advertising or classic display advertising, so they sit in the middle of search and display as a marketing channel. On the search side, you can buy via keywords and appear in the search results first with a sponsored logo, similar to placement on the shelf in a store. On the display side, you can use all the techniques described earlier in this chapter to re-target people who are thinking of buying your product or are digging into the category, not unlike the coupons some stores give you at checkout, re-targeting you to buy another item.

A special case of retail advertising networks that has grown by leaps and bounds in the last few years is app store ads. Both Google and Apple offer in-app ads, and they allow you to bid for placement in the app store on search or general placements. Similarly, this means a new messaging app could bid to appear ahead of WhatsApp to tempt people to try it, in the same way that a Unilever-owned Dove hair product could bid to appear ahead of a Procter & Gamble-owned Pantene product in a retail ad network. These arrangements can be measured just the same way as the rest of display advertising, using on off/tests, regional tests and ideally randomized, controlled A/B tests.

I expect this channel to continue evolving and developing alongside the rest of display media, but there is one big exception: these ad networks are built entirely on first-party data. That gives them the ability to use advanced targeting that aligns with both the platform rules and newly passed regulations. There will likely be more pressure over time on first-party data but it will continue to be less constrained than third-party data.

In recent years, as these retail advertising networks have grown, they have become a source of tension between advertisers and platform owners. Often, the owners squeeze a company in two ways. First, with the fee for advertising, in order to not be displaced by a competitor on the shelves of search, and second, with their own brand that competes directly. For example, Apple has iMessage and charges WhatsApp for ads. Amazon offers its own-brand solutions to many products that also have to advertise on their site. Procter & Gamble's Pantene has to compete with Walgreens's own-brand shampoos in-store and online. This tension is nothing new, as it's been seen throughout the development of advertising with offline stores. Large FMCG companies have consolidated to create negotiating power with large store chains, and the largest store chains have consolidated a higher percentage of all retail in countries like the USA to claw that negotiating power back. The internet is no different – history doesn't repeat, but it definitely rhymes.

THE FOUNDATION OF DIGITAL MARKETING

Partner-led channels are the beginning of all digital marketing. They are where the banner ad was invented by *HotWired*, and they have been at the forefront of innovation the whole way through to today, with the exciting new retail advertising networks. They are rooted in principles that date back to newspaper magazines and in-store product placement and promotion. The principles may be timeless, but the tools really have changed. You can do tremendously advanced targeting in these channels, creating win-win-wins, in which advertisers get better results, websites get better CPMs and the people using the sites receive better, more relevant ads. These wins, however, are threatened by over-zealous regulation, in my opinion, and this harms growth in a way that matters. I hope the rest of the world learns from Europe's cautionary tale here.

As you use these channels, you have to consider incrementality carefully, as there is space for fraud when you pull in large numbers of third parties. The best guard against this fraud is incrementality testing because that captures both inadvertent waste, as Netflix found under Kelly Bennett, or deliberate fraud, as Uber found under Kevin Frisch. So, these channels can deliver amazing results, but you must make sure you are carefully tracking that they actually deliver what they say they will.

13. SEARCH

Search changed everything. This channel moved the internet from a side booth at the marketing conference to centre stage, redefining marketing for the twenty-first century. Subsequently, social has taken digital marketing to another level, but search came first and remains integral. As discussed in Chapter 5, search marketing is broadly segmented into organic and paid search. Organic search is when your ads or website show up in search listings without paying for them. 'Search engine optimization' or SEO is marketing in the organic search channel. Paid search is the paid big brother of SEO. In this channel, you bid on keyword terms to appear in the search results, which is typically called 'search engine marketing' or SEM.

There is so much to write on this topic, but one major takeaway that must be highlighted is that keyword research matters. You need to know what words you want to 'rank' for, whether paid or organic. You determine these terms and ranking by looking at value, demand and supply, just like almost any economic system:

- **Value:** How valuable to you is the traffic from that word? How much is a click worth?
- **Demand:** How many people are searching for that word and how often?
- **Supply:** How many other businesses and individuals are competing to show up when users search for that word?

This point may seem basic, but if there is one consistent theme across every conversation I have had with a company, charity or friend who has asked me about SEO or SEM, it is that they have not done their keyword research up front. And if you don't know which words matter to you, how can you do anything else in search?

An interesting question is: How will AI impact search over the next ten to twenty years? The current trend of questions being answered completely in the product, without referring the user to another website or app, is likely to continue. Say, for example, you want to know the time in London. Twenty-five years ago, if you typed 'Current time in London' into a search engine, it would send you to a website to provide you with that information. Today, the search engine just shows you the time at the top of all the results. This type of result will only accelerate with AI, where, for far more complicated questions, the whole question users search for will be answered in the interface where they ask it, with no need to click a link.

This trend is better for the consumer, but it presents a problem for website and app owners. From an ad's perspective, the targeting may vary, but it seems simple that contextual ads could appear with queries answered completely in Google, or a search engine product like Google. The precise form of those ads is up for debate, but they are a likely next step in digital marketing. They will have a lot in common with search marketing, and marketers using them will benefit from understanding search marketing's history. We may move from searching specific keywords to broader topics, but search style marketing is here to stay.

Another key aspect to search that must be kept in mind is that organic and paid search can work together in harmony, feeding information between teams. Too often, SEO may be frustrating because it is so non-deterministic, and it is deprioritized by marketing teams, left to product and done badly. In an ideal world, though, SEO should be an excellent channel done well with a search marketing team who think about the channel, and its problems, holistically. To better understand the channel, its challenges and its best uses, let's first dive into some background on how it developed, and why.

A BRIEF HISTORY OF SEARCH

In the 1990s, search engines like AltaVista and, over time, directories like Yahoo! (yet another hierarchical officious oracle) were the Google and Bing of the day. During that period, links were only used by search engines for their robots, called 'spiders', to visit every page on the internet, 'crawling the web', and then adding those pages to their index. They would then tokenize the pages to figure out what they were about, breaking them down into their component words. At that stage, search engines weren't aware of site formatting, and SEO wasn't a developed profession. This meant, in large part, if you had a paper airplane website, like I did, and you wanted to rank when someone searched for 'paper airplanes' in AltaVista or Yahoo!, you could just write 'paper airplanes' 500 times below the fold in white text on a white background and you'd rank number one for that word.

Over time, search engines got smarter and capped keyword density – the number of times a keyword is included on a website – and looked at formatting of the site and more to determine ranking. This was the beginning of an arms race on content, culminating in 'cloaking', where websites would show one version to a search engine spider and a different version to a human being. Similar behaviour persists today, and if you're doing SEO, you need to recognize this is happening. The reason why is that many companies have accidentally bought a domain name with a penalty on it or have hired an unscrupulous SEO consultant who gave them short-term wins through spammy means, while hurting their long-term results. Such a consultant may have a trick Google and other search engines don't initially know about to improve your ranking, but if you want to build long-term value, beaware that Google will eventually find and close that loophole. Google will, rightly, then penalize the consultant's actions. But note these penalties affect you and can range from reducing your company's ranking to even eliminating you from the index entirely.

Another option that gained momentum in the early era of search was the human-curated directory. Initially, this was spearheaded by the Yahoo! Directory but over time DMOZ, or the Open Directory project, also emerged in this space. This approach promoted human site curation as a counter to spammy SEO. Eventually, these lost out because search is a much more convenient interface when the ranking is good enough, but in many ways, with Wikipedia and Reddit dominating so much of search today, human curation continues to play a major role.

There are two types of SEO marketers: white hat and black hat, terms taken from the world of computer hacking. A white-hat SEO is someone who does SEO using methods approved by the search engines to get sites to rank appropriately based on their content. A black-hat SEO is someone who tries to game the algorithm of search engines to get sites to rank inappropriately highly for the terms they want. Black-hat SEO techniques can be as innocuous as buying links right through to hacking sites, spam and fraud.

It was during the early period of search that Google was founded and the innovation of Page rank – which I understand references both Google co-founder Larry Page and web page (which I think is fun) – came about. Page rank was essentially a measure of a page's importance. This was determined by how many pages linked to that page *and* how many pages linked to those pages. A link from a high-value website, one with many inbound links itself, was way more valuable than a link from a website that maybe had only one link pointing to it. Amusingly, the highest Page rank page and most important site on the internet up to that time was the Yahoo! Directory. So, if you could get listed in the Yahoo! Directory, you would instantly rank highly on Google for the keyword you were shooting for.

Links at the top of a page also seemed to count for more than links at the bottom of a page. So, through luck, I ended up getting 'Alex's Paper Airplanes' listed in the Yahoo! Directory before any other paper airplane enthusiasts due solely to my name – since the list appeared in alphabetical order – and that really was how my entire career kicked off in online marketing.

Over time, Google came to dominate search. Through their near-global hegemony on the channel, they dictated a lot about how the web worked, since everyone wanted to rank on Google. Broadly, this was good because Google pushed for positive changes, which led to the field of technical SEO. For example, Google found that when users bounced back to the same search from a website, it meant Google had given them a result they hadn't thought helpful. This led to a new focus on faster page load times and placing relevant search-related content at the top of the landing page to reduce bounce rates and more.

Similarly, Google discovered that if they could get people the information they needed without them having to click on a link through the 'one box', they found the search results better because they found what they were looking for more quickly. (The one box is the little space at the top of search results that contains complete answers, images, embedded maps and more.) Webmasters, however, became frustrated with this change, since they lost out on visits to their pages. This setup became a huge source of tension, leading to anti-trust complaints and regulation in Europe, specifically targeted at the one box. Still, I believe Google has tried to produce better results for everyone; even if they aren't perfect, Google are pointed in the right direction.

As the organic search world took off, a business model was needed to fund it. This is where paid search came along. The earliest days of paid search were pioneered by Overture (or GoTo.com), which played a major role in the evolution of targeting, as discussed in Chapter 4. This company allowed you to pay for placement, so you could pick a keyword and bid to guarantee it. There was no distinguishable line for users between paid and organic then, aside from a little note explaining that they were seeing an ad when one popped up. Google took this idea and ran with it.

As mentioned, Google innovated and introduced the idea of eCPM (expected or estimated CPM, discussed in Chapter 11) and an auction. eCPM looked at how much you bid and the forecast CTR for your ad, providing an estimate of how much money you would generate for each impression. The auction then ranked the ads by order of how much money they would make Google for each impression and showed them to users in that order. This helped Google make more money, but it also showed consumers better ads, so it improved their experience too. Their other innovation in this area was the use of a second-place auction. That meant the winning bidder only paid 1c more than the second-place bidder, causing advertisers to be more willing to bid what they would actually be willing to pay to the Google AdWords interface. Further, Google added a 'quality score', which was meant to be an evaluation of the ad and advertiser's quality. This quality score allowed Google to deal with spam, fraud and low-quality sites that bid for space a lot but harmed the user experience.

These innovations led to the search world of today. There are a lot of critiques that are levelled towards Google, such as hoarding traffic rather than sending it to small websites. But, for me, the great user experience that has come from this arrangement and the alignment of Google's interests, with both its users and advertisers, is incredible. There is a big question about what comes next with generative AI. Will ten blue links appear on the page when someone searches for a word? (These are already disappearing, with images, pins on maps and more taking the place of this text.) Will websites get any traffic or value for putting information out there, or will that just be used by AI to answer a search query without sending traffic to the website? Will paid ads be included around AI-generated responses? Certainly, the channel is going to change, but paid links around our organic results will remain for a long time. There will also continue to be a way for hobbyists and professional sites and apps to get value from providing content – or they will just stop. Search will evolve, as it always has, but talk of catastrophe, for hobbyists especially, is overwrought.

KEYWORD AND QUERY RESEARCH

It doesn't matter if you are doing SEO or SEM – you must start your journey by figuring out which keywords you should be going after to achieve your North Star goal. It seems like a simple statement, but I regularly find teams do not have a list of keywords or a description of the space of keywords (often called topic now), nor any concept of how hard it will be to go after them. There is a big movement in search today to focus more on topics than on keywords, but I still believe the right place to start is keywords – the topic is just the space described by a group of keywords – and it is where I anchor my thinking at this point.

So what do I mean by 'research' and 'go after'? These aren't particularly helpful descriptions. Essentially, these ideas can be broken down into a slightly butchered supply-demand economics way of thinking. You must figure out how to:

1. Create a list of the search terms a user might search for.
2. Evaluate the supply of sites for that search.
3. Determine the user demand for that search.
4. Find the value of each search in terms of your North Star metric.

Let's inspect each of these steps further, starting with creating your list of search terms, or your keyword list.

Create a keyword list

Start by creating your keyword list. If you are lucky enough to be starting with a big site, app or product, you have some really cool options, which I cover shortly. If, however, you are starting from scratch, your job will be far harder. To begin, you have to narrow down your area of search. It's no use buying keywords about used cars when you are a travel site. So, how do you do this? Typically, there are two routes: first, use tools created by the search engine where you enter details and they create a list for you; and second, use tools you can buy that let you evaluate a competitor's website by asking for a list of keyword terms associated with a given domain. These tools are not mutually exclusive, and they should both be used to generate as large a list as possible.

If you are working for a big existing product with a lot of usage, you have more options than if you are just starting out. This is exemplified by eBay, whose affiliates generated keyword lists before the company took that role in-house in 2008 with the eBay partner network (mentioned in Chapter 9). This was an innovative, inspiring move, and an example that still impresses me twenty years later. I hope it serves as inspiration for you to innovate in this channel, and beyond, as well.

Up until 2008, a number of eBay affiliates were paid search

affiliates. For many years, they produced better results, in larger volume and at cheaper prices, than eBay's in-house SEM team. In my opinion, this was mostly because they had a better keyword list. To generate this list, the affiliates reviewed the titles of all the items on eBay (initially scraping them through the API), looking for two factors: first, the most common token strings in those titles, including single words, double words, triple words, and on; and second, which of those were most associated with bids, or the average bids per appearance of the token. They removed words like 'a' and 'the', and other similarly low-signal words, leading to a high-quality list. The list could rank by the likelihood the search word would be associated with a bid, which was an awesome proxy for likelihood to convert.

Clearly there was more to this process. For example, the affiliates could look at the age of the listings, check them over time, not just once, and so on and so forth. This was brilliant because all of eBay's sellers were optimizing to be seen in search, so they were trying to create the best words, which carried a signal of value with the list too. This process also worked in every language. Over time, however, eBay went a step further than the affiliates. They were able to use the actual search queries (as do all sites with their own big search engine now), track the action rate on those queries and use that information to generate their list. That resulted in their list being far better than the affiliates', but the process took years to get to that point. Once it was there, however, eBay banned affiliates from doing paid search, as did many other programmes around 2010.

Evaluate supply

Generally, you use the same approach to generate your keyword list for SEO and SEM. Once you have that list, your next job is to evaluate supply, or how much competition you are facing from other businesses trying to appear for that keyword. This is harder in SEO than in SEM. In SEM, you simply upload your keyword list and see the proposed bids by keyword. You will find out pretty quickly which ones have high demand and high prices, and which don't. In SEO, it is far harder; you typically have to use third-party tools to get an understanding of how many results there are for each keyword and the strength and success of those domains. For example, are you competing with Amazon.com or a local mom and pop bookstore? For a small enough set, you can hypothetically develop this keyword list manually yourself. However, generally a tool is best here for any campaign but the smallest.

Determine demand

Now that you know the supply, how do you evaluate demand? Demand for the keyword by consumers can be considered the number of searches for the keyword. Here again, SEM has an advantage. Search engines will give you an estimate of the clicks you will get for a given bid. If you put in a high suggested bid for each keyword, you will get a good ballpark estimate of how much supply there is for each word, at least relative to each other word. In many ways, though, it doesn't matter – you can also try to buy all the words or you can buy on general match, in which you allow your ad to show not just for the precise word you have entered but for similar words matched by the search engine as well. It isn't that much more work to try to appear for every word than it is for 10 percent of the words. The only caveat here is that you usually don't want to start with an enormous list. And, of course, 'enormous' is subjective – it's very different if you are Amazon versus the local bookstore, so there isn't a simple ballpark for what 'enormous' means. Regardless, you want to start with a subset and gradually build a campaign in good standing with more and more keywords over a few months, not upload 100 million words on day one.

For example, if you are trying to market a new art store in London's Marylebone neighbourhood, you can start by asking a search engine to suggest keywords based on the store website's URL, which you can upload to the search engine. You can do this for a number of other URLs for related stores in the neighbourhood, ideally stores you respect. This will give you a starting set. At this point, you can then go in and manually edit the set to make sure you feel fairly comprehensive about aspects like '[location] [descriptor]'. In this case, a comprehensive location could be Marylebone, Marylebone High Street, Bloomsbury and the like. A comprehensive descriptor could include art store, design store, interior décor and modern art. Then upload them, put a geographic limit on them, and set some bid amounts and a spend cap. Though it could be riskier, and potentially more expensive, starting broad-matched and seeing what happens will give you a wide view of what you're working with. Figure out which terms get you traffic and what you can learn from them. Consider how much traffic is there. Take your research offline too: ask people who come into the store how they found you, then iterate from there.

If you are a bigger company selling a range of products and want to scale a lacklustre SEM programme, start by looking at existing search data. You can download all the searches that happened on your onsite search tool, all the keywords your site appeared for in Google, according to search console, and all the results in your existing SEM campaigns by click volume. Next, rank each keyword or topic by number of searches, then manually review the top 1,000 to ensure they were all covered in each other's list and nothing was obviously a bad set of words for your brand (like the 'dead babies' example in Chapter 6). You can then upload the comprehensive list of unique keywords from across those sources with a special campaign for the top 1,000 words by volume to evaluate them more closely. From there, try different bids, within a campaign budget, and see how the words perform. Then iterate from there.

The approach for determining demand will be different for SEO than SEM. With SEO, you must prioritize the list more than with SEM because producing good content that will rank is expensive and time-consuming. As such, knowing where you have low supply and high demand can allow you to fill a niche, making this information super-valuable to prioritizing the list. You can mostly use the paid search tool to give you an idea of the volume of searches; it isn't perfect, but it is good for a stack rank. I learned this lesson early in my career.

When I went to university, Alex's Paper Planes was the largest paper airplane website in the world, but even in the physics department it wasn't considered 'cool'. I wanted to be cool (but also make money online), so I decided to find a new topic for a new website. This is how I landed on cocktails. I bought the domain cocktailmaking.co.uk and got a link in the Yahoo! Directory and Open Directory. Just like Alex's Paper Planes, it came up first, too, because I called it Alex's Cocktail Making, and as mentioned, the pages were in alphabetical order. After a year, I ranked number one in the UK for the term 'cocktail making', yet I was getting little traffic. I was super-confused; this had just worked for paperairplanes.co.uk – what was going on? Well, when I looked at the keyword data, it turned out people rarely searched 'cocktail making'. They searched 'cocktail recipes' instead. After another year, I retooled my keywords and ranked number one for 'cocktail recipes' in the UK. The traffic flowed in, but it was a costly mistake that wasted a year of that project.

Find the value

For valuing keywords, you must try to separate the wheat from the chaff. In an ideal scenario, you can allocate absolute monetary value to each keyword so you can determine what you should bid on each one in paid search. Then you can use that same technique to apply value for SEO. As such, this section is explained entirely through the lens of SEM, but is useful for both SEM and SEO. The best way to do this is, of course, experimentally: spend money on each word, track the results and set your bids based on them. This method, however, is just not feasible in most cases, and it is also slow. So, let's consider more practically how to set up your initial bid and then separately iterate on it.

The first concept to understand here is keyword clustering, introduced in Chapter 8 and discussed in Chapter 11. Usually, you can't get enough data on any one individual keyword, so you need to treat your keywords as groups, or clusters, that behave similarly. Here are a few examples of how:

1. User behaviour is a way to cluster keywords by how likely it is that someone will search for keyword A and keyword B in a given time period (similar to the cocktail recommendation engine explained in the in-product merchandising section in Chapter 11). You can do this as a marketer at a company like eBay or Amazon (which have with their own search engines) by analysing people's behaviour on your search engine and using it to cluster the words.

2. Another great way to cluster keywords is on a proxy for value. For example, you could cluster keywords together with a similar percentage likelihood for someone to make a purchase if they search for the word on your product. So if keyword A and keyword B both have 10 percent

purchase rate, but keywords C, D and E all have <1 percent, you should cluster those separately.

3. A third way is to look at the average purchase value for a consumer who searches for a word on your site or clicks on your site from a search engine. If you sell apparel, for example, cluster together keywords A and B if average purchase price is >$500, such as expensive shoes, and keywords C and D is <$50, including accessories, like a bracelet or tie clip.

4. A fourth way is volume of searches. Here, you can cluster together keywords in groups by how many searches happen on them and then manage those groups differently.

5. A fifth way is topic or category, such as holiday destination and holiday type, which could range from a family trip to an amusement park to a backwoods expedition. Take the apparel site example again: you could cluster together words that are all searching for shoes versus words that are searching for bracelets versus words that are searching for shirts.

Creativity and magic are crucial here. The most brilliant teams I know are incredible at understanding their list and getting the most out of it, going all the way to tailoring landing pages and more. To get started, try to first cluster on your value proxy directly. Use search data in your product and cluster the keywords based on value of conversions that came from visits started by searching those words. Then cut this off for only keywords over a certain amount of data (say one hundred searches). Second, if you don't have a direct value proxy, invest in some labelling of the keyword list and cluster them on the relevant category for your product, such as clothing, kitchenware and dinnerware if you own a department store.

When you go live, set your initial bids low and work up.

Evaluate each cluster as a bucket and consider your ROI for that cluster as a whole. Move up the bids until you get enough volume to recognize the ROI in the cluster and the comparative ROIs across the different clusters. Then rinse and repeat: expand your keyword list, evaluate new ways of clustering and have fun with it. You'll find amazing methods to get ROI and results, and you will learn some valuable insights about human behaviour and your product along the way.

SEO

Linking

In Germany, there was a famous search engine optimizer (SEO) called 'FridayNite', who wrote a book on SEO that can still be found from time to time. It was a couple of hundred pages long, nicely bound, and sold a fair few copies. Inside it, the whole book was blank except for one sentence: 'You need more links.' For the past twenty years of organic search, this was the best advice you could get (although I'd probably say more *better* links). Today, the Google team argue that links aren't that important, but empirical data suggests that they are. (I try to take a stab at squaring that circle in this section.)

Links are basically used for two purposes: first, getting a 'spider' to crawl a page; and second, showing which pages are most valuable. Getting a spider to crawl a page is crucial. If your page can't be found, then it can't be added to the web index of the search engine. If it can't be indexed, then there is no way it can be ranked. Even before Page rank was created, the number of links you had, and where they came from, mattered too, since they were the basis of whether or not your site got crawled. Later, how often you got crawled led to ranking.

Normally, spiders have a limit to how many pages they should crawl from each individual site. 'Spider traps' are a result of linking in such a way that the spiders crawl in circles. When they run in circles, they don't index the whole site because they limit how many total pages they crawl from any site. This is just one of many problems with being crawlable. With that in mind, it is important to ensure your site is crawler-friendly, and internal linking is key to making that possible, as discussed in the following paragraphs.

The second main purpose of links is to show which pages are most valuable. The pages you link to the most internally are generally the ones you are signalling as the most important to the users, and the crawlers. For example, most websites usually link to their homepage on every page of the site. You should therefore be careful about which pages you put in your navigation. You should also be willing to leverage those links. Which pages are linked to the most from outside your site tells the crawler which pages people outside your team think are most popular. Both of these – internal and external linking – are weighted by how important the page doing the linking is in the first place. If the homepage of Facebook links to your website, that is worth a lot more than if the local mom and pop shop does. So, links are a way of showing the most valuable pages in a website, both in the opinion of the website's owners and in the opinion of others. This leads to the two basic linking jobs: internal and external linking.

Internal linking

You have the most control over your internal linking. When I joined Facebook, for example, we had already launched public profiles and were working on search ranking. The company, however, was not doing well, gaining few rankings and little traffic (amusingly, TechCrunch ranked above Facebook for the word Facebook in Germany – it was that bad). I was lucky to be introduced then to Naomi Gleit, who was working with an excellent engineer, Philip Fung (pfung), on the search ranking project. Given my background in SEO, I volunteered to help.

When I analysed the site structure, it was clear our internal linking structure was telling Google that all these public profiles were not valuable. The only way you could crawl to a non-Facebook employee at the time was to click on the homepage -> about page -> blog page -> blog author -> one of their friends -> non-Facebook employee. So, the first non-Facebook employee was consistently six pages deep in the site. Unsurprisingly, Google didn't crawl these pages completely. They also didn't place great value on them because they were so many clicks away from that high-value Facebook homepage. In essence, we were telling Google these pages were low importance because we didn't link to them from an important page ourselves.

I explained this to Naomi and pfung, who understood and agreed that this was the problem. From there, we created a plan to link every profile to every page on the site within six clicks. We would do this using a combination of site maps (HTML pages which have a directory structure to navigate a whole site), linked from the footer at the bottom of each page of the site, and profile-to profile-linking, in which a profile of one user would be linked to that of another user because they were friends through the platform. We took this plan to Adam D'Angelo (CTO), Mark Zuckerberg and Dustin Moskovitz (co-founder and important leader), who were all sceptical, so much so that Dustin sent around an email asking no one to work on our proposed project.

So, we did the internal linking as a side project, testing it out only with a type of page that no longer exists, called a 'network page'. These were pages attributed to universities, like Harvard or Cambridge, high schools and even countries, and they were how Facebook had rolled out in the early years, network by network. Using the site map strategy, we were able to rank #1 or #2 for terms like Harvard and Cambridge, in some cases beating prestigious universities' own homepages. We took this back to Dustin, Adam and Mark and they greenlit our broader project. (This is one of the things I love about Meta – these leaders were willing to let us prove them wrong with a small test, and when we did, they greenlit our larger project.) Once we undertook the work, we saw a massive increase in search traffic and, commensurately, our registrations. Simple, best-practice, internal-linking strategies have been the #1 strategy I have used when helping a company do better SEO. Though they are usually met with scepticism, and are often hard to get implemented without someone who understands SEO directly working on the team, when they go through, they are normally a big win.

External linking

On external linking, the fundamental, incredible innovation of Page rank was a huge deal. The idea that you could tell what the most important sites on the internet were, based on how many links they got, and from whom, was simple and brilliant. That might sound trite, but I really believe it, and my entire career in the internet is basically thanks to that innovation and learning to ride it. So I am deeply grateful to Google personally. This innovation made the web far more useful than any directory ever could.

Most big companies don't have to think about external linking much. A site like Facebook or Instagram gets huge numbers of inbound links from valuable sites and deep into the site in the most important places. For smaller sites, there are three main considerations:

1. How many links you have.
2. Who those are from.
3. How you are linked.

Number of links is basic – you want a lot. As FridayNite wrote, get more links, or as Shawn Hogan showed, in the affiliate section, a lot of links can work. How you get more links depends on your business, but great content works across all sizes. A great content strategy, where you create articles, blog posts and so on that people want to link to and talk about, can't be beat. So, base any link-building strategy on producing and sharing content worth linking to.

In addition to superb content, as a small company, getting links boils down to talking to people and connecting with relevant friends to link to you. Perhaps, for example, your school or university alumni page will link to you, especially if you help them out with promoting their content by featuring it on your site. Basically, be a good ecosystem player. The rules change from time to time, and the lines are blurry on what it means to buy a link. For example, sometimes preparing content (like a guest blog post) for another site that links back to your site is considered link buying. But as an SMB, being a good player and caring about receiving some external links carries huge weight.

If you are a large-scale company, external linking is far harder since, typically, the volume and type of links you want are higher and more important. Here is where that content strategy comes back into play for larger organizations – it is absolutely key. Ask yourself, what is your company's area of expertise? What can you post that will attract other experts to link to it and reference it? How can you be a good player that gets cited, linked to and hence ranked? In 2025, I think Shopify is one of the most impressive big company players here: in almost any field of SMB online sales, if you search for advice, they seem to have a page that ranks highly with helpful content and a link to set up a Shopify store. Almost any other approach – such as buying links – is a fool's errand in link building that ends up with a penalty, which typically boils down to how you got the links and, most importantly, who from.

Which sites link to you is also paramount – they need to be quality. So many businesses have been undone by hiring a fly-by-night, black-hat SEO who bought spammy links. This has affected plenty of major companies. In 2013, Interflora, the global flower delivery service, was given an aggregate penalty for backlinks, and Rap Genius, the rap music-focused site and blog, was hit about the same time. Meanwhile, in 2014, Expedia lost around 25 percent of its traffic. The Expedia decline was most likely because of negative SEO, where someone tried to hurt Expedia by setting up bad links for them, which Google then penalized Expedia for. This technique is well known in the black-hat SEO community as a way to hurt a competitor. Google created the ability to disavow links in their webmaster central so you can clean up bad situations, either deliberately done by you, by a bad vendor or even by someone attempting to generate negative SEO on you and your brand. This is often an uncomfortable process and is hard to handle, so try your best not to end up in the penalty bin here. The flip side of the equation, of course, is that good-quality links are a huge deal. Early on in my career, the right link from the Yahoo! Directory made my sites rank #1 in all search engines. This is still pretty true – if you get a fundamentally authoritative domain to link to you, especially in your space, you can rank #1.

Last, how you are linked to is major. If you are the fiftieth link in a directory page, even on an authoritative domain, it won't matter much. If you are the first link on the homepage of Facebook, and the link text is the precise keyword you want to rank for, it will substantially help you. If the link is 'no followed' – meaning the link has specific markup language that tells search engines to ignore it – you will also receive little value from external linking. So, you want lots of links, you want them high up on the page that links to you, you don't want them to have the 'no follow' markup and you want them to use the keyword for which you wish to rank as the link text.

One of the most damaging actions you can take in external linking is changing your URL structure, with the most extreme case being a full domain migration, in which you change the base domain of your site, such as from thefacebook.com to facebook.com. In the worst-case scenarios, you can lose all of your traffic because Google doesn't recognize the new site as being the same as the old one. One of the most successful base domain migrations was when the *Guardian* adopted theguardian.com. (My good friend and brilliant SEO, business leader and coder Joost de Valk helped the *Guardian* get that right as a high-powered external consultant.) You need to use the right redirects and do so comprehensively through the entire site map. If you are large enough to work with Google directly on these changes, that would be ideal, but smaller companies will likely not have this option. No matter what you take away from this section, though, my key advice is, if you are not sure what you are doing and SEO matters to you, do not do a domain migration. Ever!

Though I've explained the great benefits of external linking, some readers may still wonder why linking is so important considering recent revelations. Particularly, they might ask why links matter if Google uses behavioural data from the Chrome browser, a detail that they even emphasized in court during their 2024 antitrust trial. The only behavioural data that is not search tends to come from clicking on links or direct navigating to bookmarks or remembered URLs. Given that, links remain important, and quality links in prominent positions on high-traffic websites matter even more than in the early days of Page rank. As such, it is totally reasonable for Google to be using links less in determining ranking directly but for links to still be really important, because they determine non-search navigational behaviour, and that is used in ranking. For what it is worth, empirically in 2024 all my conversations with SEO colleagues and actions I have taken myself, for Meta and other engagements, suggest that linking is still extremely important for ranking. To bring it all back to FridayNite's canonical book on the subject, 'You need more links!'

Content

Whenever I have taken on SEO consulting gigs or talked to colleagues internally, people seem shocked that I talk so much about keywords, research and linking *before* I get to content. The line goes that 'content is king' but, bluntly, I don't buy that. Though, as described in the previous section, great content is important, it is far less important than the other SEO best practices discussed thus far. Granted, if you have a site that has high authority with Google, that has been built up through getting good links, in high volume around your topic, then mediocre content with lots of the right links about keywords with low competition and high value will still crush it at SEO.

Awesome content with none of these linking elements, on the other hand, will fail completely. And even if your content is amazing, it is nearly impossible to create excellent SEO quickly from a fresh start because you first need to build reputation and authority in your topic area. That said, once you've got the basics down, *of course* content matters and, as stated, great content can help you get great links.

In the early days of SEO, content was simple. Keyword density equalled ranking, so you just wanted to make sure you stuffed that keyword you wanted to rank for everywhere you could in the page. How you did it didn't matter. While the white text on a white background three pages below the fold was a great trick, as time went by, search engines got smarter, and rightly so. Keyword density mattered still, but too much was as bad as too little. Search engines started to improve semantic understanding with the ability to scan and 'understand' the site, so content needed to make sense. Meanwhile, people trying to game the system began creating gibberish sites made with something called a Markov chain to simulate language in a way search engines, mostly, couldn't detect. The arms race between such spammers and other bad actors and search engines kept escalating, and continues to do so.

For large companies, though, the watershed moment on spamming with content came in 2006 when bmw.de was delisted by the Google spam team for 'cloaking', discussed earlier in the chapter. This was the first time I was aware of a major brand being eliminated from Google. For such an iconic German brand to disappear from search results was a big deal beyond just the SEO community. Obviously, there are fly-by-night SEO agencies, spammers and black hats still trying to deceive Google around content, but hopefully, if you are reading this book, you are a serious marketer. And serious marketing requires a sustainable approach that will not expose you, or your clients, to sudden catastrophic loss. Any agency or person in your team suggesting 'workarounds' or otherwise should be avoided.

Now that we're beyond the days of keyword density and we aren't going to resort to black-hat tactics, what is the best approach for SEO regarding content? There are two that are particularly useful: writing content for the user and employing an SEO best-practice copilot, such as the Yoast plugin to WordPress. When writing content for the user, remember search engines are working to be more useful for the people using them.

So the more you can write for the end user of your product, the better aligned you will be for the direction of travel of search.

Producing content that has been useful to a user, within the constraints of caring about what you want to rank for, will consistently deliver results. If you want to see what a great content programme looks like, find a topic you love and start searching online. As an example, while I researched how to write and publish a book, I was impressed by the depth of content about self-publishing and selling books online that Shopify kept turning up, which makes sense for an online store. The best-ranking site in the search results was Reedsy, a site that connects authors and editors. Reedsy features blog article upon blog article about every topic related to writing or publishing a book (traditional and self-publishing), and at every turn as I had another question, they had already answered it.

I don't know how they did this so well, but it appears to me they first employ people who intimately know and care about the subject, causing the articles to be thorough, informative and easy to understand. They must also understand the logic that people would run through to publish a book in terms of questions. Second, at the same time they must have had a good SEO-aware editor working with the website publishers, bringing keyword insights to the subject matter experts, and great linking strategies.

Great SEO-aware editors are so valuable. These folks know how to look at keyword data and understand important, growing trends, like recognizing that cerulean, for example, is a growing topic area in fashion. They then feed those trends through to site authors as topic areas to dig into. Some of the very best SEO editors get ahead of stories, knowing the potential results of sports matches, elections and other events, with content prepared and ready to go, ahead of time. This type of behaviour works well for small and mid-sized businesses, or large businesses like Shopify or Stripe with a smaller target audience, such as SMB owners versus the entire general population. The best content tends to win links as it helps people, and with a site like Reedsy, they have huge numbers of potential and actual authors linking deep into the articles that helped them, which is a wonderful vote of confidence for the value of the content.

On employing an SEO best-practice copilot, there are many excellent products out there today. Historically, I was always a fan of yoast.com, produced by the wonderful Marieke and Joost de Valk, which recently changed ownership, but there are others. And in the future there will continue to be services that give you advice on optimizing the content you write for the keywords you want to rank for. Many newsrooms now have proprietary versions of this type of product in-house too. If you have that support in place, all you need to focus on is a way to discipline yourself and your team, or set up your product to regularly produce lots of content focused on what you want to rank for. Take inspiration from the Reedsy programme described, or some other programme you have found truly impressive in a space you care about. If you can make that content your biggest focus, because you've taken the SEO basics off the table, you will put yourself ahead of most of your competitors.

If I wanted to go deeper here, I could discuss user-generated content (UGC) tactics and what can be learned from Reddit; Google's love of reviews (when done right) and how that's employed by large e-commerce sites to great success; image content; image search; alternative tags and much, much more. But this is not a book just about SEO, and the richness and depth of SEO content on the web is so fantastic, I couldn't cover it all here. So just remember, if you avoid spammy black-hat tactics, create a content programme where you write for the end user and use a good SEO copilot tool for that writing, you'll go far with content for SEO.

Technical SEO

This final section on SEO and organic search is about technical SEO, the nuts and bolts of how you build the site in code. I've placed it here in the chapter on purpose. Too often, this area dominates the conversation about SEO: what type of redirect should I use? How should I set up sitemaps in xml? What should I put in my header tag? Though these questions may be important to an extent, the reason I have put this section last is that technical SEO is the least important aspect of organic search. Even if your technical SEO is completely on point, if you have not done your keyword research and you rank #1 for a keyword with low search volume, or that is unrelated to your field, you'll be very unhappy. If you have a few good-quality links to your site on the right keyword, you can muck up almost anything and Google will still show you high up in the rankings, just without a description and using the most common text linking to you (at least at the time of writing). This holds true even if you were to tell a search engine to not crawl and index your site, which is done by including a 'noindex' tag on robots.txt, the file that alerts search engines to what they are allowed to do on your site. Don't get me wrong, technical SEO does matter, but it matters the least. It also blocks people from focusing on doing SEO because it can be overwhelming to think about, and often SEO blogs, talks and agencies discuss technical SEO *first*, scaring people off.

So, the question then is, how can you best approach technical SEO? If you are technical yourself, it's worth taking the time to better understand how it works – visit the blogs and the discussion boards and you'll pick it up fast (*Search Engine Land*

and *Search Engine Journal* are still great places to start). Briefly, though, there are a few main considerations:

1. Redirects – You need to have the right redirects. Sites get redesigned all the time, but even if you fix all the internal links so they still work properly, you can't fix external links on other people's sites. To handle this potential problem, you need to redirect the old URL to where the new one is located, or you will lose all value from those inbound links. Use a permanent (301) redirect every time you move content. Make sure the redirect works – if you aren't careful, content management systems sometimes make mistakes on redirects because there is such a wide range of them available.

2. Markup – Markup is the actual code that a browser or spider receives from your site. Discipline is necessary for your markup on your page. Use the appropriate markup tags and put the keywords you want to rank for in those tags. Make sure the language is phrased in a way a human would actually use and appreciate, not just in a way a search engine crawler would latch onto. If you have a title for your page, use <TITLE>. Try to use headings and subheadings, via <H> tags in HTML, and always add alternative text describing the images, both of which help human accessibility and SEO. Computers love structured data and there is a correlation between such data and better SEO results. My rule of thumb is to use the markup that makes sense for your site, in a way that would help your site be more accessible for a person who is blind and uses a computer site reader. If you do that, you are writing content for the user, which generally works well for search and is resilient to changes in what search engines value over the long term.

3. Robots.txt – Ensure robots.txt allows the right bots and pages to be indexed. This is simple but daunting, especially since, if done improperly, it can be a huge source of issues. In short, make sure your site is indexable. (When I do pro-bono consulting for small charities, I find a shockingly large number of them are doing badly at SEO because they ban their site from being indexed by mistake.) To do this, it doesn't get more complicated than writing 'user-agent: *' on the first line of robots.txt (this means all user agents) and 'disallow:' on the second line (this means disallow nothing). You can also usually add your sitemap in there with 'sitemap: <insert url here including domain name>', and if you have one – which you should – link to it there.

4. URL structure – You need a URL structure that is readable for humans, not just bots, and features keywords, not just lots of '?' and '&' and other special characters. Of course, any human or machine outside of your company will never be able to definitively interpret the meaning of a URL, but it helps search engines and users when they are intuitive. Engineers hate this piece of advice and lots of URLs don't follow this format, but the people who use your product and search engines love human-readable URLs that make sense to them. For example, having the word 'store' in the URL if it links to the store section of your site or using keywords about the page or part of the title of an article are helpful for the user.

5. Sitemaps – To make your site crawlable with internal links, a sitemap helps bots find all your pages, and you should therefore have one in place. In my opinion you should have both an HTML and an XML sitemap (XML sitemaps are a file or set of files on your server which list all your pages for bots to use, HTML is browsable by

humans). Most content management systems (CMS) can now create both sitemaps for you out of the box. The technical specifications for XML sitemaps are simple, though, so read them over and then review your sitemap to make sure it follows the same format and specs. It is easy to eyeball and find most major errors that could be lurking there. To compare your sitemap to others, you can type in, say, www.facebook.com/robots.txt, or the equivalent for any top-level domain, to your browser. There, you will see the link to their sitemap and can open it and see how it is coded.

There are more aspects of technical SEO I could write about, but those big five will take you a long way, and they will help you avoid issues if you ever change your URLs or domain. When my team at Meta took over an e-commerce product, for example, we had plans to change the URL structure to be more Google-friendly. We wanted to do this because Google's search function did not recognize the site as e-commerce, but we could rank better for e-commerce-related terms by getting those terms in the URL structure.

In this case, the belief was that placing the word 'shop' into the URL structure would flag the site as e-commerce, so we created www.meta.com/shop/. Another leader at Meta was concerned that this move deprioritized the e-commerce functionality because we were 'burying' it in a subdirectory. In fact, we thought the shopping functionality was the most important aspect of the website. We were even redesigning the homepage to put all the items for sale right at the top of the page. By creating a cleaner URL structure that would be readable by humans and search engines alike, it would be flagged as a shop, and when users clicked on an individual item the URL would make clear to them, too, that they were in a shop.

This misunderstanding was easy to resolve – my colleague was reasonable, and we sorted it out with one senior conversation. The experience, however, was striking to me, as it showed that some leaders at Meta didn't fully understand SEO best practices, even though they were so essential to our work. Those leaders believed that the SEO changes were either bad or unnecessary. Because I am a search engine opitimizer, I can cut through at the most senior levels and make sure those changes happen when needed. But when I wasn't in a senior position, it was far harder for me and my teams because I would have to explain these tactics to my own leaders, and they would have to weigh them up against other escalations before making an argument for them.

I try to keep current on SEO, as it was my first online marketing passion, and from what I hear from friends in the space, this misunderstanding by leadership is common. I am lucky to work where I do and have the colleagues I have, because, unless SEO is completely core to your company, generally internal politics makes SEO near impossible to do well, especially at a big company. This is not because these leaders are trying to hurt the company or your performance, it's just that they are not well versed enough in SEO to judge certain actions that could prove to be useful, or necessary.

So, if you are a leader who has SEO as part of their remit and you don't fully understand it, get close to your SEO person and learn their frustrations. Listen to what they have to say about where the company is being silly about their SEO, then give them air cover to fix those issues and track the results. Generally, the results will be spectacular – since big companies so often make SEO impossible, if they support it instead, they will almost immediately see a positive change. (If you are at a small company, be grateful you won't have to deal with this layer of complexity!)

If you are not technical enough to dig into the five considerations mentioned, then there are two other approaches I strongly suggest: first, get a site audit from a reputable firm and actually listen to what they say, or if your business is big enough, hire your own expert in-house (and listen to them too!). Second, implement a technical SEO monitoring copilot (just like in the section on content).

For a site audit, the best SEO partners are likely to come through recommendations and referrals. As discussed with best hiring practices in Chapter 9, hire an agency or employee in this space who has previously worked for companies where SEO has been integral to their success. Ensure they worked for those companies a long enough time to have actually played a part in making that success happen and to signal they were competent enough to stay employed. For an SEO-monitoring copilot, there are multiple tools on the internet today to help. BrightEdge and Semrush, for example, are great products with advanced tools, but you should do your own research for what might be best for you.

In summary, don't let technical SEO terrify you – it's not that important. Still, it does matter, so try to get the five considerations suggested right. If those are too much for you, or you feel you need additional support, get a technical SEO audit from a reputable agency or in-house expert, listen to them and implement the recommendations. If your SEO person has huge internal frustrations, understand what they are, ask them the most important issue and give them air cover to fix it. The results will likely be good. Finally, going forward, use one of the reputable technical SEO tools on the market to monitor your site and warn you if you do something wrong.

SEM

Valuing your keywords to determine bids

As discussed in Chapter 8, as with all channels, marginal return is important when you look at SEM. You need to know your ROI for the last dollar you spend, not the *average* dollar. Buying on the biggest paid channels in digital marketing tends to behave like a lot of economic theory, even in practice. Remember, there are diminishing return curves such that the more you spend, the harder it is to make returns with that last dollar. The paid search ad systems get you the easy wins first, including those users searching for words that indicate they are right at the bottom of your marketing funnel. The more you try to spend, the harder you have to market to convince people who are searching for words further away from the action stage of the funnel. How you then choose to allocate your dollars is key.

Just as you must think about cross-channel allocation in regard to marginal, incremental return, with search you must think about cross-*keyword* allocation. To help, keyword clustering has become a standard tool in the industry. Clustering keywords that have similar attributes, as described earlier in the chapter, is especially important in SEM. Few words have enough searches in a reasonable time period for you to make decisions on how to bid on them individually. It usually takes hundreds or thousands of searches in the time period you are using to receive maybe tens of clicks and get to a reasonably confident decision about how valuable those clicks are to you.

The number of searches and clicks varies dramatically. If you are selling a product with a long and complicated consideration process, like a new washing machine, you might be happy if you get one conversion for a thousand clicks. If you are selling something less expensive that has a shorter consideration process, like a last-minute dinner reservation, you might expect one conversion for every ten clicks. This also varies based on where the users are in the funnel – the keyword 'buy washing machine now' or 'dinner reservation in Burlingame tonight' will have higher conversions than 'what should I look for in a new washing machine' or 'great restaurants in the bay area'.

Finally, your keywords may have plenty of searches and high enough conversion rates but also be expensive. Selling a washing machine, for example, usually costs more than getting a dinner reservation, just as keywords lower in the marketing funnel cost more than those higher in the funnel. Spending enough on every keyword to get the data you need to value what those keywords are worth may therefore be prohibitively expensive. As such, there are many variables for what can be considered enough volume by keyword and why you might want to analyse multiple similar keywords at once to make decisions. The most important few (including sparsity of clicks, conversions or total expense) call for handling most keywords in groups, not individually.

Keyword clustering to bid keywords in groups

You need to create clusters that include enough data to make decisions. In the paid search industry, we found those groups needed to behave similarly so we could optimize them as a whole, rather than treating each word individually, since we had enough data on each bucket. By creating clusters of keywords that behaved similarly, they could be treated almost as independent channels, allowing us to better allocate our budget between them. We tried lots of approaches to clustering: the category people bought in, the gender of the buyer, the value of the items bought, the locations people bought, and more. Luckily, almost every cluster worked and almost everything was interrelated. However, that means there's no silver bullet. You need to take the time to develop and explore these clusters and work on your budget allocation from there. This work really matters, and it is a lot of fun.

You can use modern bidding tools, and even search engines themselves, to automatically create keyword clusters; they do an amazing job and are often completely automated so you don't see the intricacies of how they work. In the 2000s, it paid to be an expert at keyword clustering, but now if you use the right tools, including Google's own, you can hand this duty over and don't need as much detailed knowledge here any more. That said, today's automated keyword clusters aren't creative in the way a human developing these groupings can be. These tools won't come up with clever ways to look at your keyword targeting list or suggest new independent variables that you haven't fed to them on which to do the clustering and budget allocation. So, if you want an edge here, get creative in how you think about variables, such as:

1. Independence – You want variables that are not closely correlated. To do this, above all, you need to uncover the behavioural attributes of the keywords, such as high converting versus low converting, or high average revenue per user (ARPU) of converting users versus low ARPU of converting users. At the same time, you might want look at who converted. For example, in America, age and wealth are pretty closely correlated variables, so adding wealth when you already cluster on age won't be that independent. Wealth and shirt size, however, are likely fairly independent variables, so adding in shirt size when you already use wealth will gain you more power in your clustering. You could even cluster all words without enough data to make a decision into a cluster (which is an

independent variable in itself – how much people search for the word).

2. Meaningful behavioural variance – There needs to be a real range in actions taken and value of actions across the variable you are looking to cluster for. Conversion rate is a great one because there are clearly a lot of low-converting words and a lot of high-converting words. Age is good too – younger buyers have an obviously different buying mix than older buyers. A variable like shirt size, however, while useful for independence, is not so useful for behavioural variance. Unless the site specializes in, or skew towards, certain sizes it won't add anything useful. Yes, people buy different sizes, but everyone buys clothes.

3. Scoring words on those variables – In general, scoring words on variables can be difficult, and this is a huge thing I struggle with in marketing. At Meta, my team created wonderful segments and clusters of keywords through research in concept. But when we got to the point of saying, 'How will we do this in practice?', we came to a standstill because the ability to actually target, segment or score words or users on those variables doesn't exist. As such, you have to think hard about how you will append the data and only suggest variables where it is possible to score words on them. I call this targeting-aware segmentation – don't create segmentation that cannot actually be implemented in practice. So a good data foundation is key when you score words on variables.

Another theoretical example may help bring this idea to life: If you are a book publishing company with thousands of titles, you might have tens of keywords per book, but hundreds or thousands of keywords per category. With keywords per book, there will be some high-volume words that can probably be managed individually, especially for blockbusters with huge followings, like the Harry Potter books. Most books, however, will have few searches, and you would need to decide what to bid on them.

For example, you could cluster keywords by intent through inspecting and labelling them. If someone searches for 'buy click here by alex schultz', then that will be highly valuable and get a higher bid, whereas if someone searches for 'when did alex schultz write click here', that will be low intent and should get a low bid. You could also cluster keywords by the price of the books – a keyword for a $10 novel would be clustered differently than a $50 coffeetable book – or by a hardback versus a paperback, at which point category probably matters (business books, for example, might convert faster than reference books).

You could start by labelling these keywords manually, or with a little assistance from AI, and then analysing those clusters. The keyword groups overlap, so you might get multiple uplifts for, say, a specific search, like 'where can I buy a hardback copy of business book click here by alex schultz'. 'Where can I buy' would be lower on the marketing funnel than the keyword for a 'hardback' or 'business book'. This specific search might happen only once a year, but across a portfolio of 1,000 or 10,000 books, each cluster might happen thousands of times, so together, they can tell you what to bid on a rare keyword. Here would be an example of the keyword clusters to consider within that approach:

1. Buying intent (i.e., includes 'where can I buy').
2. Desire for a hardback.
3. Searching for a specific title.
4. Business book category.

Whether you use modern bidding tools to help you develop clusters, create them on your own, or use some combination of both approaches, you must still keep your goals in mind. This is where incremental return comes back into play.

Incremental return in SEM

Not surprisingly, incremental return is also important when you look at these SEM channels. Search, unfortunately, has never been great at running user-level tests, which is why I suggest running on/off tests geographically to see if conversions follow the trend you would expect based on what you attribute to paid search. As discussed in Chapter 8, on marginal and incremental returns, from this test you can uncover your incremental return, not just your tracked and attributed return. Search is the primary channel where I use this technique, as other channels let me do the more powerful technique of A/B testing at the user level.

So, as with all paid channels, you need to think about marginal and incremental returns. You will get the highest ROI with clusters of keywords that give you the same marginal return. In theory, you would do this at the individual keyword level, but few keywords have enough volume associated with them, which is why, in practice, you cluster them together. Most bidding tools and search engines will automate this process for you now, but there is value to be had in being creative with the data on which you segment and what you feed into their bidding systems.

BIDDING ON YOUR OWN BRAND NAME

Back when I started out in affiliates, we were all about SEM. Affiliate programmes allowed you to buy the brand name of the company you were an affiliate for in SEM. This resulted in the homepage for the word 'eBay' having multiple paid ads, all pointing to the eBay homepage and all taking credit for traffic eBay would have gained anyway. This wasn't just eBay, though; every major brand out there with an affiliate programme was doing the same thing. Personally, this was great for me. While still at college, I figured out I could do this as well, and if I paid more at night than during the day – a practice now called day parting and automated in most good campaign tools and the Google system – I could get higher conversion rates and make more money by outbidding my competition. (This was another part of my earliest digital marketing efforts that helped me pay for college.)

Shortly after I joined eBay in 2004 most affiliate programmes, including eBay, banned this practice. Clearly, the affiliates were not adding any unique value in buying such obvious keywords. At that point, however, the question arose, 'Should we buy our brand search term at all?' And so began one of the great debates of paid search that, twenty years in for me, is still not truly settled. I touch upon this concept in Chapters 5 and 8, but I want to remind you of my opinion here: broadly speaking, you should not bid on your own brand in search. If a potential customer is so deep in the conversion funnel that they are searching for a specific brand, they are very likely going to convert, whether they are shown a search ad or not, and they are just as likely to see that brand at the top of the search results without the brand having to buy an ad. I am, however, always open to being convinced otherwise by experimentation.

The only large-scale public experiment I am aware of in this area is a study I brought up in the Introduction, called 'Consumer Heterogeneity and Paid Search Effectiveness: A Large-Scale Field Experiment', that was performed by eBay's former chief economist Steve Tadelis. Tadelis used the tools I advocate for in this book to test for incrementality, and he wrote up the results in this academic study, which is well worth a read. One specific example he researched was how incremental bidding on the word 'eBay' was for the company. He had questioned the incrementality of paid search and emphasized how important it is to run experiments, not just look at post-click tracking, as discussed throughout the preceding chapters. He showed that, if you don't focus on incrementality, you can waste a lot of money paying for conversions you would have received anyway. The bidding by eBay on its brand name was found to be no different – they would have made those conversions anyway. This is another reason the guiding principle of *incremental results are everything* is so important to keep in mind.

Buying your own brand name as a keyword skews your results for two main reasons: first, it is usually cheap for you to buy your own brand name; and second, it drives a huge volume of clicks and conversions. So, if you were to do this and then check your averages for your overall campaign, without splitting out your brand name, your CPAs will look lower and your conversion volumes higher, making your overall work seem deceptively good. Numerous times during my career, I have also found a brand keyword that *accidentally* got included in non-brand keyword campaigns. The effect on the campaign's results usually starts small, but they gradually become skewed. You must therefore always keep an eye on whether you have brand keywords in your campaign by manually reviewing your highest-volume keywords often. And if you do, you need to split them out in reporting. Buying your own brand keyword also makes your campaigns less incremental, so when you run your periodic incrementality testing, your performance will be way lower than without the keyword involved.

In short, buying your own brand name in search is non-incremental; customers looking for your brand were going to buy from you anyway, and your site is likely at the top of the list in organic search anyhow. So why is this still a great debate?

Well, you will never be the only result on the search page when someone searches for your brand, both organically and, in some cases, in paid search. Increasing your share of the search result page can, because of this, result in incremental conversions. We have experimentally proven this for our brands in a few situations and, even though for years I banned us from buying our brand terms, we now buy them sometimes.

There shouldn't be a hard and fast rule, but buying your own brand name should be a deliberate decision. If someone is searching for your specific brand, they are probably far down the marketing funnel and at the action stage, and they likely see you in organic search. Any conversions you get will not be particularly incremental. You aren't the only result on the search page, though, so sometimes you should buy your brand name to protect yourself from competitors stealing your customers away. If you take this approach, run experiments to determine how incremental the impact is and report the data for brand search terms separately from the rest of your campaign; otherwise, they will skew your results.

Tomorrow's campaigns

As discussed, the trend in search today, and in paid ads more generally, is something along the lines of 'Jesus take the wheel' or at least 'broad match, smart bidding and AI ads take the wheel'. You might think that, given all my hard-won experience down the years, I would be against automation or would argue to not embrace it, and instead continue to personally tweak and optimize all your paid search campaigns like an artisanal chef. Though, as you may have picked up by now, I feel quite the contrary.

In my experience, these systems work. If you feed the right data into the automated bidding systems so they know the value of the conversions you are giving them, which users you want to show ads to, and which you want to avoid, you will get great results. At Meta, this means mostly exclusion and un-targeting; since so much of the web uses our products, we want to show ads only to those people who are not currently active on our services. We've worked for years to optimize how we train systems to show our ads to the people we want to resurrect or acquire and not our existing users, who include the majority of people online at this point. (Note, the situation is different for our e-commerce work on selling virtual-reality, mixed-reality and augmented-reality devices because they don't have billions of users yet – un-targeting is less important with a smaller pool of users. In this case, we want to feed through purchase actions tied to the click ID from Google into the system and attach the value of those purchases so Google will work on finding us more high-value conversions.)

So, there are three questions to consider with these automated campaigns: what data does the system need to make the right decisions for you? How do you send that data to that system obeying all privacy laws? And how do you double-check that the campaign is giving you incremental conversion, not conversions you would have got otherwise? For the last question, the key is to keep on incrementality testing. Run user-level randomized controlled tests where you can. Where you can't, match markets at the state or country level and turn off ads in one versus the other, then observe the results. If all else fails, just run pre/post tests where you turn your campaign on and off completely. From there, you can see what happens to your topline performance and if marketing is delivering nothing through that channel.

In a way, that's the crux of this entire chapter, leading us back to the second guiding principle: incremental results are everything, and that holds true across all forms of search. If automated AI campaigns get you that incrementality, awesome.

If brand keyword bidding gives it to you, awesome. Don't just follow dogma. Do your own testing. And don't forget how crucial testing is to your success. It's easy to waste money and time if you aren't uncovering the real results.

14. SOCIAL

Social is the current pinnacle of online advertising, where search, social and partner ads all compete for advertising dollars. In part, this is because it combines the best aspects of all the other channels. It lets you bring together creativity in content, conversion and targeting and shepherd customers through the marketing funnel, from awareness to intention. With social you can work on your own or with partners. You can operate for free, or pay for premiums. It democratizes online marketing tools unlike any other channel, such that small businesses paying $100 a month in ads can play on the same footing as corporate giants spending $100m.

And of course, the channel is huge. Over 10 million businesses buy ads on Meta properties today, and hundreds of millions have a business presence. Social is also highly competitive, with multiple giants, like TikTok, Facebook, YouTube and Instagram, to name just a few. That competition pushes innovation on tools for businesses and consumers. Above all, though, social is the channel where the guiding principle that *incremental results are everything* is most true and most measurable with user-level AB tests.

There will be continual innovation in this space, and companies that take advantage of each new format and channel that opens up will gain a lead over their competitors that is hard to close. The journey of social has been to become more immersive, from text to photos to video to even worlds now, like Roblox, the 3D social and gaming platform. The technology has gone from simple ranking to machine learning to AI agents bringing you what is most relevant for your business and goals, and even creating the content itself. Social media is not done evolving either. There are many platforms competing for the space, and this is great news for any business that wants to take advantage of social's continued evolution.

SOCIAL CHANNELS

Social can be divided into three main categories:

1. Organic social – In organic social, you post content and get distribution on your own (some folks call this 'owned media').
2. Creator marketing – In this category, you partner with someone else who is good at organic social.
3. Paid social – Just like in paid search, here you buy ads in the social media channel.

For organic social, the single most important quality is to be interesting. No matter what the algorithm optimizes for, companies want engaged, happy users who keep using their product. Time and time again, companies have tried to fake it, and this just doesn't work. You can't be interesting without authenticity, which makes all the difference. Part of being authentic is to think of the channel first. Too many people use the exact same content across social channels or, even worse, just upload some corporate website video and expect to succeed. This is a lost cause.

In organic social, you also need to stay engaged. Every piece of content you produce can't be perfect and go viral, but the number of times you step up to the plate matters, and engaging in the comments with your audience matters. Organic social is a game of slugging percentage – how many home runs you get, not your batting average. The value of a home run is basically uncapped in social – the right piece of content can get seen 100 million times and change the trajectory of your company, for good or ill.

Creator marketing is all about leveraging people who are geniuses at social to help take you to the next level of your digital marketing. But beware: just because someone is a social media star with a large following doesn't mean they are social geniuses. When you select who to work with in this channel, the absolute core to success, again, is authenticity. Ask, does it make sense for your brand to work with this creator? The launch of our RayBan Meta glasses, for example, was creator-first, as was the launch of Threads, a Twitter-like platform from Meta. The results of both were spectacular, in large part because the creators were the right ones for the products we were promoting. The hardest part for me as a CMO working with creator marketing is the loss of control. This can be scary, as it can go wrong and backfire, but it's the only way to get the most out of the brilliant, talented creators out there. There are creator-first options for every business, small or large, and the right partnership can be transformational.

Paid social media is built around user-level targeting. Here, you show ads to logged-in users associated with a user ID they've had for years at a time, whereas with search you roughly target a keyword ID. Fundamentally, that means social media is better set up for both driving and measuring incremental results. With social, you can create audiences at all levels in the marketing funnel, using creative that speaks to them. In the process, you can move folks from literally being unaware of your product through to getting them to take a direct response action, even in-line in the product, which is how TikTok, Meta and others build a checkout function inside their apps. It all boils down to integrating appropriately with the social platforms, trusting the algorithm primarily and tweaking its targeting where you have an advantage. But before we get to the details of paid social, let's start with the organic category.

ORGANIC SOCIAL

When you think about social media, remember that the value of the right post or interaction is potentially uncapped. In rare cases, the wrong social can also be worth negative points to the same extent, so capping the downside matters. I like to think of this channel as 'interesting squared'. Your distribution is related to how interesting and engaging users find your content. Every social platform tries to distribute content their users will love, so distribution is related to being interesting. At the same time, the likelihood that you will convince someone to take an action is related to how interesting you are. So, if the total actions you create are equal to the amount you are distributed times how convincing you are, and both of those are correlated with how interesting you are, you get to 'interesting squared'. This is why results in social media can be so discontinuous – either you have a hit or you don't.

The best brands on organic social are both engaged and engaging. Today, companies like the language learning app Duolingo (discussed in detail later in the chapter) do an incredible job here. Duolingo's iconic green owl mascot chases users around on social to complete their lessons for the day. It is funny and authentic, and it gets the app distribution and awareness it would never have otherwise.

To be engaging and interesting, you have to use the current channels as they exist, not as you want them to exist. For example, you should shoot videos vertically, not horizontally, for phones, where many users will be viewing your content. Or on Instagram Reels, TikTok and YouTube Shorts, the videos should be short form, not ten-minute long speeches. You must optimize to the platform and format as it won't change itself for you.

Content-wise, you need to move at the speed of culture. As trends emerge, jump on them and engage with them. In 2024, for example, there was a massive trend of older creators at old school institutions, like the National Trust in the UK – a beloved institution that manages hundreds of stately homes and more – poking fun at themselves using Gen Z catchphrases to describe their business. This generally started with the script from one satirical viral hit on TikTok where a creator called Jools Lebron said her makeup for work was 'very demure, very mindful'. It was a super-funny and sharp satire on makeup creators and etiquette experts of old. The posts that were inspired by this trend were self-aware and authentic, native to the platforms in format, and moved with the speed of culture on a new breaking trend.

I believe the breakout here was a video promoting Fyfield Manor in Oxfordshire. The owner, Christine Brown, takes one Gen Z social media hit after another and wanders around the grounds of the 880-year-old B&B, using them to describe parts as being 'demure' or having 'rizz' in a way that made people young and old fall about laughing. This really built awareness of her business and inspired lots of other institutions to try this humorous approach, with a lot of success. It also shows how social can be hugely effective even for small businesses – you don't have to have massive marketing budgets to have a massive viral hit!

To measure organic social, you need to consider the following:

1. Do you even get seen? (impressions and reach)
2. Do you get engagement? (comments and likes)
3. Is the message on strategy? (manual scoring)

Luckily, all social platforms have the reporting to allow you to see and understand these steps. So, let's work through some examples to see how organic social works in action, and how its success can be properly gauged.

Growing the top of the funnel as a new brand

The blender company Blendtec started an incredible campaign in 2006 on YouTube, appropriately titled 'Will It Blend?' The core reasoning behind the campaign was that, though consumers were buying plenty of blenders in the aughts, many didn't know about Blendtec's. To gain awareness, Blendtec created a TV show-style ad in which a host, Blendtec founder Tom Dickson, would take items, usually improbable ones, and ask, 'Will it blend?' before putting them in the blender and blending them to find out. They blended iPhones, iPads, Glow Sticks and even tried a crowbar (it did not blend).

This campaign did everything right. These videos were seen, and they engaged with and stayed on their core message, consistently driving increased awareness of the existing brand. They were completely relevant to the channel. The campaign shot videos in a horizontal format and at an average length that was in line with the typical YouTube videos of the time. The show was authentic too, featuring the company's product at its centre and a host who took obvious pride in the surprising strength of the product. The top video of the campaign reached 19 million views at last count, broke awareness of Blendtec in the United States, and even landed segments on mainstream TV. It is worth remembering that, when this campaign was huge (the peak video came out in 2010), the internet was still quite small in the USA. The campaign would have surely gotten larger still, were it to have happened today.

Taking users through the whole funnel

As discussed in Chapter 5, in 2012, about six years after Blendtec's first success, Dollar Shave Club created a whole company off the back of one successful social media viral video, which they uploaded to YouTube and Facebook. At that point in the company's evolution, Dollar Shave Club was a subscription service that sold razors through the mail. The video they produced – one continuous shot, featuring CEO Mike Dubin, often talking directly into the camera, explaining their business model with deadpan humour and theatrical flare – received almost 30 million views on YouTube. Not only was it engaging, but the video solidified their brand and awareness of the category – the company went through the roof.

Though BlendTec did a great job with their campaign, Dollar Shave Club's was almost revolutionary, and they were able to keep this surge in awareness alive with great paid social media marketing. This channel helped them capture folks who were hearing about the company through the buzz of the video, then shepherded them down the funnel with ads. During this time, every social media site showed ads for Dollar Shave Club, which emphasized the product's price and drove conversion. These ads were placed by Dollar Shave Club based on lists of their existing customers that they uploaded to sites like Facebook, known as custom audiences, which were then expanded via lookalike audiences by asking Facebook, Instagram and other social media platforms to find similar consumers.

This approach allowed Dollar Shave Club to capture the awareness they were creating, build a booming business and then successfully sell it to Unilever in 2016 for a billion dollars. As this story shows, by coupling viral marketing success with strong paid advertising, you can convert the demand into leads, which is incredibly important, especially if you're in the process of building your brand.

Authenticity and distribution through the funnel

Duolingo is my favourite current example in the 2020s of a brand creating incredibly engaging campaigns for organic social. It is a successful publicly traded company, a status that often makes it far harder for companies to take risks in their marketing creative, and yet it has irreverent, brilliant social media campaigns. The campaigns are centred on their logo, and now iconic mascot, the Duolingo green owl. The app has a multi-year history of impactful marketing, starting with You-Tube videos in the 2010s. The company's VP of growth from that time, Gina Gotthilf, has been interviewed for several great videos explaining their growth strategies during this period.

According to Gotthilf, Duolingo optimized on leveraging great product-led growth techniques, focusing on notifications that remind people to come back to the app and do their daily language lesson. During the 2010s, they built their brand through notifications from the nagging, aggressive teacher – the owl! Duolingo executives, such as head of product Cem Kansu, publicly say Duolingo 'love being unhinged with our owl'. (I strongly encourage you to watch Gotthilf's videos and interviews, particularly her interview on 20VC, for insights on how Duolingo used product-led marketing to huge success.) The company had an incredible existing platform of product-led growth tools and general growth marketing, but they still had a lack of awareness compared to their potential opportunity.

On social media, Duolingo have taken their marketing game to the next level. For example, they comment on users' posts in a fun way. When users complain about the owl chasing them via notifications on their phone, the Duolingo owl shows up and chases them on social too, chiding them to do their lessons in a tongue-in-cheek way. This has become a running joke, and users will make such posts just to get these interactions. The mascot provides Duolingo with a series of opportunities to be at the batting plate for a viral success. They have a history of viral PR stunts with their mascot, including the most recent in 2025, when they ran a whole campaign focused on the concept that the owl was dead, which was 'unhinged' and engaging, both on social media and in the press. They have used that same branding and made funny short-form videos for TikTok and Instagram Reels. In my opinion, they were the first brand to fully nail this approach when short-form videos emerged as a fully fledged social media format.

Now Duolingo are branching out with creator collaborations, such as a collaboration with the TV show *Squid Game* from Netflix and the release of its second season. They have millions of followers on Instagram and TikTok, and they are building awareness with more humour, in an authentic way for their brand. The results are stunning: in the five years from 2015 to 2020, they approximately doubled their monthly active users; from 2020 to 2025, they seem to have grown five fold in monthly active users, with revenue following. Some of this increase was no doubt a result of the COVID-19 pandemic, during which so many people were stuck inside, looking for ways to keep their brains active, but a lot seems to have unlocked subsequently, correlating with their excellent social media marketing strategy.

Be interesting – it matters

All three of the preceding examples prove the point that for organic social, consistently engaging and interesting content matters. Blendtec and Duolingo, in particular, gained more and more engagement and distribution with their social media over time. They had to work at it to get results, though – it wasn't overnight success. The likelihood of convincing people to do something is related to how interesting you, your brand or your campaign are. Distribution is also proportional to how interesting something is, as is conversion, which leads us back to the idea of total conversions being proportional to 'interesting squared'. As such, results can scale exponentially from social media, helping you add huge amounts of value to your company when done right.

Companies in a range of industries – from mid-sized manufacturers like Blendtec, in the 2000s, to startups like Dollar Shave Club, in the 2010s, to multi-billion-dollar tech companies like Duolingo, in the 2020s – have made organic social a huge driver of growth. As time has gone on, the top example for each decade has gotten better, revealing what a truly excellent organic social strategy looks like today:

1. **Engage consistently and constantly.** Give yourself opportunities to have viral moments (Blendtec and Duolingo did this well).

2. **Ensure you are authentic and true to your brand.** Nothing fails harder on social than inauthenticity.

3. **Focus on your funnel problem.** All three of these companies had awareness issues and grew the top of their marketing funnel in response.

4. **Stay on message.** Don't just chase any engagement – chase the right engagement.

5. **Capture the demand.** Duolingo and especially Dollar Shave Club did an incredible job here, capturing the awareness they were driving with paid ads and turning it into customers.

Organic social is an incredible medium, but it takes classic creativity in brand marketing to get outsized successes in this channel. It is particularly powerful at the top of the funnel, and I hope these examples inspire you, just as they inspire me.

CREATOR MARKETING

Despite the success of Blendtec, Dollar Shave Club and Duolingo, being creative in this way is not for everyone. Personally, I'm better at creative with data and targeting; I don't think I will ever be brilliant at the sort of creativity shown by the teams at those companies. Of course, you can hire incredibly talented creative people who can augment your areas of expertise by bringing those skills to your team. But today, many of the most creative people on social media are completely independent, drumming up their own business and working for themselves as creators. This presents an incredible opportunity for marketers to work with content creators who have directly demonstrated their talent at social media through purely Darwinian selection in a public setting. It is also super-exciting that every niche has its own creator ecosystem, so there is usually a creator for any company at any scale, from the local shopping expert to the archaeology genius to the health and wellness guru to the massive international superstar and beyond.

Some of the greatest successes during my time as CMO, although I didn't personally drive them, have been related to working with creators. The launch of RayBan Meta glasses, for example, was led by Shachar Scott (VP of marketing at Reality Labs, our hardware division). The success of Instagram's Threads app was the result of wonderful work by many teams, including our creator partnerships teams led by Charles Porch and Sibyl Goldman (VPs of partnerships for Meta). Both launches were huge successes, and the creator partnerships were among the key drivers, beyond the products themselves being great. Many marketers I have talked to, though, find creator marketing scary, so I hope to demystify it here. In short, it is not alchemy. There is a process, and once you have it down, you can rinse and repeat and get fantastic results.

In creator marketing, creators represent your brand and your campaign instead of you. Typically, you pay some creators to post content around your campaign with reasonable constraints that you've put in place, and hope you land the campaign so well that it goes viral beyond them. Letting go of control like this can be terrifying for many brands, legal teams and CEOs. And, truth be told, if not approached correctly, it can go horribly wrong. But some of the best brands in the world – from luxury brands like LVMH to brands shooting for everyday purchase prices like Coca-Cola – have embraced creator campaigns that have had huge distribution and been completely on brand, time and time again.

There are a few key pieces to make creator marketing work:

1. Treat the creators like agencies and give them a brief that is simple and punchy.
2. Move at the speed of culture, and that means *fast*.
3. Select the right creators.
4. Be comfortable losing control, and know that if you do this right, you will.
5. Understand measurement is hard, but measure what you can.

Let's explore each of these pieces in detail.

The brief

In any successful creator campaign, there is always a brief, and it is usually beautifully simple. A marketing brief is a concise document outlining campaign objectives, target audience, key messaging and performance metrics to guide the development and execution of a focused marketing strategy. A good brief is a boring concept but the core to great creative. Coca-Cola has done wonderful work around the 'Share a Coke' campaign. The brief is very simple: Coke's audience is, give or take, everyone, and they asked creators to create content that showcases the joy of sharing a Coke with someone. It is easy to understand how creators can do work around that one simple phrase. The 'Coke Creation' campaign in 2023 was another simple concept brilliantly executed. It took an idea that would be super-uncomfortable for any brand – people playing with the logo – and made it a campaign. Instead of correcting local interpretations of the Coca-Cola logo, they worked with the VML advertising agency to embrace them, taking the versions made by local artists and creators and distributing and celebrating them.

Simple briefs are always best, if at all possible, for campaigns big and small. The Coke brief above was simple and created great work. The brief for our RayBan Meta campaign basically stated, 'show what the glasses can do in a cool way,' and then listed the four main features we wanted emphasized: listening to music, calling, asking AI questions and taking photos and video. The magic was then in selecting creators who would be good at interpreting that brief in a cool way.

There is, however, a tension here. As a marketing leader, I want our creative to all stay on brand, and I am scared that giving up control to a creator could lead to mistakes, for which I would be held accountable. Meanwhile, creators want to be free to interpret our brief as they see fit. They know if they are inauthentic, they will lose their follower base, and along with it, their source of income and success. This is a healthy tension, and it can work to your advantage. As I discuss further, a clear process with strict turnaround times to give a creator a 'yes' or 'no' on a potential posting is crucial. The default can be that they get to post if you don't reply, and that you have a high bar for saying no, which gives them the freedom they need and you the necessary oversight. This is particularly important considering how fast creators must move to capture trends and cultural shifts.

Moving at the speed of culture

For these campaigns to succeed, creators need to be able to jump on trends and media cycles that last days or even mere hours. For most creators, this is one of their specialties, and how they likely got successful in the first place. Survival of the fittest in the creator ecosystem has optimized for a set of people who can do this properly, and to your benefit. Large companies, on the other hand, aren't used to moving that fast. As mentioned, they will want to maintain some level of control over people they are paying for work that will be tagged as an #ad from them. Many is the great creator idea that has been strangled by the committees of BigCo™.

So how do you avoid this potential issue? It comes down to boring BigCo™ pre-work and alignment. Above everyone else, the key folks you need to align as a CMO or marketer are your management and legal teams. This must be done first, up front and ahead of time, so everyone is on the same page going into the campaign. Second, you need to have an agreed approval process for any work the creator will post. Third, a service-level agreement (SLA) laying out the turnaround time from all parties involved, including the CMO for approvals, must be agreed ahead of the campaign. Finally, the resources must be put in place to deliver on that SLA. Remember, though, approvals are approvals. If either party says 'no' to an idea, you need a plan to handle that. Similarly, if a creator goes too far in a campaign and doesn't accept feedback, you need a plan to handle that as well. You can't plan for each situation in advance, but you can plan for the general concept of what they will produce as they represent your brand.

Depending on your company, those review processes can be light. Some companies consider review as simple as a disclaimer that the company claims no control over what creators say, do or produce. Most companies require some review of the creator's content related to their brand before they post it, but they can usually keep it to a minimum. Since it's an endorsed third party making statements, not a company-owned and operated entity making statements, there is a sense of distance between the creator and the brand. Keeping it 'light' is the operative word here – consider yes or no approvals in this space, not creative feedback. That said, taking into account what the creator has been working on, don't hesitate to share thoughts to inform their *next* piece of creative – but don't try to frame-edit. If you do, it won't appear genuine, and it will slow you down, which is the exact opposite of what you're looking for from partnering with a creator.

So to move fast in BigCo™, remember: plan ahead. Have a process. Have SLAs. Keep feedback simple. And get permission from management ahead of time for taking risks. Then if the risks pay off, with excellent results and no major scandals, you'll find you can get lighter and lighter, allowing you to move faster and faster. That's where the real magic happens, as you gain trust and build results.

Selecting the right creators

In addition to getting set up so that you are aligned with creators and able to work in a flexible way at the speed of culture, you also need to make sure the creators are right for your brand. That makes the process far easier and great results far more likely. There are three key questions to ask when deciding on the right creators:

1. Are they big enough?
2. Are they brand-aligned?
3. Are they campaign-aligned?

Not every creator needs to have the social media following of a Shakira or Lionel Messi to work for you, but they should be popular enough to drive the campaign. Know the scale you need and then pitch to creators at that scale. With brand alignment, consider the creators that LVMH might pick for their campaigns versus those Coke might pick – the overlap is limited. If you are Dior, for example, make sure your creator is on brand, either in high-end fashion or respected in that world. Dior might be tempted to pick someone who is extremely famous, but if they never produce content around high-end fashion, then there's no point in collaborating with them. Campaign alignment is similar to brand alignment, though in a way this can also flip the last point on its head. For example, a campaign juxtaposing Oscar the Grouch with Dior fashion might be buzzworthy, cheeky and a huge success. That approach is, of course, totally cool, but the alignment should be a deliberate decision. If you want a creator amplifying Paris Fashion Week, for example, they should be there and be good at real-time summarizing in their existing work – even if they are Oscar the Grouch. The devil here is in the details of vetting and doing the hard work to align with the creator, not explaining what the work should be to them.

Losing control

If it all comes together well, then you will lose control. Paid creation, in time, becomes organic creation, with other creators copying your paid creators and trends – instead of jumping on a trend, you are riding it like a wave. In my career, I have only experienced this situation once at scale, during the launch of our RayBan Meta glasses in 2023. My role in this campaign was making space for it to work; giving the team senior approval and air cover from any other execs; providing fast approvals;

aligning my peers and management and taking responsibility if it all went south, which thankfully it didn't.

We were working with 100–200 creators, including three huge accounts. The huge accounts produced and posted first-person-shot music videos using the RayBan Meta glasses. These were epic: essentially, full ads from creative geniuses with tens of millions of followers combined. These videos had more input from the team and oversight than the next wave of creators. That next wave was a set of 100–200 creators kicking out their own versions of a first-person filmed experience that fitted with their particular style and audience. My team did a brilliant job of picking creators for whom these videos would make sense. For many of them, their artistic lens was more important than being a big name personality, meaning the camera didn't have to be focused on them the whole time. They also invited the audience into the experience by showing them experiences from their viewpoint through the glasses, like a musician on stage or an athlete competing. As CMO, I had no creative input in any of these videos, just the right to say no if I was worried about the content. However, the team did such a great job, nothing came to me that I wanted to say no to.

Then the campaign took on a life of its own. We saw creators on TikTok, who we were not working with, who wanted to create these types of videos themselves. They started buying their own glasses and creating 'Get Ready With Me' (GRWM) videos in the mirror using the RayBan Meta glasses. The trend went on for a month or so and got far higher reach than the creators we paid to get it started. The glasses themselves sold far above our expectations. As mentioned, you can't make this happen without a great product, but the viral campaign sparked by creator marketing and Shachar Scott's brilliant team were part of why we got to the heights of sales we achieved.

Measuring it all

OK, so famously I'm the numbers nerd of Meta, not just the CMO, and measuring all these moving parts of creator marketing is hard, but critical to receiving support to continue in this channel. You need to measure what you can, and then explain what you can't. You should *not* push measurement into places it can't do the job. So, in this space, I come back to my two key points about organic social: you have to get reach and you need to be on strategy. Tracking the distribution achieved through your organic social efforts, both reach and frequency, can provide an understanding of your creator marketing campaign's success. This data is available in all good social media monitoring tools and in the interfaces of the big social media companies. With any creator collaboration, they should report those metrics back to you as part of the relationship.

For social you don't control, you can only use proxies. Consider the number of content pieces you didn't create yourself, the average reach of creator and how engaged users were with that content. You can use engagement as a proxy for reach, using your own data to equate one like to X viewers on average. That approach provides only a rough estimate, though, and that is all you will get here. You should then also perform a second level of measurement, scoring the content on its strategy alignment (a simple yes or no) and giving a percentage score of all the posts being on message. It is easy to have huge but irrelevant reach with a trend, so you need to do this work to know if the trend was just big, or big *and* helpful. The last necessary measurement is sentiment – is it trending positive or negative? In general, you can argue for advanced AI-based sentiment analysis, but that's usually a waste. It's easier to just score sentiment as broadly positive, neutral or negative, which will get you 90 percent-plus of what you need for this type of work.

Beyond that, you can really only do pre/post measurements. You can't control the distribution of organic social, nor can you measure clicks on your website from organic social or visits to your app. For our viral RayBan Meta glasses campaign, I can't to this day tell you how much the organic social drove, or really if we caused it to happen. I just know it was big, and we had huge jumps in all our key metrics in the parts of the world where it happened and where we were selling the glasses, so I'm happy to attribute a lot of value to that campaign. As I discuss further later in the chapter, I believe that because I am trusted with the rigour on measuring everything that can be measured well, my team can hit a point where we actually run out of tools for measurement, but we are given the benefit of the doubt if we say creator marketing really matters, as it did in this case.

PAID SOCIAL

Paid social is the current pinnacle of all forms of online advertising where social, search and partner ads are all competing for advertising dollars. It is the most recent form of advertising to evolve at scale, and it brings together pretty much everything I have written about in the preceding chapters into one channel. As of 2025, social media – including YouTube, Facebook, Instagram, TikTok, Snapchat, X and LinkedIn – has overtaken search to become the largest marketing channel on Earth. Being brilliant at this channel is key to being successful in modern marketing. My goal here in exploring paid social is to explain how all you have learned in this book thus far comes together to form a coherent advertising plan on social media.

Paid social started with banner ads. Even as late as 2007, MySpace and Facebook were running banners, skyscrapers and, in the case of MySpace, even full takeovers of the homepage.

Facebook first launched flyers, which were like little university noticeboards, and then a much more advanced ad platform, which is the basis of most social media advertising today, in an overblown event in New York in November 2007, just days before I joined the company. As the system has evolved, the basics have stayed constant. Social media lets you target ads based on people's profiles, data and what they are doing at that moment. Every iteration has worked on making these ads more relevant and personalized. Paid social is better than contextual advertising because people are more than the page they are looking at, or whatever they are doing online at that precise moment. It is also better for users because, unlike banner ads that were generic and lowest common denominator, people get ads that are relevant to them, making them less annoying and jarring.

As I said at the start of the book, I joined Facebook because I believed it would be huge, a revolution in modern marketing that would help people understand the incremental impact of their marketing efforts and give everyone targeting superpowers that only big companies could afford in the past. In many ways, this has played out. Facebook, now Meta, has billions of active users. We have designed lift studies that allow you to understand the incremental value of your advertising on our platforms and, typically, show you the value well beyond just the last click attribution.

This value creation for advertisers has, in turn, allowed Meta to become a meaningful advertising player and created a huge boon for SMBs, of which more than 10 million globally are advertising through our services every month. As a result of the return on ad spend (ROAS) we are delivering to our advertisers, Meta has created an over $100 billion a year advertising business. That said, the long-term holdouts still aren't where I'd like them to be, and brand advertising has done less than I'd hoped. However, as internet connection speeds have improved and memory has become cheaper, there has been a major shift to video online (video now accounts for >50 percent of time users spend on Instagram and Facebook). In future, this trend will likely continue and may well attract more brand dollars and long-term thinking, while encouraging measurement innovation. But the jury is still out.

Meanwhile, some of paid social's results have been greater than I had hoped for, or ones that I hadn't even thought of. The one that has been the greatest revelation to me, as a gay man, is how gay-targeted businesses and products have thrived due to new opportunities brought about by social media. I love my rainbow flip-flops and T-shirts bought from ads targeted at me as a gay man. I am also inspired by how the Terrence Higgins Trust – a British charity focused on sexual health and HIV awareness and services – has used Facebook ads to find the cheapest route to help people identify if they have HIV and get into treatment. They run ads offering free HIV testing in communities that are over-indexed for HIV in the UK, such as men who have sex with men or people of West African roots. People then opt in to take those tests. If they find pre-symptomatic HIV, they can get themselves into treatment with the result that their viral load becomes so low it cannot be detected. In doing so, they can halt the spread of this terrible disease. This wouldn't be possible without the ability to target the communities where undetected HIV is over-indexed. As a result, the Terrence Higgins Trust is improving lives, stopping the spread of HIV and contributing to hopefully removing community transmission of HIV by 2030 in the UK.

Interestingly, this great public health tool is under threat since well-meaning but, in my opinion, misguided campaigners have campaigned effectively against targeting on 'sensitive categories'. Some laws have been passed and generally media and informal government pressure has been brought to bear because of this. As a result, social media and targeted advertising companies have moved away from targeting in that area, as they don't want to risk brand harm and problematic government interactions. I understand the anti-targeting impulse, but as a gay man and data scientist, I believe the good uses of targeting with ads outweigh the bad discriminatory behaviour. These include awareness of, and access to, LGBTQ+-friendly products; businesses optimizing for the LGBTQ+ community and the enablement of more LGBTQ+ businesses to thrive because they can find an audience online. I believe online targeted ads, especially on social media, are a net positive for society. Yes, we should regulate and police the issues, but we are going too far and are in danger of throwing the baby out with the bathwater. It will be interesting to see how this plays out in the decades to come.

Outcomes and data

The place to start with paid social is the same as any other channel – being clear about what you want to achieve. This sounds basic but, strangely, teams and individuals often think about this foundational point too late in their ad campaigns – I call this 'ready, fire, aim'. Clearly define your North Star goal, and the North Star metric that measures it, from the start of any campaign. Ask yourself, do I want app installs? Do I want leads for our sales team? Do I want registrations? Do I want purchases? Do I care how much revenue is associated with each one of these? Every major social media service now has different outcomes you can optimize for. You can optimize for leads, app installs and conversions by telling the system what you are optimizing for. The most successful campaigns take these actions up front, maximizing their chances of success.

These considerations lead to data. Once you know what you are optimizing for, you want to feed data (obtained with appropriate consent) from your service into the social media ad system which can then optimize for you. Again, this process is often taken lightly and not done correctly. Our excellent head of sales, Nicola Mendelsohn, and I still meet with top advertisers we've worked with for a decade and more to ask them to improve implementation of these data feeds. For what it's worth, I get the same requests from our internal teams for how my teams use our systems. Great work here is hard – the systems keep evolving and getting better, and you may miss changes and updates. Don't feel bad if you haven't done it well, just keep focused on continually improving. To help, you must send all conversions well tagged and make sure to append value data. Let's look more closely at both.

Send conversions

For sending all conversions, the web evolves. This used to be as simple as throwing up a pixel on the conversion landing page, after which the third party would use that cookie data to track conversions. This system was always flawed, but good enough. Today, cookie deprecation is widespread, and it can't be relied on any more. As a result, you need to do more work. You must put various conversion APIs and user-consent dialogues in place to send data. Since specific advice in this area quickly goes out of date, focus on the factors you can control, such as:

1. Hiring a great technical agency which can ideally manage this process for you.
2. Developing an excellent relationship between that agency and the team that implements tracking for you.
3. Making sure you hire marketers who are experienced in this area, allowing them to ask the right questions and validate that the implementation is done well.
4. Revisiting this process periodically.

I, for example, leverage the Cannes Ad Festival as the time each year to hear how our vendors think we are executing on these integrations and ask for follow-ups explicitly outlining where we're falling short. It is important that you send all conversions, though, and not just those that come from a click from the social media service. Why? First, the service needs to be able to model what a user who will convert looks like, and to do that, it needs to see as many converting users as possible. Second, for measurement, if you want more than just post click (which you should), then you need conversions passed without a click associated with them.

Append value data

Append value data means add data to an existing conversion signal that says how much it is worth to you in dollars. It sounds straightforward. For example, someone who buys something on your site is worth X and you simply send that value through. Easy, right? Well, it can get super-complicated quickly. A lot of questions arise when appending data – here are just a few:

- Since you don't know the value of an app install, registration or lead when they happen, you must get a sale completed or see users active for some length of time to predict how much revenue they will generate in their lifetime. Say you run a small car dealership and you get a lead for a test drive: Do they make the purchase? Do they finance the car too, driving up their value?

- The value of a simple purchase is way more complicated than the actual purchase price. You have to figure out the cost of goods (COGs) so you can subtract it from the purchase price and understand the actual profit.

An example would be the difference between selling a case of Diet Coke (low margin) versus a bottle of wine (high margin) at an online grocer.

- Is this an item that is easy to sell, or one where you have a full warehouse you need to shift? As an example, a friend who worked at a large retailer told me that when they stocked the wrong goods for a season, they would sell them at a massive discount just to get them out of the warehouse. That meant the value of the ad that sold them was far more valuable than classic ROI because they were just not selling otherwise, and space needed to be cleared. So, either the goods sold or were landfill.

- Did that purchase result in a user coming back who had been inactive for a year, leading to a resurrection associated with LTV? At Facebook, for example, if we can get a user who has been absent a long time to return and now keeps using our services again, that is way more valuable than a single session.

Each system is different, but most allow you to add value when a conversion happens, and some let you send value data delayed, which I hope becomes standard over time. This is where real magic can happen on driving ROAS for your campaigns and being a super-effective marketing organization. So, do as good a job as possible when you start but realize you must keep iterating.

For example, think about a simple purchase as an online retailer, such as a customer buying a throw cushion. You could send through the purchase value only, say, $30. But if you consider if the customer is a new user or a resurrection, you have better data to work with and send. If the user is a resurrection, send through an LTV value, which might be $300 or more. The user ID should have last active time associated with it in your database, allowing you to quickly recognize if they are new or returning.

This should be easy for your tech teams to implement, even if they say it is hard, which is another example of where a little technical skill goes a long way. You can start with the average LTV, but then you can analyse the data further, like modelling the LTV of everyone who made a purchase of the same value. In doing so, you will get a little bit better at appending data and smarter about how to share it. This growth is valuable because the more information you give the system, obtained with appropriate consent, the better decisions it can make to find you the most valuable outcomes.

Then there are businesses that thrive on actions that do not have a purchase associated with them. These may include an app install (say, for an online game), leads (like those for a local car dealership) or sign up (such as for social media companies like Facebook). In those cases, how do you send through an LTV? Again, you can start by sending an average LTV for every previous user who took that action. But you can get smarter as well. For example, consider the following:

- You can use geography to send different predicted values for LTV, so ask what country, state or city the user is from. The USA has far higher LTVs than, say, India, and a wealthy state like California probably has higher LTVs than Mississippi.
- For registration and lead-generating forms, people who show more intent and fill out more optional fields are usually more valuable. Look into how much information the users filled out on these forms.
- Users of different phones will have different LTVs as well. For example, today an iPhone user is usually

more valuable than an Android user. So ask, what type of phone were they on for an app install – a high-end smartphone or basic phone – and how do similar users rank in LTV?

Your goal here isn't to be perfect. Even after a year, we at Meta can't tell you an individual user's exact LTV, but we can accurately predict pretty much any bucket of 1,000 users. We do so by looking at high-value data points for predicting LTV with the previous questions and considerations discussed. Are users from an expensive state or an inexpensive one? Are they using expensive or cheap technology? Are they showing high intent to convert or not?

You can ask the same questions and track the same data. Anything you can do to teach the systems you are buying from what you are looking for will get you better ROAS. The systems offered by big social media companies are powerful but only as good as the information you give them. This comes back to the old 'garbage in, garbage out' adage. The details matter, so work hard on them, but don't let the perfect be the enemy of the good, and don't let yourself be overwhelmed. Be creative and go for it!

Data and targeting

Targeting is a balance of targeting and un-targeting users. You want to tell the systems you buy ads from when you want to show a user an ad. But once the users have converted, you want to get them out of your targeting set so you don't end up wasting money on them. Teams typically focus a lot on targeting users but not enough on clearing those people out that they should no longer be targeting. As targeting has evolved, it has become increasingly easier to just give data to the ad systems (like Meta,

YouTube, Google and others) and let them optimize for you according to your instructions. The systems are getting better and better, a trend that will only continue.

As discussed, these systems are, however, only as good as the data you give them. So, you can gain an edge by being thoughtful about the data you are sending through, versus people who are just doing the average job. You can make your targeting a little bit better each time, and a little bit better than everyone else, if you put your mind to it.

Above all, the best question to ask yourself here is, what do we know more about than the machine does? If you have done a good job of competently implementing tracking and data sharing, the answer should be very little. And if that's the case, it is important to accept that fact as you figure out how to improve. As mentioned, I didn't initially trust the auto-optimization systems and believed we, as human marketers, should be able to beat them. I fought this trend, but time and again, as we tested auto-optimization, I found that giving up control on the actual targeting, while feeding the systems the most data technically and legally possible to do ranking, was, and remains, the best way forward.

With that in mind, it is important to structure your ad accounts appropriately. Generally, a clean structure is based on the meaningful segments of your company and campaigns. Examples of meaningful segmentations include:

- **Brand.** Meta, for example, places Facebook, Instagram and WhatsApp in different accounts.
- **Country.** Different countries should also be segmented into different accounts.
- **Category of sale.** This might include home and garden versus apparel for a retailer, or romance versus science fiction for a bookseller.

- **User state**. Where users are in the funnel matters, so re-targeting people who have a full shopping cart should be a different campaign than prospecting for new users.

- **Goal**. There are different goals depending on the sought-after action, so buying an ad as a business, for example, versus registering as a consumer is totally separate.

The ad systems of all the major players tend to have a structure of accounts and campaigns which enables you to perform this sort of segmentation. This allows you to apply changes like adding targeting or associating data at each level: the account, campaign or ad. The systems are structured to follow a flow from account to campaign to targeting and then to the ad. If your marketing campaigns are structured in a way that makes it easy for you to manage them, and for the platform's ad system to understand them, then you will set yourself up for success. As you start to run and scale your campaign, you will learn more about what is uniquely true for you, and how your campaigns are behaving with the systems you are buying from. At that point, evolve your campaigns further. I was recently at a dinner where a client noted they had just audited their ad accounts with us and had over 280 active. This made no sense for the campaigns they were running, and they were looking for our help to clean it up. Clean account structure is really important, and it easily degrades. Without a clean structure, you end up bidding against yourself, struggling with reporting and generally operating a marketing programme that is a total mess. Keeping your accounts in order may seem simple – and in many ways it is – but it is a consistent issue for many companies and it often isn't done right.

One trick to try when a targeting approach just isn't working is to start a completely clean account that only focuses on the new behaviour. Say you are a book publisher starting a campaign to sell audio books, but you have only sold hard copies in the past, so your targeting is not landing as you'd hoped. Creating a new account for that segment might help. Sometimes, big systems and algorithms can learn your campaigns almost too well, and you might need to have a clean slate to add in a new behaviour.

Exclusion and inclusion

When targeting in paid social, it is important to think about exclusion as well. Who do you *not* want to target? Where do you *not* want your ads to appear? Why? There are often simple parameters or aspects of your marketing that you know and that the system could learn directly from the data you provide, but it would be *very* expensive for it to learn on its own.

On a user level, consider country and geography. For example, if your service is only available in, say, France, then you want to stop the system buying everywhere *but* France. The system would quickly learn that other countries don't drive conversions, but you would be spending a lot of money on ads in other countries before it figured this out. The best targeting is, as discussed, always behavioural. As the awesome Ani Kortikar on my team always says, we don't do targeting, we do un-targeting and run the largest un-targeting team on the internet. We mostly spend direct response dollars on bottom-of-the-funnel conversions for our main platforms – Instagram, Facebook and WhatsApp – and, in doing so, we know who already uses them. It would cost an ad system, even our own, a lot to learn that information.

To that end, we try to tag in the systems, using whatever tool they prefer, the list of people they shouldn't show ads to. This can be done via pixels or conversion APIs or by uploading lists of identifiers. Each service has different options and more are emerging, so we focus on the technical implementation being good and we push on that with our partners. Obviously, every part of this targeting and un-targeting has to strictly adhere to all privacy regulations and policies that your company is subject to or has committed to.

On a placement level, un-targeting is rare. Placement is more a question of high ROI versus low ROI. If the systems do a poor job of optimizing for placement, you can give them a helping hand by separating campaigns out and bidding different amounts in the different accounts or campaigns. Sometimes you do want to un-target completely, either out of brand safety concerns or because you truly don't see performance. That is usually easy to do, as you can switch off sites and placements during campaigns. On the whole, though, I advise against this move as it just harms conversions, and you can probably act more creatively to make the sites, channels and placements work out.

Guaranteeing inclusion is probably the place where you have the least leverage in these modern ad systems, but again it doesn't mean you shouldn't try to teach the system based on information you can provide, or at least give it a start in the right direction. As discussed in Chapter 4, in the basics section on targeting, behavioural targeting beats demographic targeting every day because it gives users the most relevant experiences. Even in something as basic as geography, there are Americans living in the UK who will buy something from a US company, even if you'd by nature exclude the UK from your targeting. My experience at eBay showed me that there are women who buy men's products either for themselves or as gifts for their spouse and vice versa.

The place that any company will have an advantage over an ad system is not simple demographics, but more proprietary information, which tends to be behavioural data. With that in mind, consider uploading lists of lookalike audiences. You can obviously select these based on credentials from your database of customers and their behavioural information. This data could come from your highest-value consumers, or from an area where you'd explicitly like to get more customers. Similarly, you can take the same approach with the pixel or conversion API. In that case, you choose which signals you send over and which consumers you would tag as high value versus low value, both based on having appropriate consent. Again, you can craft this behavioural data to flag the customers you want and exclude the ones you don't. Beyond this approach, try avoiding base demographics, unless you have a skewed or unusual product that never gets gifted and only has customers and users in a tight demographic base.

Today, targeting in paid social is mostly about teaching the systems to optimize. Think hard about structuring your accounts correctly, both on account level and on campaign level within the account, based on results. If you are going to try to be clever with targeting – which, generally, big firms with enough resources should be – think about what you know that the ad system doesn't or would take a long time and a lot of money to learn. Within that data, behavioural data is the most valuable to optimize against. Be limited in the demographic data you use, saving it primarily for geographic exclusion of the places you don't sell your product or service, or where it isn't available.

Ad formats and creative

Unlike search marketing, creative is an area with huge opportunities in social media. High level, you want your ad creative to be native and fit the channel in which it is appearing. To this day, this is the number one piece of advice we put out in all our marketing materials for the Meta paid social products. The top outcome of our presence at Cannes in the past three years is that people who buy Reels (vertical, sound on, shortform video) better understand the presentation of the creative. We've hammered the points that they must upload the video in 9:16 format, the dimensions of a phone screen; do it vertically so the orientation matches the phone's screen; and have the sound on, since people watch Reels with sound and a weird quiet ad break usually loses out unless you are somehow being clever. This is not a new ad format at this point, and these aren't low-sophistication advertisers we are talking to. So, though this advice might seem basic, it is the single most important aspect here, and it generally is surprisingly poorly done.

Keep in mind, creative is the first place where AI is truly revolutionary. At the time of writing this book, over 4 million active advertisers already use Meta's AI creative tools, launched in May 2024. They let small businesses create many versions of the same ad, as it allows them to easily work with formatting. For example, they can take an ad designed for a horizontal placement in newsfeed and transform it into a vertical short-form video with sound for Reels. The tools are creating an abundance of ads, where advertisers are making more of them and getting more performance through that variance. They are also scaling creatives to do more with existing tools, such as Photoshop. Finally, they are allowing people who couldn't afford a creative agency to do better work than they ever did before. Creative will continue to be a field of massive impact for AI.

So, your ad should be native to the channel, and AI is helping people create ads that are native to the channel, driving great results. But how do you find what being native to the channel means to begin with? In terms of practical tips, first, use the channel yourself. Observe the trends that are going well organically. Pay attention to which ads are showing up for you and what the ones with the most obvious engagement look like. Check out what the most successful advertisers in the industry are doing as well. Second, look at the best practices companies like Meta are putting out there. We put a lot of work into making sure we are sharing what works, as do our competitors. We benefit when you upload the most effective creative, too, so there is a good alignment of incentives here. Finally, make sure you hire an agency that has real case studies of producing actual results in native ad formats and can give you good explanations of how they make sure their creative fits the placement it is being run in.

Of course, in addition to creative that natively fits the placement or channel you are using, your creative needs to be eye-catching! It must also follow the rules of the differentiated channel and pop as much as possible. To do this, the design of the ad and the creative concept must be spot-on. From a design perspective, all companies put limits on what you can do. Though this may seem unfair, it makes sense. If there were no limitations, bright flashing lights and inappropriate content would make up a significant portion of the ads for the lowest-common-denominator products and arbitrage affiliates. You can, however, learn a lot from the policies. Keep in mind they are there for a couple of possible reasons. First, it's essentially a question of taste – the company may just not want certain styles of ads on their service. Second, if ads work but are long-term detrimental to the channel, causing people to be ad-blind or even churn from a service completely, then it's not worth it. You need to take these points into account in your creative as well.

So, what tends to work? A clear call to action is of the utmost importance. In many cases, the ad system has this call to action built into the ad format for you, but even if it does, you want to try different words in the call-to-action button. The button, icon or image should be bright and prominent, with simple words people understand, like 'buy now', and not uninterpretable graphics. (Never forget the big green button and the big green button test!) You also want an eye-catching graphic, whether video or static. Video or animation can help here, as can colour, to help make that creative pop.

In terms of a creative concept, this is where there is space to differentiate your paid social campaigns and do something special. For most of the meat-and-potatoes campaigns, you should use standard creative: uploading your catalogue if you are an e-commerce retailer, for example, or having good call to actions, along with excellent photography and imagery. When push comes to shove, the standards aren't all that exciting from a creative standpoint, but executing on them really well is incredibly effective.

Club Med has done a brilliant job pulling all of these elements together. As a travel and tourism company, they deliver premium all-inclusive holidays for families across their sixty-five award-winning resorts and locations worldwide. Among other outlets and methods, Club Med advertise through Meta, using a particular Meta ad format for catalogue ads for travel. In these ads, a travel advertiser like Club Med can upload their catalogue of holidays available, with compelling imagery of each, and then the Meta ad system dynamically optimizes them to show resorts to potential customers based on their travel and destination plans. Thus, Club Med, and other similar travel companies, leverage totally native creative, eye-catching imagery – and all the first- and third-party data Meta has – to show these ads to the right person at the right time.

Club Med's North Star goal was booking and sales, and the only filter they placed on the targeting was to limit to people in the UK aged 35–55, who were their target growth audience. Previously, they had set up their ads manually. But by leveraging this native creative and automatic optimization, they ended up with 58 percent lower cost per incremental web-initiated checkout, and 41 percent lower cost per entry in their booking engine compared to their previous campaigns. This is an example of how, by leveraging the latest formats available and compelling creative, a company can drive results.

Measurement

In the end, your success in paid social, just as with the other channels, relies on your measurement capabilities. Fundamentally, social media is best positioned to measure incrementality, using lift studies with user holdouts. (Please do not use last click and allow cross-channel conversion stealing – you will undervalue paid social, overvalue search marketing and not drive the most ROAS for your company!) Most platforms offer these studies as standard now, along with industry auditing and vetting so you can trust they are doing them right. We tend to do these studies a lot when we buy ads in social media and then back them up with validating geographic matched market testing, as explained in Chapter 7, on measurement. I use a cross-channel approach here to evaluate how incremental paid social is versus those other channels. So far, and yes, I know I am biased, I have found social is undercounted by last-click tracking and search overcounted. This finding aligns with what most big players advise you to do for measurement. But the right way to do this is not to just listen to me or to assume all the value is in the last click. Instead, do the appropriate holdouts and find out for yourself.

A brilliant example of measurement in paid social can be found in the iconic sports eyewear brand Oakley. In fact, Oakley have all the elements of paid social down and really know how to work the channel. They created their stunning creative and imagery in the correct format for the social media platform they were using. This was vertically shot video for capturing users with sound on, looking at short-form video across feed, Reels and shorts, which are the leading social media formats at this time. They then set up a test campaign to measure the impact of changing the optimization objective. In this case, they compared two test groups: 'advantage+ shopping campaign' versus 'advantage+ shopping campaign' using the 'awareness object-ive'. The awareness objective was based on an upper-funnel brand campaign on top of having the system optimize for sales as is standard in an advantage+ shopping campaign. Oakley leveraged the native lift studies that are part of Meta's offering but, essentially, all social media platforms offer a similar form of lift study. (This is another advantage of social media because all the users are logged in.)

The native element of running the advantage+ shopping campaign with sales-optimized ads is that a 'shop now' button is added natively, and the system takes the sales data from the advertiser as the objective to optimize against. The second test group was a full-funnel campaign – using the integrated sales-optimized creative and leveraging optimization against both awareness and sales objectives – and created a 64 percent lower cost per incremental purchase versus the usual direct response campaign. The campaign also drove a 96 percent lower cost per search versus their normal direct response campaigns because of the integrated awareness objective. Their experience pulls together targeting, developing creative native to the social media platform, leveraging the latest ad formats, relying on auto-optimization from the ads system and measuring incre-mentality. Oakley drove every level from awareness to action through the AIDA funnel with stunning results, while showing what it looks like to pull together all the capabilities that modern digital marketing delivers in the leading channel of our time, social media.

The future

So where is this paid social channel going in the long run? I do worry about not enough people standing up for the value of online behavioural advertising which, in the end, is the foundation of social media advertising. As discussed, I strongly believe it provides users with a better, more enjoyable experience. I also believe it helps businesses exist that couldn't otherwise, improving and growing the economy, and providing jobs, especially in SMBs. We will eventually reach an equilibrium here – this form of advertising is here to stay, as it provides so much value. In all the work I have done, people prefer it to the alternatives. Regulation has passed, and continues to pass, so the nature of paid social will shift, but we should all hope it doesn't hurt consumers more than it helps them.

In the future, I believe more AI will be used to rank the ads and less data will be used. Conversions will go more first party, happening within the social media sites. We are already seeing this play out. Regulations have come, constraining the use of data, especially in Europe, and the various social media companies are adhering to them. At the same time, you see YouTube, Snapchat, Meta and other major players in this space making more revenue, clearly able to do more with less data. For example, deep integrations with commerce platforms like Shopify are almost standard across all social media companies. TikTok is pushing hard into e-commerce on site around the world. And Meta has created shops in Facebook and Instagram, as well as a huge business around 'click to messaging' – all of these conversions are inside the first-party ecosystem.

This evolution will allow companies to get great ROAS, drive sales and find happy clients. The tools will get better for creative, as well, integrating generative AI to develop ads and targeting. In the long run, users and businesses will have agents that can chat to each other to solve their clients' and end users' needs. There is an exciting, cutting-edge future ahead for the best online marketing channel ever created.

4

SUMMING UP

15. AI

'It is impossible to predict the future, and all attempts to do so in any detail appear ludicrous within a very few years.' So said Arthur C. Clarke in his brilliant 1962 collection of essays, *Profiles of the Future*. With those words in mind, I enter this chapter with trepidation. That said, I've exposed myself to plenty of room for scorn in this book thus far, so, in for a penny, in for a pound!

Every conference I attend today is dominated by AI. Every conversation I have with other marketers cannot escape a discussion of AI's impact on our job. Luminaries as brilliant as Tony Blair have written long books on how leaders should leverage the incredible future offered up by AI, so rather than broad prognostications, I am going to try to be more practical. Here, I provide insight into my experiences of working with AI at one of the leading tech companies, and how I see AI technology changing marketing tactically. Before I dig into the main part of the chapter, though, a baseline understanding of AI is necessary for context on how this is all playing out in marketing today.

AI FUNDAMENTALS

As I write early in the book, a little technical understanding is useful for using online and digital tools, so here I'd like to share, in a super-high-level way, how I look at AI. A good way to think about AI is:

1. **Data** – The fuel for the AI training. Data can take many forms, from general web content through to specific

structured data sets, such as maths queries with correct answers.

2. **Algorithms** – This is a catch-all for the actual AI software research and programming.

3. **Compute** – The data centres in which the AI is trained, filled with the famous Nvidia chips or their counterparts, like Trainium from Amazon or TPUs from Alphabet.

There are two different types of AI data centre:

1. **Training data centre** – These mega data centres use the amount of energy necessary to power some cities and towns, or more. They train the base models, the original model underlying all subsequent use cases and sub models distilled from them. The latest one Meta is building in 2025 is roughly the size of Manhattan in Louisiana.

2. **Inference data centre** – These data centres are individually smaller and cheaper than the training data centres today, but there will be many more of them in total. The models and tools that are built and produced in training are run here – this is where the AI action happens. Production AI models are getting smaller and smaller, enabled by open source because people can optimize them as they see fit. For example, Meta's Llama system, our base large language model, is open source and has been used to show just how small a device these AI models can run on, including a computer or phone. (It's worth noting, the human brain runs on just 20 watts of power, which is way less power than a PC.) Over time, this trend is likely to continue, as more AI runs outside of data centres.

There are currently three layers in producing an AI model:

1. **Training** – The initial process of teaching a model on a big data set.

2. **Fine-tuning** – Adapting a pre-trained model to a specific set of actions or tasks you want it to complete and ways you want it to behave.

3. **Distillation** – Creating a smaller model which has learned from a larger, more complicated model, to do similar work but far more cheaply. Llama has proven to be excellent here, allowing these models to run on smaller devices, such as a phone.

Because of how AI is produced today, AI models are frozen in time – they don't learn and adapt in real time. They run based on context windows, a feature that acts as memory for the interactions the AI is having or the data it wants to access. AI can use online and digital tools and query the internet or associated databases for information. But the fundamental models, as of the time of writing in 2025, don't update themselves in the way a brain does, continually creating new synapses and changing the weights of a given synapse. One day, however, this will change, and once AI is able to learn in real time, the impact will be incredible.

To use a modern AI model, you must send it a prompt that tells it what to do. But describing what to do in a way that consistently gets you the answers you are looking for can be extremely difficult. This has led to a major new field opening up called 'prompt engineering', which aims to ensure users are able to consistently get their desired results. In many ways, the future of white-collar work will revolve around prompting AI, providing explanations to AI so it can fine-tune its actions and results, or checking if an AI got something right. This may be as little as five to ten years down the line. Humans will still be bringing creative thinking and problem-solving to the table, which, today at least, is not a field in which AI has made easy progress. But don't be mistaken, AI is already here, and it's here to stay.

AI IS ALREADY HERE

In 2025, AI has already revolutionized my job and that of any other digital marketer. Looking at social media specifically, I don't think folks realize how disruptive AI has been. One specific example is TikTok and short-form video. Short-form video is a different form of social media than what we have seen in the past. Historically, all social media centred around what we call 'connected content' in which users see content from an account they have friended or followed. TikTok ignored this idea completely, showing users content from accounts they don't follow, which we call unconnected content. Instead, what users are shown is based on a semantic understanding of that content, the users themselves and what they are interested in right now. Over time they expanded into both connected content with a follow graph and friends and family content with contact importing, messaging and people you may know, similar to how Facebook moved towards them by adding public content and then unconnected content to their feeds.

Meta and YouTube started from behind here but have caught up and, in some respects, overtaken in this area. In the process, we had to implement modern AI to be core to the ranking. Modern AI allows semantic understanding, so the AI recognizes what the videos are about from watching them and looking at their meta data, such as who is viewing them and what other videos they view. As a result, the AI forms an understanding of the videos available. In turn, the AI learns about the person watching the videos. Who are they, what do they typically like and what does their current session say about them?

This last point is interesting because some days I want to turn up and see videos of comedians. Other days, I might want to check out recipes to plan dinners for the week. The AI systems used by YouTube, Meta, TikTok and others recognize how I engage with the first few videos when I open the app, and from there show me videos based on my current mood. Our systems could not do this even five years ago. And not only can they do this now, but most of the time users spend on Instagram and, I believe, social media as a whole is now based on this form of content ranking. It is a complete revolution.

Similarly, ads ranking has been completely and quietly revolutionized by AI in the last five years. Meta experienced two notable issues a few years back. First we pivoted to short-form video without first focusing on monetization. This move, however, was based on our standard behaviour, so when a new social media format emerges, we can move fast enough to respond to it. Second, Apple rolled out App Tracking Transparency, its new privacy framework. This referred to conversion measurement for personalization as 'tracking' in a scary way that encouraged users to opt out. Meanwhile, however, Apple buried its own conversion measurement and optimization in a settings menu called 'Personalization'. This was obviously a brilliant business move but, in my opinion, deeply cynical because tracking is scarier as a word than personalization, and popping up a dialogue is more prominent than a setting in a system menu. By 2024, however, just two years later, our revenue growth had surged and aggressive expense management efforts had taken hold. The main source of our ability to overcome these obstacles was not some clever new way of getting hold of data – it was doing more with less data. We were able to so by deploying modern AI-based ranking systems and tools throughout our ads stack. That means anyone using Meta's ads technology today to drive conversions is leveraging modern AI at scale. This is true for most digital ad vendors at this point, and it is clearly a multi-billion-dollar business for us.

These are just two examples, as there are many places where AI has fundamentally changed the world already. Take coding copilots, AI that can check and debug code you've written. I first heard about them in 2021 at a dinner with Alex Wang, the CEO of Scale AI, and Nat Friedman, CEO at the time of GitHub inside Microsoft. Fast-forward three years and any developer who wasn't using coding copilot was around 20 percent less productive. Four million businesses in 2025 were using AI creative tools to design their ads on Meta's properties. E-discovery in law firms leveraging AI has given paralegals superpowers. The examples continue on and on. This is not a field of pure hype – AI has completely transformed my company in the last five years, and if it hasn't transformed yours yet, it is only a matter of time.

AI IS A THRESHOLD TECHNOLOGY

AI is not deployed until it reaches a threshold where it is useful, and from that point its deployment accelerates dramatically. Short-form video in social media is a perfect example. Meta was not oblivious to TikTok and ByteDance trying to succeed in the West as they had in China. They simply weren't able to at first, but they kept iterating and iterating until one day they got the ranking working well enough to engage and retain users. At that point, they deployed a massive marketing budget, mostly direct response, leveraging all the best practices (those I have shared throughout the book), and scaled tremendously. The moment they crossed the threshold of 'good enough' the whole of social media was disrupted, forcing Meta, YouTube and Snapchat to launch their own versions of the product and try to catch up. This moment wouldn't have happened without AI ranking.

A second example of AI as a threshold technology is Meta's internal work on content moderation. As a company, we have around 40,000 human reviewers and billions of dollars of spend on content moderation. This is only a fraction of what we would have needed ten years ago to do the same job, but we have specially trained classifiers (AI tools to classify content) to help with each category of content moderation. The way we look at both our human reviewers and classifiers is to analyse them on precision (what percentage of decisions they get right) and recall (how much of a given content violation they find). Precision and recall can be plotted on two axes, as shown below:

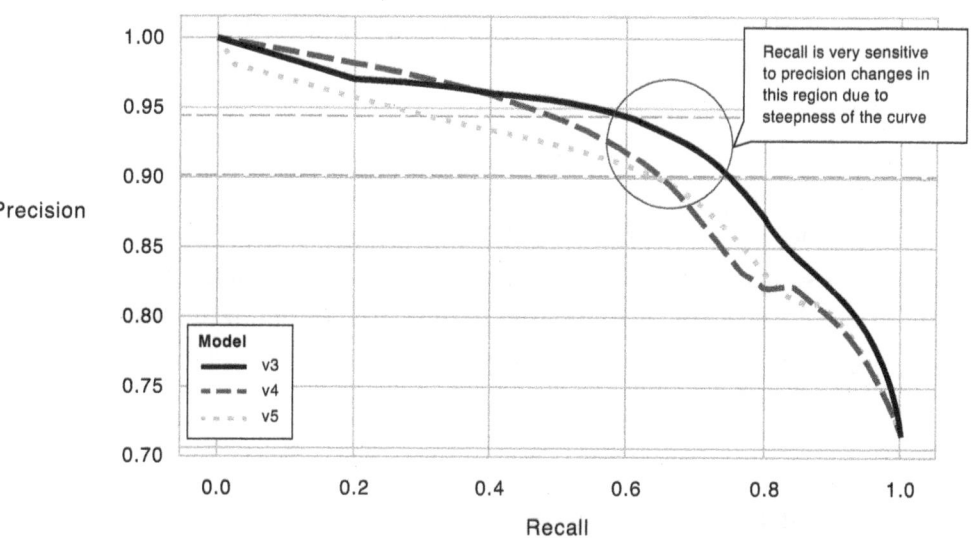

Precision versus recall

As models improve, the curves shown should push up and to the right on the chart. You can see this is happening with the specific example here. What is interesting, though, is that companies are now looking at curves like these on multiple tasks; the one I am currently closest to is content moderation. We are scoring the modern AI models versus our existing customized models and human raters. Until, at the target precision or recall, the new model has a lower recall or precision, we will not use it for a task. When it crosses the line, we will replace the task with the model. This means the experience of the roll-out will be sudden, even if the improvements have been gradual and iterated over years.

The first example here shows how something totally new is being made possible and created by AI. The second example shows AI replacing older machine learning or humans executing a task. There is a third case, which is likely to be more prevalent, and is big already – the previously mentioned AI copilots, such as those used in coding. (Microsoft has even branded their version of this assistant 'Copilot'.) In this case, AI augments a human worker's skills, making them far more effective than someone who doesn't use AI, and enabling them to do multiples of the work they could do without it. In coding in 2025, the software industry is talking about getting AI as good as a mid-tier engineer. But even for senior engineers we are seeing AI use accelerate their productivity across the field. As mentioned, this is likely to happen in many white-collar fields in the coming few years, not least with AI serving as a tool for producing creative in marketing.

AVERAGE DATA GIVES AVERAGE OUTCOMES

As I work in my role as head of analytics for Meta, one thing I look at is how good AI is at various tasks that are performed by humans today. I have described how by looking at precision and recall curves. In the specific example of content moderation, we have been doing something similar for years with machine learning. Even though neural networks are massively different from, say, random forest models (an older form of machine learning or AI from a decade and more ago), the way we analyse them is not, and neither is the impact of training data. What we have found is that AI can only currently get slightly better than its training data, even if you give it large volumes to train on. To get expert-level outcomes, or better than expert-level outcomes, you need expert-level training data, i.e., an average engineer telling you how to code something is non-expert; a twenty-year veteran engineer telling you how to code something is expert-level data.

This makes sense – when you learn a new skill from an expert, for example, you usually have the chance to get to a higher level than if you learn from a mid-level person in any field. Of course, not all experts are good at teaching, and not all experts are good at producing data for AI to learn from, so there are many parallels. This fact is being reflected in the field of data labelling, where more and more expensive, higher-quality labels and data sets are being sought out.

TODAY, INTELLIGENCE IS OUR BIGGEST LIMITING FACTOR

So much of what we do today is basic, repetitive work that we currently cannot give to a computer. Benedict Evans, the tech analyst and newsletter author I refer to earlier in the book, introduced me to a brilliant analogy that applies here: if the internal combustion engine gives humanity access to infinite horses (horsepower), then AI gives us access to infinite interns. In fact, AI is getting better than interns. For example, in 2025 many people in tech think AI will be able to reach the capabilities in coding of a mid-level developer at any large tech company, but the concept still holds. The intelligence just becomes greater. It is a useful thought experiment to try and understand what we would do if we had intelligence too cheap to meter, or charge for, a phrase I hear a lot in Silicon Valley. As marketers we'd create more ads, we'd optimize landing pages, we'd try to create one-to-one experiences for our customers and much, much more.

FOR NOW, AI ISN'T CREATIVE

For now, though, that intelligence can only do what we tell it to do. It cannot be creative or come up with new ideas and concepts that are not already in its training data. Even today's progress on reasoning where an AI improves its error rates and ability to answer questions by debating with itself is not creativity – I would call it algorithm improvement. Creativity consistently seems the space where human input in the systems will be the most valuable as they get better. I often think of the sci-fi novel *Player of Games* by Iain Banks as the optimal view of an AI-led civilization, one in which humans are cared for by benevolent machines, and we all get to create, live life and have fun – it is well worth a read. One day, AI will be creative, but I'll be shocked if that happens in five years.

MOVE TO WHERE THE AI PUCK IS GOING

Sam Altman, CEO of OpenAI, has said there are two fundamental strategies in AI: build for where AI is today or build assuming AI innovation continues to keep pace. In his opinion, if you do strategy one, AI will 'steamroll you', and I couldn't agree more. So how do you think about where AI may be headed? The framework I use is mirroring AI to chip development. I trained in the semiconductor physics department at Cambridge for my master's. My experience there was that we always knew the next couple of breakthroughs that would come, but we didn't know what would work three or four breakthroughs out, which was the field of fundamental research.

The exceptional *Chip War: The Fight for the World's Most Critical Technology* by Chris Miller runs through the history of chip development and its geopolitical ramifications incredibly well, culminating in the Graphics Processing Units (GPUs) being used to train AI today. It explains how original circuit boards were big and bulky, and gradually innovations – like drawing on a semiconductor wafer with acid-resistant pen and then acid-etching them – made them smaller. They then moved to printing on the chips through photolithography, making the projections even smaller through better imaging. With each innovation, the chips got smaller and better.

I have that same feeling when I interact with AI development. At the end of 2024, it was clear that larger models, better data, agentic behaviour (allowing AI models to act as agents) and the beginnings of reasoning would be on the agenda for 2025. Some of those developments had already begun by the end of January 2025, including demonstrations of agentic behaviour and reasoning. Some of them are just being built, like larger data centres that reach up to 1 gigawatt in power, which may cause huge steps up in performance, as the natural conclusion of OpenAI's 'Scaling Laws for Neural Language Models' argues, and their attempt to spend $100 billions on data centres suggests. Or these centres may prove we have reached diminishing returns, as others believe.

The way to stay up to speed with this rapid evolution is to read blog posts of leading companies in this space, like Meta, OpenAI, Anthropic and Google, and watch videos featuring their CEOs and leaders of their AI teams talking about where they're headed. We are all sharing information, and you can keep up to speed by paying attention to the trends and changes currently happening. In a fast-moving field like this one, there's a real chance you can give yourself an edge before someone like me packages up the talking points and turns them into sales and marketing material for the masses.

AI ENABLES AN AUDIENCE OF ONE

Hopefully this chapter is giving you a reasonable theoretical background for where AI is going. Practically, though, what does it all mean for marketers? In many ways, marketing can be thought of as sales, at scale. Marketers talk to large groups of people at once, trying to convince them to take an action. Of course, it would be way better if each of those individuals within that group could have a salesperson talk to them directly, who knows them personally. If they are looking for a vacation, that salesperson remembers their past vacations, and customizes their recommendation for price, location and type of holiday. In marketing, this is often referred to as an audience of one. We truly have the ability, at least within the limits of a thought experiment, to show the right ad to the right person at the right time. We have unlimited intelligence, run on cheap, distilled models, that can think about what to say to an individual to present them with the best opportunity your product can offer them.

To prepare for this possibility at all scales of business, you need to have your data in a shape where the AI can consume it in the future. AI needs more structured data, so you will do better if you have a well-structured customer database to train the AI. As a small business, this database can be as simple as a list of people who have purchased from your shop or stayed at your small hotel, with contact details and details of what they bought. This simply scales up for a large enterprise. A huge travel company like Expedia or Booking.com needs the same information, just with which hotel layered in, and details like loyalty programmes. A huge online retailer like Amazon or Target needs a database of every purchase users made and when, and their contact details, to run their business, and they can use parts of that, where they have the appropriate consent, for training. Over time, AI will get better at consuming totally unstructured data. Today, AI is already brilliant at taking a large, unstructured data set, like a book such as this one, and simplifying it into an easy-to-consume format. It's possible that in the future AI may not even need a well-structured data set to consume and analyse it.

So, get started using the tools already out there. I am proud that Meta offers amazing tools like business AI agents, which can start a conversation with a potential customer over Whats-App and be utilized by businesses both big and small. We have over a million businesses using AI creative tools today to run ads. Try these out! If you are advanced in your use of AI, we offer the whole of Llama for enterprises to adopt and, privately, completely customize. We are not alone – there are so many tools out there, and you don't have to just try ours, of course. Get out and experiment. And, as a marketer, hold the North Star in your head that we will finally be able to truly show the right creative to the right person at the right time, even so far as having infinite salespeople to talk to customers one-to-one.

16. PARTING THOUGHTS

The two guiding principles of the book have hopefully come through strongly by now:

Tools evolve, but principles are timeless: History doesn't repeat, but it rhymes. By now, you know that tools may change but principles remain constant, and I hope I have shown you why. As we work on the cutting-edge channels of today, it is important to remember that every classic marketing channel was once cutting edge too, often sparked by a technological breakthrough, like television or radio. Those channels rose up and permanently changed how marketing was done, with their marketers becoming the disrupters and then the establishment. What was groundbreaking has become classic.

Incremental results are everything: In the marketing industry, measurement has always been a struggle, as well documented up to a hundred years ago in classic marketing books like Claude Hopkins's *Scientific Advertising* and Rosser Reeves's *Reality in Advertising*. Today, we look for incrementality in online marketing that soap marketers figured out how to deliver decades ago through geographic testing and scale through media mix modelling (MMM). Measurement isn't the enemy of marketing – it is the way we understand if we did the right thing. At a larger company, it is the language by which we get support and funding. Incrementality measurement is the holy grail here, which great digital marketing can provide.

My key wish is that we could integrate the knowledge from the classic channels into online marketing – knowledge that, in our naivety, we sometimes ignore – and that the cutting-edge channels could be integrated into the mainstream more quickly. My hope is that this is already happening today, as we see more CMOs like me, who grew up a digital native, filling senior roles in the industry, and that maybe this book can help a little bit in moving the process along. At the same time, for the future, when new channels come along that I didn't grow up with, I hope anyone who reads this book can give me a nudge to accept them faster!

I also want to reiterate how deeply I believe in marketing. Marketing matters, growth matters, and I worry sometimes that we, as marketers, are too ashamed of our craft. At industry events, and in general, we tend to platform marketing critics, not those who celebrate our impact. We shy away from simply talking about results and sales and dress our actions up in meaning beyond them. Though this may be laudable, I often feel it ignores the core value of marketing. Still, it's something to consider. For example, Steve Harrison's *Can't Sell Won't Sell: Advertising, Politics and Culture Wars. Why Adland Has Stopped Selling and Started Saving the World* is a compelling read if you want to be challenged about the industry by someone willing to swim against the tide. He points out that in a lot of public marketing forums we have forgotten to say that marketing exists to sell, and this is bleeding through into everything we do, harming our industry. (I don't agree with everything in the book, as I feel you probably shouldn't with good books.)

Connecting consumers to consumption accelerates growth. That is a good thing. It improves people's lives by helping them consume things they like, want or need, and by creating jobs making and selling those products and services. I believe that is something to be deeply proud of, and I also worry that if we who practise marketing don't make that point loudly and proudly, no one will make it for us.

Over-regulation can remove the value we add and hamper

our ability to improve people's lives over amorphous fears with no counter voice. Online marketers and digital natives tend to be less prevalent in the industry bodies that influence policy, partly because the previous generation in any field doesn't easily welcome the next. And if those of us who grew up digital natives don't wake up, in the next five to ten years we could end up with an online marketing world that is much poorer for it. That would make our jobs less enjoyable, harm economic growth, and mean consumers discover fewer products that could surprise and delight them. In short, it would be a shame.

That said, today online marketing is thriving, so much so that friends, colleagues and acquaintances continuously ask me for a recommendation on a book that would introduce them to this world. The fact that I just didn't have one I felt I could recommend became an impetus to writing this book. I wanted to set out how I think about the main channels at a high level and how to operate as an online marketer. I hope I have achieved that, and feel that I have – I hope you do too.

If there are just a few takeaways you leave with after closing this book, remember the following:

1. **The basics matter.** Sweat the details on them.
2. **Be clear on your goals and metrics**. Have one key North Star goal and stick to it.
3. **Own that outcome.** Make sure your impact is incremental.
4. **A little technical skill goes a long way.** Make the effort to gain that skill – it's within reach.
5. **Good marketing can't fix a bad product.** But when good marketing and a good product are combined, magic happens.
6. **Direct response marketing is a game of inches**. And you have to fight for every inch.

Above all, nothing is more important than making it easier for a potential customer to do what you believe will improve their lives through your product. Make them aware of the opportunity and show them the value you will give them. When they've decided, shorten the path to conversion and make it frictionless. Do everything you can to help them on their way, often by getting out of their way, and the results will reward you fully.

Bibliography

Banks, Iain M., *The Player of Games: A Culture Novel* (Orbit, 1989)

Blake, Thomas, Nosko, Chris and Tadelis, Steven, 'Consumer Heterogeneity and Paid Search Effectiveness: A Large-scale Field Experiment' (*Econometrica, Journal of the Econometric Society*, 2015)

Clarke, Arthur C., *Profiles of the Future: An Inquiry into the Limits of the Possible* (Phoenix, 2000)

FridayNite's SEO book

Harrison, Steve, *Can't Sell Won't Sell: Advertising, Politics and Culture Wars. Why Adland Has Stopped Selling and Started Saving the World* (Adworld Press, 2020)

Hopkins, Claude, *Scientific Advertising* (Merchant Books, 2014)

Humby, Clive, Hunt, Terry and Phillips, Tim, *Scoring Points: How Tesco Continues to Win Customer Loyalty* (Kogan Page, 2008)

Miller, Chris, *Chip War: The Fight for the World's Most Critical Technology* (Simon & Schuster, 2023)

Ogilvy, David, *Ogilvy on Advertising* (Welbeck Publishing, 2007)

Penenberg, Adam L., *Viral Loop: From Facebook to Twitter, How Today's Smartest Businesses Grow Themselves* (Hachette Books, 2009)

Reeves, Rosser, *Reality in Advertising* (Widener Classics, 2015)

Acknowledgements

Any endeavour like this takes a lot of support from a lot of people. Firstly, my mum and dad, who have put up with my intensity and drive for so long and without whom nothing would be possible, and my boyfriend, Mark, whose pride in me makes me believe in myself, even when I lack self-confidence – he inspired me to get my first draft done. My closest colleagues, Naomi and Javi, who on one sunny day in the Felbrigg Hall tea shop pushed me to make this book happen, and my wonderful team members, far too many to name, but with a special thanks to Denise, Brady and Brian. In terms of learning from the industry, no one has done more for me than David Yuan of Tidemark, through his TCV Customer Acquisition Forum, and Marcus Tandler, through the SEO G50, where I met many of the brilliant leaders in this book.

Thank you to all those who proofread this book and gave me suggestions, especially my dear friends Tim Junio and Joost de Valk. They were the first to read the manuscript and tell me, in their inimitable style, I had some work to do, but they thought it was good, and they had learned something, encouraging me to move forward. Thank you to Ani and Aswin for their brilliant presentation on our direct response marketing, which inspired me to go back and attack the manuscript once more after I had already completed the second revision. I deeply appreciate Kelly Bennett taking the time to talk to me about his revolutionary approach at Netflix and I hope I have done it some service. My many thanks to the editorial team of Alex, Talia and Zach and my Meta partners Jon and Nissa who have held my hand throughout getting this live. My thanks to my dear friend of twenty years, Brendan, for believing in me and introducing me to Hachette, and to David Shelley for running with the project! Finally, thanks to Mark, Lori and Heidi for giving me permission to pursue this project: I have wanted to write this book for a decade and to get the chance to do it while still at Meta is a dream.

Index

Page numbers in **bold** refer to figures.

AI (*cont.*)
    intelligence 349–50
    marketing impacts 352–3
    models 343
    outcomes 348–9
    paid social 337, 338
    precision 347–8, **347**, 348–9
    production layers 343
    prompt engineering 343
    ranking systems 345–6, 346–7
    recall 347–8, **347**, 348–9
    search 259, 264, 297–9
    semantic understanding 344–5
    and social media 344–5, 346–7
    strategies 350–1
    as threshold technology 346–8, **347**
    training 341, 343, 348–9, 352
    training data centres 342
aims, of book 8–12
Airbnb 5
algorithmic recommendation units
    196
algorithms 189, 342, 350
AltaVista 260
Altman, Sam 350–1
Amazon 5, 229
    conversion rates 208
    in-house skills 161–3
    recommendation engine 193
    retail advertising network 254–5
Amazon Marketplace 139
anecdotes 121
animations 94
anti-targeting movement 320–1
anti-tech regulation 2
API (application programming
    interface) 48, 63, 67
Apple 166, 208, 256
apps, push notifications 6
attention, competition for 91
authenticity 309

automation 297–9
auto-optimization 67–8, 327
auto-optimizing campaigns 66–8
awards 85
awareness 28, 28–9, **28**, 29, 31, 32, 35,
    72
awareness creation 182, 305–8, 309,
    336

backlinks 277
back-testing 119, 138–40
Banks, Iain 350
banner ads 81, 90, 201–2, 230, 237–8,
    318
banner advertising networks 10
basics, the, importance of 12–13,
    19–20, 355
behavioural creative 87–8, 96
behavioural data 206, 330–1
behavioural metrics 117
behavioural personalization 87–8
behavioural targeting 52–3, 54, 56–61,
    58, **59**, 61–2, 62–3, 64–5, 330
Bennett, Kelly 84, 96, 229, 232, 257
best practices
    implementing 19
    measurement 107–8
    targeting 67
better decisions analytics campaign
    108–10
Bezos, Jeff 121
bidding engines 156
big green button test 85–6, 210–11
Blair, Tony 341
BlendTec 305, 306
Booking.com 140
bottom-line goal metrics 102
bounce rate signal 196
brand awareness 35, 182, 305–8, 309,
    336
brand distinctiveness 112

RAISING READERS
Books Build Bright Futures

Dear Reader,

We'd love your attention for one more page to tell you about the crisis in children's reading, and what we can all do.

Studies have shown that reading for fun is the **single biggest predictor of a child's future success** – more than family circumstance, parents' educational background or income. It improves academic results, mental health, wealth, communication skills and ambition.

The number of children reading for fun is in rapid decline. Young people have a lot of competition for their time, and a worryingly high number do not have a single book at home.

Our business works extensively with schools, libraries and literacy charities, but here are some ways we can all raise more readers:

- Reading to children for just 10 minutes a day makes a difference
- Don't give up if your children aren't regular readers – there will be books for them!
- Visit bookshops and libraries to get recommendations
- Encourage them to listen to audiobooks
- Support school libraries
- Give books as gifts

Thank you for reading.
www.JoinRaisingReaders.com